Bolivia Tried to Kill Us- A Year Trekking and Travelling in South America.

By Tony Hastie- with Amanda Briggs-Hastie.
Illustrations by Iris Maertens.

Copyright © Tony Hastie 2015

For my sister Sandy. Editor extraordinaire, sounding board and full time English tutor.

Table of Contents

1- How on earth did we wind up here?......6
2- Bed bugs, buses and waterfalls 15
3- Dogs we have met......20
4- A stark contrast......40
5- The Fitzroy range beckons 51
6- The Carretera Austral 64
7- To pole or not to pole? 82
8- Adventures in Pucon......94
9- The lone cactus......106
10- A tale of two valleys......116
11- Bolivia tried to kill us......123
12- Drama in Colca Canyon......147
13- Scenery, archaeology and techno 156
14- The best trek we've ever done......170
15- Sun, surf...and boobies 195
16- Rainy season sucks!......208
17- Protest in Bogota 209
18- A mud hell 222
19- Hot enough for ya? 237
20- Bikes we have pushed 251
21- The in-laws 259
22- Knackeragua 276
23- Epilogue 289
24- Other interesting stuff......292

1- How on earth did we wind up here?

Leblon, Rio de Janeiro, Brazil

It's Sunday morning, 11am, 35°C (95°F). Breakfast was beer.

For the last two hours we've been standing in the exact same spot, crushed shoulder to shoulder with a estimated thirty thousand Brazilians, sweating buckets in the sweltering heat, snorting diesel fumes from the rear end of an unserviced truck, and being mentally tortured by the same song, blaring full volume from a gigantic sound system installed on said vehicle, over and over...and over. I look at Amanda and no words are needed: this is *not* how we had envisaged Carnival. How on earth did we wind up here?

Here's how...

We are not by any means born travellers. But that's not to say we haven't done a bit. In 1992, in my early twenties I headed off into the wide blue yonder for two years; like most Kiwis my age on their "big OE". That's nineties talk for *Overseas Experience*, a term we Kiwis use to refer to young people heading out to see the world for the first time- usually to the United Kingdom. Unlike most that made the trip, I almost completely forgot to visit the rest of Europe, only making a quick jaunt to Scandinavia and spending a drunken week at the beer festival in Munich, Germany. Why did I not travel more? I joined a cricket club, then a rugby club and the rest is history. Based in Norwich, England, I did manage to see a lot of East Anglia, some of which I was sober enough to remember. That, however, is another story.

In 1999 Amanda, who's a Brit, decided to spend her gap year in New Zealand (a gap year is Brit talk for an "OE") which is where we met and fell in love. When we met, I was living in a newly purchased house with seventies decor and a fridge full of beer.

Initially she thought I was shy, and a bit weird. Luckily the fridge full of beer managed to assist in overcoming these hurdles. What were my first impressions of her? She was HOT! I really am that shallow.

After a four year romance we jetted off to the UK to get married. A quick honeymoon in Italy followed, and then it was back home to reality. We hunkered down and worked for the next ten years, managing to acquire some rental properties along the way, but saving absolutely no cash.

So, Amanda's gap year turned into more of a gap decade.

It was just before a 12 hour overnight orienteering event in Wanaka, New Zealand, that we were competing in to celebrate our eighth wedding anniversary (who said romance is dead!) that the travel seeds were replanted. Sitting in the pub having a pre-race drink, Amanda 'popped the question' she had apparently asked several times before. This time it seems I was actually listening.

"Shall we go travelling?"

My answer shocked the both of us:

"OK."

And so the planning began. Before the end of the night I had plotted a route starting at the bottom of South America and ending in Alaska. It's a pity my navigation wasn't up to this standard in the race that followed.

Why was I suddenly saying yes to uprooting my whole life and hitting the road? We both needed a break from work; that was clear. After 16 years with the same company I was bored. And after ten years in her job, Amanda needed de-stressing. But how serious were we?

For the next three months we umm-ed and ahh-ed and kept spending. Were we really prepared to give up successful careers to go gallivanting off around the world? How much would it all cost? Did we really want to leave our cushy lifestyle behind and live out of a backpack in some developing country for an entire year? Or were we too old for this shit?

At 43, I certainly didn't *feel* old but it did dawn on me quite early on that I was (feasibly) old enough to be the father of most of the travellers we would meet. It would be fair to say that after my initial enthusiasm, I was quite reluctant to commit to the two-years-from-now date Amanda had set. But then that all changed.

I was happily plodding away in my workshop one day when two of my workmates popped in and started measuring it up.

"What are you doing?"

"We're measuring up how much pallet racking we need to fill this space," one replied. "You're moving over to the other factory."

"Over my dead body!"

After a discussion with the boss where he eventually agreed it would be easier to kill me than move me, my workmates stopped measuring and I resumed normal duties in the workshop I'd become so attached to.

"Let's see how this arrangement goes and re-evaluate it in a year or so," I suggested.

So now the trip was not only well and truly on; the "maybe in two years" departure date we'd be contemplating had become 14 months. If I was going to move, it wouldn't be across town to the other factory, it would be across the world.

Could we save enough in 14 months? The initial research on my ambitious length-of-the-Americas trip was quickly cut back to South and maybe Central America. The USA and Canada were going to be just too expensive. And so the saving began...

For twelve months we pretty much didn't have a life outside work. I wrote up a budget and came up with an amount I thought we would need. I spent every waking moment reading travel books, plotting routes...reading more travel books. I now knew more about South America than Simon Bolivar did. (Google him!) Amanda, busy at work, trusted me to have it all sorted. I really enjoyed the planning stage for some reason and was strangely sad when it finally came to action.

> Amanda-.May I point out that the agreement here was for Tony to do all the planning and I would learn Spanish!

Everything was on track; we were close to our savings target and our plans were coming together. I was starting to wind down a little, ready for the big trip and then the hinges came off the plan...literally. Two months before our planned departure date, we discovered a wayward tenant had completely trashed one of our rental properties. Amanda's initial thoughts were "That's it, our trip is over." ***"Bugger that!"*** was my reaction and I booked airline tickets that day. We now had a deadline. Two months to completely renovate a property for as little cash as possible- and have it re-rented before we left. There was only one thing we could do; move in and get to work. On October the 30th (Amanda's birthday), with our own home rented out, we did just that. When

Amanda saw the house (she hadn't yet, I'd done the evicting), she cried. The mice living in the oven were her shoulder to lean on. Not the best birthday present Amanda has ever received from me...but not the worst either!

> Amanda- No, not the worst. That would be the romantic book "Living with allergies" he gave me in our first year together.

For six weeks we hunkered down. Our routine started at 6am: wake up and go to work. Get home at 5pm and go to work on the house. Finish about midnight. Weekends were different. We could wake up, stay home and work! We worked bloody hard. We also received a lot of help from friends and family. I for one remember with fondness the countless lasagnes supplied by one particular friend...and the therapeutic kitchen demolition enjoyed by another. Even the neighbours got in on the act. One lady, who had every right to hate us for renting our house out to a complete moron, supplied us with curry. We didn't have to cook for six weeks...which was just as well; we had no kitchen.

This house was the seventies-decor-house mentioned earlier; both my first home, and the first place in which Amanda and I lived together, so it was especially hard for us to see it in the state we found it. It was much easier to do a good job of its *second* renovation in eight years. (Amanda made me promise to get rid of the seventies pink Formica kitchen bench top and other icons before she agreed to move in the first time). We eventually had it returned to its former glory. No, even better than it was before.

Carefully screened tenants moved in before Christmas and a professional property manager (Mum!) was put in place to ensure nothing like this ever happened again. We left New Zealand in January 2013, as planned. After a brief stay in Scotland, mid-winter, to visit Amanda's family, we decided to opt for a relaxing start to our holiday after the hard work and stress of the last few months: Rio de Janeiro's carnival.

Back to Rio...

Heat exhaustion or carbon monoxide poisoning? It's hard to predict which will kill us first. Six million people live in Rio. Two million more are visiting for the same reasons we are. Quite a crowd! Coming from New Zealand, a country with a total population of four and a half million, it's easy to feel overwhelmed.

Shoulder to shoulder people, sweltering heat, diesel fumes, the same song on repeat and it's official, we've had enough. Amanda is on the verge of a panic attack.

"I need to get out of this crowd right now," she whispers.

Easier said than done. There's a wall of people as far as the eye can see in every direction.

"What's Portuguese for excuse me please?" I ask her.

"No Idea. I doubt they'd move for us anyway, even if they could."

There's only one thing for it: aggression! It's an emergency situation after all. A lifetime of playing (and more recently watching) rugby is about to pay off. Amanda latches onto my waist, I put my shoulder down and we head for the nearest side street. No quarter given…none asked for. Fifteen minutes later we break free of the masses and can once again breathe. It feels good to be back on the field, breaking tackles again after many years in retirement.

We haven't eaten since the breakfast beer over three hours ago, so next on the agenda is lunch. Now well clear of the *bloco* (street party), we spot a nice little restaurant and secure ourselves a table for a well-earned sit down. Not half an hour later we again find ourselves in the middle of the party. The parade has turned the corner and come to a stop right outside our peaceful lunch spot. Rio is taunting us! A chain goes up over the entrance and two employees stand guard, shielding us and others from the onslaught of people requiring the toilet. And there we have to sit for another two hours, waiting for the crowd to disperse. During this time the restaurant does a roaring trade with their policy: "if you want the toilet, you buy a beer." Finally, after a six hour excursion just to get something to eat, we manage to escape back to the comfort of our air conditioning. It's been an interesting first day at carnival.

Over the next few days we try and avoid getting stuck in such a large crowd again, preferring to watch the activities from a distance. Drunken people attempting to navigate slippery surfaces are very funny to watch: that's the conclusion I reach whilst sitting on a rocky outcrop at the end of Ipanema beach, people watching. It was one of those "I've walked onto a slippery surface and fallen over, so I'll get up and try it again because I haven't learned my lesson" kind of scenarios. A scene that also amuses me considerably is the obviously very drunk and very happy local, laying in the surf and laughing hysterically every time a wave washes over him, talking to each one as it approaches. Maybe he *has* learned his lesson on the rocky outcrop and simply decided to stay down.

We don't need long to experience Rio's carnival and four days after we arrive, we're ready to wind things up with a visit to the world famous samba parade at the aptly named Sambadrome. Getting there is the first challenge. With impromptu *blocos* popping up everywhere, public transport is a nightmare as authorities attempt to re-route buses around the masses. The scheduled bus doesn't turn up so we start walking. After about 45 minutes we spot another bus. A quick check with Google Maps confirms this one is also going to the Ipanema train station.

Amanda- *Google Maps* was an absolute godsend to help with navigational issues, especially in less than desirable areas which normally required "walking with purpose." We bought local sim cards in every country we went to (-apart from Nicaragua, where foreigners aren't permitted to buy them) so we always had a decent enough connection to use it. A bonus in Rio was the transport information provided, which was not available in any other country we visited.

We are finally dropped off at a train station...but it's not Ipanema! It seems there's a large party going on there already. We do manage to get on a train heading for the Sambadrome; unfortunately it misses our station altogether! This turns out to be a bit of a blessing in disguise. When we disembark we find ourselves out the back of the Sambadrome where 'paraders' are putting on their costumes and the massive floats are being lined up in preparation for entrance into the kilometre long parade runway. We have arrived via the tradesmen's entrance!

Walking down amongst the samba schools and all the markets catering to the 'tradies' last minute food and drink needs before the big show, we decide to stop and get some last minute supplies ourselves. Happily we bump into an English speaking vendor.

"Two bottles of water please." Amanda asks.

"Why you drink water? IT'S CARNIVAL!!!" shouts the vendor.

"Do you want the sale or not mate?" I mutter in my Kiwi accent.

Luckily, as I would soon find out, throughout South America, even the English speakers couldn't understand a word I said.

At 9pm we finally take our positions in the cheap seats, happy to be sitting down after a four hour journey to get here. And we wait.

Neither words, nor picture can really describe how awesome this spectacle is; it simply needs to be seen to be truly appreciated. Even from our super cheap US$30 seats we're able to take in the atmosphere as the colourful costumes of the dancers and floats make their way down the runway. They defy belief. As an added bonus we can watch live proceedings on the big screen while we wait for it to get to us.

> Amanda- Well, honestly I think Tone could've at least *tried* to describe it for you, Reader! So let me give it a go...
>
> I remember thinking that the carnival floats and the thousands of dancers that passed us were so crazily big, colourful, elaborate and extravagant that it was hard to believe they existed in real life. It was the kind of spectacle that only exists in Disney movies, or computer-generated graphics in movies, because no-one could really afford to build and co-ordinate such an amazing show in reality- could they?
>
> The one float that really took my breath away was made up of three lorries. The first two were connected and carried four full-length water slides- the open ones with bumps that you might find in a water park. The very end of each angled up, and would easily launch whoever was crazy enough to go down it high into the air. Driving about five metres in front of the slide, the third lorry featured a giant splash pool into which the sliders would 'land.' In between the vehicles was nothing more than road, and any misjudgement or speeding up by the splash pool driver could've been disastrous. Dozens of half naked sliders- or maybe acrobats is a better description- were flying down the water slide, being catapulted into the air, landing in the splash-pool (thankfully!) and then jumping out, running back, climbing the ladder, and doing it all again, over and over.

> Meanwhile the float was elaborately decorated, including the live "decorations"- bejewelled samba dancers, wearing even less than the sliders, except for their feathers, and followed by thousands of other costumed performers, all dancing to the same samba tunes. Nuts and awesome at the same time!

At 4am we've had enough, and we've still only seen six of the eight samba schools dance. With every school getting an hour and a half on the runway to work their magic, and having only a five minute planned routine to the same song, it gets quite repetitive towards the end. The show isn't due to finish until well after 6am. We head back to the train station and board what can only be described as the "gringo" train. Like us, most foreigners just can't go the distance. There isn't a local to be seen.

And there isn't a single person to be seen when we exit the train station either. After the constant barrage of people, to walk out onto completely deserted streets is quite an eerie feeling. Not really the situation you like to find yourself in in a city with more than its fair share of crime. We quickly flag down the first taxi we see, and the dangers of Rio at night became more apparent; in the twenty minute taxi ride home, not once does the driver stop at a red light! Luckily it's only taken us an hour for the return journey and we are tucked up in bed just as the sun comes up.

After a day at the beach and another good night's sleep, we grab a bus out of town... finally escaping the madness. And it was mad. I have no idea when- or even if- most people slept. At 43, and after enjoying a considerable amount of drinking in my youth, I find I no longer have the stamina −or the desire− to get continuously drunk and stay out all night. These days, a night out involving alcohol usually leads to the following week being a total write off. So in hindsight, carnival in Rio was probably not the place for me. In my twenties it would have been AWESOME...and I most certainly would have been robbed!

2- Bed bugs, buses and waterfalls

Unfortunately, Brazil is too expensive for us to hang around in for long so we decide to jump on a bus to the world famous Iguazu falls on the border with Argentina and Paraguay. According to my research it's a must see before we leave the country- and I've done a lot of research!

Arriving in Foz do Iguacu we have to wait a couple of days for the torrential rain to stop before we can head out to see the Brazilian side of this highly rated natural attraction. This gives me time to get over a case of *elephantfeetitis*. My feet have swelled considerably on my first ever long distance bus ride. Don't attempt an 18 hour bus ride in jandals, folks.

> Amanda- It's all about your elephant feet! What about my 120 bloody bed bug bites??

Yep, in only the second hostel of our travels (and our first stay in dorm rooms) Amanda wakes up one morning looking very spotty indeed. Faced with the proof Amanda represents, the hostel owners are hugely apologetic and swing into action to help out as best they can. Armed with the complementary antihistamine cream we retire to our new digs, the room of the owner's niece, to better assess what we're dealing with. After an hour of cream application and bite counting we throw all our stuff into a dryer...apparently 60°C (140°F) kills these little blighters. After a thorough search of both of our backpacks, we finally give ourselves the all clear.

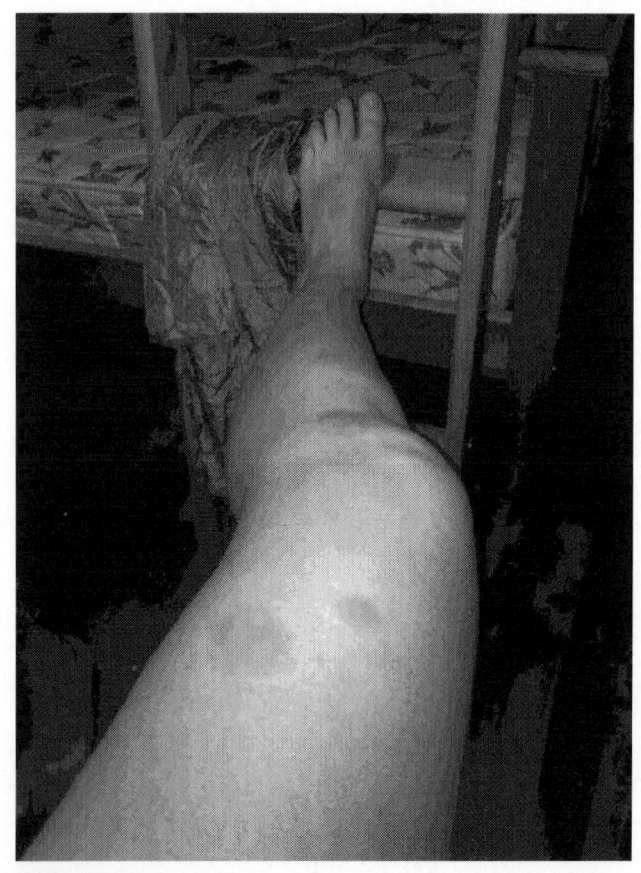

Amanda- And so begins my nightly search for bed bugs…and my mental battle against "mind bugs."

Hopefully a trip to one of the seven natural wonders of the world will take her mind off the itching.

I love a good waterfall so I'm like a pig in shit when we finally get to walk the trails and take in the Brazilian side of Iguazu falls. Nothing I've ever seen can compare to the sheer power of one of these waterfalls, aptly named the Devil's Throat. We're standing at the bottom of the falls, only metres away from it, and the roar is deafening. Falling in here would be certain death. Nothing I say here can really do it justice. Photos fail miserably to capture the falls in their full glory. I doubt I will ever see anything like this for the rest of my life. Tomorrow though, it's Argentinean Iguazu's turn to shine.

Having found that bus prices are cheaper to Buenos Aires from Foz do Iguacu, Brazil, than they are from Puerto Iguazu, Argentina, we decide to stay in Foz another night and sign up for a day tour to the Argentinean side of the falls. Talking to an elderly German traveller who did the trip independently the day before confirms to us the value, and the ease, of proceeding this way.

Our first stop on this guided tour of the Argentinean part of the falls is the top of the Devil's Throat.

"Et eez like ze beginning of ze vorld," our German friend told us last night.

He is not wrong. It is simply breath taking. Amanda is reduced to tears at the sheer magnificence of Mother Nature. Not that anyone notices; we are all thoroughly drenched within seconds of arriving on the platform.

More trails, more falls…closer proximity to the action; it makes a great day out on the Brazilian side the day before seem a bit ordinary. The tour guide is slightly annoying as we are rushed everywhere, obviously on a tight schedule, but it's a small price to pay for a great spectacle. All waterfalls we view for the rest of time will have to be pretty special to get the nod from us:

"It's good, but it's not as good as Iguazu."

Happy to have put the falls on the itinerary, it's time now to head south. The Patagonian trekking season is already half over and we want to take full advantage of the remainder of it. The first leg of our journey is an 18 hour bus ride to Buenos Aires. It is not without excitement. Our first border crossing on a bus is shambolic to say the least. After a very hot 5km walk with full packs, we hit the station and board the bus. Five minutes later we're at the Brazilian border. Off bus; queue for immigration; back on bus; heading for Argentina. Five minutes later it's off the bus again at the Argentinean border, this time with all our gear -which goes through an x-ray machine that no one seems to be watching.

During this lengthy procedure something odd catches my eye. She's tall, slim and blond, has VERY large, obviously surgically enhanced breasts, and a MASSIVE, obviously surgically enhanced bum. Her facial features are the strange part... I am intrigued. As fate would have it we end up sharing the same immigration officer and I take a sneaky peek at her departure card. My suspicions are confirmed. Her name is Leon.

After spending two hours at the border we are finally able to sit back and relax on the bus as it wheels its way to Buenos Aires. Until we get a flat tyre that is. As the tyre is being changed, a North American backpacker screams...

"OH MY GOD! IT'S A TORNADO!"

We look out the window and, sure enough, a mini tornado is bearing down on us. Now, a tornado might seem like something to worry about if you're from a place where they occur with some frequency, but this is my first ever live sighting. I stare fascinated as it hits the bus and gives us a bit of a shake. The men changing the tyre stop only briefly to brace themselves. And just like that the excitement is over, the wheel is changed and we are once again on our way.

It appears the only casualty of the tornado is the air conditioning which has packed it in. But for some unexplained reason we spend the next six hours seemingly travelling at a snail's pace, mysteriously stopping at every petrol station we see. Is there something we should know? Finally, at about four o'clock in the morning, the driver finds what he has been searching for- a replacement bus. We are duly transferred onto it and arrive in Buenos Aires four hours later than scheduled, but in one piece.

Luckily, the flight we catch from Buenos Aires to Ushuaia a few days later is drama free.

3- Dogs we have met

    Being unaware of anywhere in South America, let alone the world, where you are able to hire dogs to take for a walk, I am somewhat surprised when the following conversation actually takes place:
Yoshi: "Did you hire those dogs?"
Tony: "Yes."
Yoshi: "Where did you hire them from?"
Tony: "There's a dog hire kiosk at the start of the trail."
Yoshi: "Ahhh ok, great."
    There is no denying that there are plenty of dogs in South America. There is however a very small percentage of dog hire kiosks. Zero percent in fact. There's really no need as you can have a dog of "your own" in almost every town you visit. When it comes to dogs, South America offers you a bit of everything. Some are wild and aggressive, most are inquisitive. All roam the streets, sometimes in packs of ten or more. Breeding at will. Where are their owners? Around; *if* they have them.
    Throughout a year of travel we met a lot of dogs. Some of the more memorable ones include 'Limpy Poo Fur,' the dog who would accompany us part of the way on the Huayhuash trail in Peru (more on that later); and our Colombian guard dog 'No Name,' who guided us safely past machete-wielding locals and what could easily have been (but probably weren't) cocaine-processing factories. Also in Colombia, a dog taking a horse for a walk is one of the funniest things I have ever seen.
    And then there are the ones who are memorable for all the wrong reasons. Like the dog that bit me twice in Huaraz, Peru. The first time I was caught unawares; I walked happily past a dog sitting on the pavement, as I'd done countless times before. He waited for me to pass then got me from behind. Ten days later after returning from a trek, I walked past the same dog, a little

more wary this time. I even turned to watch him for a good five metres after we had walked past. Then as soon as I turned my back on him, BAM; he was latched onto my leg again. It was a Mexican (-ok, South American) stand-off after that- neither of us was prepared to back down. But I decided he had much bigger teeth than I, so I threw my bottle of water at him. That did not end the stand-off though; it took Amanda and her impersonation of an angry dog to shift him. I was quite scared of her too! Thankfully neither of these bites drew blood and I happily avoided a series of rabies injections.

Finally, there is the dog that did his best to piss on my backpack whilst we were waiting for a bus in the small Chilean town of Santa Lucia. Luckily I stopped him mid flow before serious wetness occurred. Undeterred, he moved on to Amanda's backpack. She was ready for him, shooing him away before he even got his leg up.

> Amanda- He didn't do his best to piss on it, he did piss on it! When your entire life is in your backpack this is very upsetting indeed!

None of the aforementioned dogs, however, compare to the first two dogs that befriended us, and who would end up accompanying us for five days on our first, and one of our favourite treks in South America. This is their story...and ours...

YAY! Patagonia!

Ushuaia, Argentina bills itself The World's Most Southerly City. What *isn't* mentioned in any tourist brochure is that it's actually quite an unattractive place, with far too many cars all trying to get up the same street. Being the hub for cruises to Antarctica, it's also tourist hell. But, location, location, location, or so the saying goes. The surrounding area takes in some of the most rugged, pristine wilderness in the world. It's a real shame to leave after only a short trek to the local glacier behind the town, but our plans involve heading further south and we have the very weather window we need to do it. Our plan is to walk the five day Dientes de Navarino trek that starts across the Beagle channel in the tiny Chilean town of Puerto Williams.

The only thing we know about Puerto Williams is that it's small. With that in mind, we decide to do our shopping in Ushuaia the evening before we leave. We find a good sized supermarket and enter excitedly, happy to be buying expedition food again after such a long time. A frustrating hour later we leave the store completely disheartened, carrying a bunch of packet pastas and rice. It's certainly not the selection of trek food we are used to.

Aware of the tight regulations on carrying fresh food across the border to Chile, we depart the next day on the boat across the Beagle channel with only this depressing array of food to our names, pinning our hopes on Puerto Williams now to provide us with something to please the taste buds. My mood doesn't improve as we are extorted US$100 each for the 45 minute trip. But it's a beautiful day; it's looking good for the rest of the week and the scenery is fantastic, so it's hard to stay grumpy for long.

Our first contact with the locals on this remote island is with the lone border official. Amanda decides on a pre-emptive strike-style border crossing and hits him with it straight away:

"Do you want to see our passports?"

"No."

"We have some food; do you want to check it?"

He risks a quick glance into the bag, gives it a bit of a shuffle then loses interest.

"Welcome to Chile."

The second local we meet is the bus driver. We board the bus and are whisked 20 very scenic kilometres along the coast to Puerto Williams. With the hustle and bustle of the big cities of Brazil and Argentina now well and truly behind us, and glorious wilderness all around, I start to relax for the first time in our travels.

Even immigration is a breeze. We're dropped off at the local police station/immigration office for the official Chilean entry formalities. About 20 minutes later the immigration official arrives and opens up the building. Soon it is our turn to officially arrive in Chile.

"Where are you staying?" the duty officer asks.

Amanda tells her.

"I know them," she says.

And with that she picks up the phone and calls the hostel owners, instructing them to come and pick us up. Yep, this is my kind of town!

It doesn't take long for our ride to get here and they welcome us by giving us an extensive tour of town. That takes all of five minutes. What strikes me immediately is the amount of firewood in people's gardens here. There are dozens of people out chopping it and adding to already large piles. And this is the middle of summer. Obviously preparing for a long harsh winter already, these people take their firewood seriously; around here it's not a hobby (as it was with my father), it's a way of life. Dad, who is no longer with us, would've loved it here; his version of heaven.

Tour over, we arrive at our 'hostel' and settle into our room. We later find out it's a family member's room, the whole family having moved out to live in the tiny garage for the summer in order to take paying customers. They even wake up at 3am to make sure the fire is stoked. That's service! Comfortably settled, we decide to hit town, to start making preparations for our trek. There's no time to lose; by all accounts the weather doesn't stay good around here for long. Our first stop is the local restaurant for a spot of lunch. Amanda asks to see a menu.

"The menu today is chicken," the waiter informs us.

OK, chicken it is then!

While we're waiting for our food, I am introduced to what is apparently a Chilean institution. Eighties rock and pop video medleys on the TV, continuously. There's no playing one song in its entirety going on here!

After lunch we get busy. We head to the police station to register our trek plan and then decide to pick up a few last minute goodies from the supermarket. Once again the selection is disappointing but we do manage to acquire fresh bread and salami. Our last stop is the local camping store where we purchase a crude map, upload some GPS waypoints (a bonus we weren't expecting) and get the latest local weather.

"It looks good today," the shopkeeper says. "But it can change very quickly here."

Very helpful, thanks. His words are reiterated when we arrive back at the hostel and bump into a couple of Australians who have just completed the trail.

"Yeah, we started the trek on a gloriously sunny day as well," Aussie Bloke says. "Then we woke up on day two and there was half a metre of snow outside the tent."

Cough, bullshit…is my first thought. Aussie Bloke seemingly reads my mind and whips out the camera to back up his story. Shit, this is hard core…is my second. Are we fully prepared for conditions like these? Amanda, who feels the cold a lot more than I do, goes to bed worrying whether she's packed enough warm clothes.

Dientes de Navarino; day 1

Having done most of our packing the night before, we wake up, grab our last decent breakfast for five days and walk out into glorious sunshine. Amanda's jersey dilemma continues; is she carrying too much weight now? Will it be a case of the jersey that broke the camel's back?

It's a leisurely old start, with a 20 minute walk along the road to the start of the trail. As we approach the trail head we spot three very menacing looking dogs. A quick scout of the area reveals no owner so it's action stations. Back when we were preparing to travel, Amanda was so busy at work she didn't have the time to spare to get the suggested rabies shots. I did, but I left it a bit late and I wasn't tested to see if it had worked. My doctor assured me it had. If a dog was to bite me, I'd have three days to get to a hospital and get the necessary injections without having to get a blood booster. Amanda would have one day to get to a hospital but would need a blood booster that not all hospitals are able to supply; not ideal in such a remote part of the world. She would probably die a slow and painful death.

Amanda- Thanks!

With this in mind, we practised our "rabies drill" in the few days before we travelled.

"DOG!" one of us would yell.

Amanda would then run and jump on my back. I would assume a frontal attack position and attempt to ward the dog off, kicking out with my legs, taking any bites that might occur and therefore saving Amanda's life.(You're welcome!)

An infallible plan...

...in practice. However, a lot harder with full packs on. We approach cautiously. So do the dogs. We pass the point of no return, needing to get past them to start heading up the trail. They let us pass unmolested, and start to follow us up the hill.

About halfway to the top of the hill we have two problems. Problem one is a fitness problem. I hark back to the days when I considered training for this and didn't follow through. This is the first time we've carried full packs on a trail for as long as the both of us remember, travelling light on the occasional adventure race we entered, or going car camping. Oh well, at least *this* will be getting us fit for the trekking to come. Problem two is a dog problem. One of the dogs who couldn't hack the pace has retreated. The other two aren't so easily deterred. We've tried everything to make them turn around, but to no avail. Too tired to care anymore we give up, thinking they'll probably go home when they get hungry.

It's a tough old climb from sea level to the top of the 610 metre high *Cerro Bandera* (literally, "flag hill"). A huge Chilean flag resides here as a result of the countless border conflicts this region once had. Basically, it's a big "Up yours Argentina, we won this one!" The view is astounding from here and the weight of our packs and our aching legs are temporarily forgotten as we take it all in.

Pressing on along the ridge line, we start bumping into a few people who have decided to walk out from Puerto Williams for the day. In the distance we also spot a couple with larger backpacks on, walking towards us. They must have done the trek in reverse. Great! Some inside info! But no, as we watch they seem to find what they are looking for, turn around and start walking away from us again. Eventually they stop for a break and we catch them up. Michael and Jo from the UK have decided to have a go at this trail with no prior experience and have been having a few navigation issues. I'm not surprised; the trail is poorly marked and we're having trouble staying on it at times too. I'm happy I've brought my GPS as backup, that's for sure.

We press on, following the trail when we can, or being guided by the occasional well-hidden cairn (piles of rocks trekkers build for trail markers) when the trail fails us. Eventually we reach a stream, and decide that the grassy area beside it is the perfect place for lunch. It's not long before Michael and Jo catch up. They have a day walker with them. We hold a quick conference.

"Where to from here?" Michael asks.

"Anybody's guess," I reply, "but I reckon it's through those trees just there for a start."

For the next 15 minutes Amanda and I listen as rustling and swearing emanates from the trees. Finishing lunch we decide to go and join the fun. I quickly realise what all the swearing was about:

"Bollocks! This isn't the trail!"

It's clear that we've all missed a marker somewhere, but how far back is anybody's guess. Never one for backtracking, I fight my way through the trees to a clearing, look up and spot Michael, Jo and Day Walker halfway up a near-vertical rock scramble. Holy shit! Navigation 101: if in doubt, stay high! We follow their lead up the face of the rock, not an easy task with a full pack on; its sole purpose, it seems, is to cause its wearer to overbalance and fall backwards.

Amanda and I are experienced at this kind of thing though. She is forever following me on my little "shortcuts" that, nine times out of ten, take longer than the time I am trying to save.

> Amanda- And usually involve climbing sheer rock faces with no equipment!

We soon catch up and pass Michael and Jo, wishing them luck for the rest of the day's navigation. The look on Michael's face suggests they'll need more than luck, as he clings precariously to the final rock lying between him and safety.

Once again it's just the four of us. Us and our two canine companions. Who, despite our best efforts, are still with us. But it's not long until we catch up to Day Walker, who's stopped for a rest. We start walking together and when we reach a fork in the trail which will lead her back to town, and us, further into the wilderness, we try and get rid of our canine companions once and for all. Amanda slips Day Walker some of our precious salami and we say our goodbyes. Day Walker calls the dogs, shows them the salami and then walks off. They don't move a muscle! She walks back and tries again. No, they're not that stupid...they know where their next meal is coming from. Day Walker gives up and walks off eating our salami. We walk on with our inseparable companions.

It's been a long, hot day and we're happy when we finally spot camp. With only one tent already up, it's also the kind of crowd we like, a small one. The dogs run ahead and introduce themselves to the tent's sole occupant, who lets out an almighty scream as they appear at her doorway. And that's how we meet Annie the French Canadian Super Trekker. We make a dinner date then go about putting our tent up for the first time in the wilderness. Having only put it up a couple of times in the lounge at home to see if it all fits together, there's certainly room for improvement.

Over dinner Annie tells us of her trekking feats. She's done more trails in New Zealand than we have and has been all around the world walking whichever trails she's decided on for that particular trip. We fully realise her super trek powers when I enquire how long it took her to get to camp today. We're no slouches but she's blasted our time out of the water. We also discover her kryptonite, as she breaks her newly acquired Spork (a cross between a spoon and a fork) on the goo she calls dinner, served up in her folding bowl. She's human after all. Finally the dogs get a feed, not from us, still standing firm; Annie's remaining goo is hungrily scoffed.

Just as we're finishing up, Michael and Jo walk into camp. They get set up and sit down to cook a meal and Amanda walks over to welcome them while I do the dishes and prepare to hit the sack. I'm bushed and looking forward to bed. Suddenly I hear fits of laughter. Michael and Jo, having made a last minute decision to walk this trail, purchased all their gear in Ushuaia- not known for its selection, that's for sure. Amanda's having a great laugh at their expense. Their tent is suffering much verbal abuse, as is most of their other gear. Luckily, they're taking it well.

With no new arrivals at the campsite, everybody settles down to a blissfully peaceful first night on the Dientes trail. The dogs settle down just outside our tent.

Day 2

Something I noticed as I walked into camp yesterday was that there was no obvious way out, apart from back the way we'd come. Unless you consider the old adage 'the only way is up.' Upon further inspection it's confirmed; the only way out of here without backtracking is to scramble up the local waterfall. Annie is long gone and the dogs have decided to go with her. We sit down for breakfast and watch Michael and Jo as they climb out of camp. We get going shortly after, and it's not long before we're shrouded in an icy cold mist as we climb away from the Laguna Del Salto campsite. Navigation is once again a challenge. With no marked trail, we rely heavily on cairns to show us the way. That's easier said than done though, as Amanda sums up in the quote of the century:

"It's hard to find a pile of rocks...in a pile of rocks."

Some cairns are more helpful than others. Having overtaken Michael and Jo, we take it upon ourselves to start dismantling some of the less helpful ones, in an effort to help Michael and Jo avoid the navigation issues we're having. There are cairns in every direction and only one trail, after all. Today is the day we find out that the limited and apparently brand new signage on the trail is grossly inaccurate. This is well depicted by a sign that points us straight up one of the craggy peaks of the Dientes mountain range we've been circumnavigating.

From all the trail descriptions I've read whilst researching this trek, today's trail is supposed to offer the best scenery. Trudging through snow up to our knees at times, seeing the Dientes range close up is a nice little taster. Unfortunately though, menacing cloud doesn't allow for the view I wanted to see. Cape Horn remains shrouded. Annie and the dogs inadvertently play guide at times as we follow human and dog prints through the snow and, after a relatively short day, we're at the campsite. Annie has been there for hours.

It's an exposed site by the shores of Lago Escondida but Annie assures us she's checked further down the valley and found the alternative to be more swimming pool than campsite. So we start setting up camp here. There isn't a breath of wind at the moment but we decide to take measures in case it picks up during the night. There are plenty of rocks nearby so we decide to build a defensive wall around the tent. This also serves as good exercise to keep us warm as the cold, damp mist attempts to permeate us to the core. Pretty soon I get sick of this and decide that a fire's a better way to keep warm, so I go off to find some wood. When I get back Amanda's defensive wall has grown considerably. The Great Wall of Chile

Once the fire is roaring we invite Michael, Jo and Annie over to share its warmth. Annie brings her boots and socks over to join mine, already drying by the fire, and Jo brings The Pot. While she boils up some water to make some pasta I can't help but stare at it. It's a medium sized saucepan with a big thick glass lid! I now realise what all the laughter was about the evening before. I see things a little differently though and develop a new respect for

Michael and Jo. Obviously they have purposely handicapped themselves, thinking this trail is a bit easy. Then I spot the cheese and can't help but ask the question Amanda has probably already covered in her gentle ribbing session.

"How much cheese is that?"

"A kilo," Michael replies.

"That's half the weight of our tent!"

"I like cheese."

I steal another glance at The Pot but remain silent.

It's a pleasant evening; like-minded people sitting by the fire, making conversation and taking in the occasional view of the lake and surrounding mountains when the clouds allow. After spending most of the evening trying to push themselves in front of us and steal the fire's heat, the dogs finally get the opportunity to warm up as we all head off to bed.

Day 3

With the fire long out, I wake to a very funny scene. The dogs, like our tent, are covered in ice! Amanda is a little concerned but I assure her they're from here and this is summer for them, so they'll be well used to it.

Annie walks off as we're having breakfast, this time only one of the dogs goes with her; the other will be our companion for the day. It's not long before we head out after her. Michael and Jo give themselves a well earned sleep-in, the rigours of carrying The Pot and a kilo of cheese obviously catching up with them.

In keeping with trekking law, with shoes and socks warm and dry from the fire the night before, we come to a stream within five minutes. Our feet are cold and wet seconds later.

More fantastically desolate scenery, beaver dams, and being the furthest south I will ever walk (S 55'01.355 W 067'43.406) are the highlights of a very short day three.

Our four-legged friends are reunited that afternoon at camp...and one of the dogs decides to help me search out a good site for the tent. I spot a good place and walk over to investigate further. Said dog runs ahead to potential site and alerts me to the dangers of a human poo sitting on the exact site I thought would be good...by eating it! I name him Poo Breath.

We finally take pity on the dogs and decide to feed them some of the meagre rations we have with us. Poo Breath hungrily gobbles the half a snack bar we give him; the other takes a sniff and turns up his nose. His name becomes Fussy. Fussy and Poo

Breath are officially welcomed into the campfire community as we spend the rest of the afternoon and evening basking in the fire's warmth.

Funnily enough, Fussy seems a lot more welcome than Poo Breath after I explain to everyone how Poo Breath got his name. Amanda is worried about them being outside again all night and suggests one of them (preferably Fussy) joins us in the tent. Good sense prevails and we decide against it.

It's taken a few days to get a bedding preparation system going but we've finally got it down to a tee. It's quite an easy system. Amanda sets up the inside of the tent. Full stop. It is simply too small for me to do anything but sleep in. Evening proceedings are as follows: having set up the air mattresses, sleeping bags and silk liners, Amanda pops into the tent and gets herself ready for bed. Once she's ready it's my turn. She hands my sleeping gear out to me; I undress and hand my "trekking attire" into her; she shoves this into a dry bag that I use for a pillow. This leaves me standing in the cold, dressed in only long johns and a thermal top for what seems like an age. I then get the "ready" call. This is where it gets a bit weird. I enter the tent feet first in a strange shuffling motion and Amanda guides my feet into the silk liner which is laying on the unzipped sleeping bag. She then zips the sleeping bag up and I am snugly cocooned for the night. God help me if I need the toilet quickly. Diarrhoea and this system do not mix. I will not elaborate.

Day 4

After washing out my long johns as best I can and draping them over my backpack to dry, we hit the trail. Luckily the sun is out and my sleeping attire will be dry and back in action tonight. You've got to do what you've got to do.

Fussy has gone off with Annie and again we have the pleasure of Poo Breath's company. Both the trail- and any markings- are nonexistent so we try following our faithful companion. It turns out he is as clueless as we, so we finally resort to the GPS and manage to arrive at a crucial marker post. This is where we turn off and start our ascent of 850 metre Paso Virginia. The mud begins, and with it, Amanda's worst nightmare. We are knee deep in mud for the majority of the climb, a tough ask with our full packs and three days walking already in the legs. I love it anyway; it reminds me of the New Zealand bush.

It's always a nice feeling to be walking on solid ground and at the top, we're able to do just that. Only 850 metres above sea level and this is a desolate, barren landscape. After walking over this moon-like surface for a while, we find that the trail markers seem to abruptly end at a cliff. We back track, but not finding an alternative, we arrive back at the cliff side markers and stare disbelievingly at the scenario they present.

We have to go down THAT??

Shit. It's time for a rest. I dump my pack and walk along the cliff top, still not quite believing that we have to go down a near-vertical drop to get to the lake below. But there's no doubt about it. Resigning ourselves, we begin mental preparations for this scary descent. I'm not afraid of heights, but since sliding off the roof at home some years ago, onto the roof of a van, then sliding off that onto the ground, I am *definitely* afraid of falling from them!

About five metres into the descent, things become a little heated. I want to get this over and done with as quickly as possible.

"Why the hell are you stopping?" I shout tensely at Amanda.

"I'm scared!" she yells back, "and so's the bloody dog! It won't move; I'm scared I'll trip over it."They're not the only ones. Amanda, frustrated with continuously having to push the dog forward, and annoyed with me yelling at her, finally takes measures into her own hands, flops down on her arse and starts sliding safely down the scree. Just like that, terror has turned to fun and I quickly follow suit. Over the worst, we stand up and traverse to the right in order to avoid the menacing cliffs I was so concerned about. Then it's a short and very cool scree-run to the bottom. Looking up from the lake's edge, we still don't quite believe what we've just done.

    With the worst of a very long day behind us, we enjoy a well marked and maintained trail all the way to camp, which we almost overshoot in our enthusiasm. Luckily, Annie has put a marker towel out for us. She seems *very* happy to see us this afternoon: It doesn't take long to see why.

    Yoshi from Japan has been lost for three days. In his joy at finally finding the trail again -and a human being into the bargain- he has talked at Annie continuously from the moment she arrived. Jumping at the chance to escape, she quickly offers to help Amanda put up the tent. Now it's my turn to listen. Going into my *listening-without-actually-listening* mode, (perfected on Amanda over the years, much to her annoyance) all I need to do is stand there, attempting the odd comment when I sense he may be losing steam. My ears do perk up though when he tells me how he's been making cairns to make it easier for other trekkers to follow the trail.

"So, you've been lost for three days and making cairns all that time?" I ask.

"Yes."

"Great!"

Luckily my sarcasm is completely lost on him and his attention turns to the dogs. He makes a commitment to keep a look out for dog hire kiosks in the future.

At 4pm, and after many hints, he decides he'd better get on his way. His destination is Puerto Williams but I have no doubt he could end up almost anywhere. It's hard to be concerned, as he happily walks off; you kind of get the feeling he'll be alright, no matter what the wilderness throws at him.

We are, however, a little worried about Michael and Jo. We could see them in the distance when we started the climb and, having eaten most of the cheese by now, their pace should've been a lot quicker. So it's a worry when dusk approaches and they still haven't arrived. Amanda takes Annie's towel marker one step further and pops out some wilderness signs she learned at Girl Guides so our trekking friends don't miss the campsite.

> Amanda- Ha! Mock me if you must but I bet Bear Grylls would appreciate my wilderness skills!

Right on dusk I shoot back up the trail to the lake to see if they've made it down the cliff yet. There's no sign of them but, being confident that they're intelligent human beings, I assume they won't be trying that descent in the dark and go back to camp to report that we won't be sharing the bonfire with them tonight.

Amanda is devastated! Completely sick of packet pasta, she was hoping to trade Michael something for some cheese. Our tent? Her sleeping bag? Me?? That's how desperate she is; unable to face packet pasta again, she gives the dogs a bonus meal tonight. All jokes aside, concern for our friends accompanies us to bed.

Amanda has an especially restless sleep. The past four days she has raved about our fancy blow up sleeping mats to anyone who would listen. They are AWESOME, but not so good when you drag a backpack over one and manage to tear a four inch hole in it. (This mat-related crisis marks the start of a near-comical series of disasters for Amanda; ironically, it seems like everything she raves about ends up falling apart.) Half-heartedly I offer her my mat and am very happy when she refuses. I am older and more vulnerable to the rigours of a hard sleeping surface, after all.

Day 5
With supplies running low, we decide the best thing we can do is walk out today as planned and alert the police to our missing friends. We hit the trail early. Poo Breath is our companion once again and Fussy races to catch up to Annie, already striding off into the distance.

It's not long before the well-trodden trail we're following completely disappears and we're guessing once again. Tired and ready for civilisation and the luxuries it brings, I consult the GPS for the last time on this expedition. Although we can see the road in the distance, I stubbornly drag us up a hill rather than down it, hoping to come across a trail that will take us down to the road, avoiding the swampy farmland on the way. Given all that this trail's thrown at us, I wonder why it still surprises me that the GPS marker is simply a fence post and a trail is nowhere to be seen. Amanda, sick of following me uphill, makes an executive decision and heads straight for the road.

Trudging around swamps, and sometimes through them, we finally road-walk the remaining eight kilometres back to Puerto Williams. The final day is without doubt the most uninspiring part of the last five. 200 metres from town, the first car we see offers us a ride. No thanks, I think we can manage the rest. Poo Breath spots his mates and is off to tell them about his adventures.

We head straight to the police station to let them know we're out safely, as required, and pass on our concerns about Michael and Jo. We leave a message for them with the police, hoping they'll show at a restaurant we've agreed to meet Annie at for dinner. The police also promise to send out a search party if our friends aren't here by the morning.

As we're walking back to the hostel for a well-earned shower, we spot Fussy! He runs over, obviously excited to see us, so we decide to buy him something to eat. We walk out of the store with what is best described as an unknown meat-like substance as he sniffs around eagerly. Amanda unwraps it and puts it on the ground. Fussy, living up to his name, sniffs it once and walks away, apparently disappointed. A local, looking on, literally falls out of her car laughing. Luckily she's not driving at the time.

A little before 8pm we walk over to the restaurant we've agreed to meet Annie at.

"Oh my God! YOU'RE ALIVE!!" Amanda screams as she spots Michael and Jo walking up the road.

There are hugs all around.

Michael and Jo, obviously not ones to shirk on a dinner date, have put in a mammoth ten hour trek to be here, knowing that we'd be worried. Over dinner they tell us where they went wrong, obviously missing the post our GPS led us to.

"We started following someone's footprints," Michael says. "And before you know it we were lost"

"And we were too stubborn to turn around," Jo adds.

Foot prints? Lost? Amanda, Annie and I look at each other.

"Yoshi!" we all burst out at the same time, dissolving into fits of uncontrollable laughter.

Hopelessly lost, and with darkness approaching, they made the sensible decision to set up camp. Running low on gas they even used the water they'd boiled their pasta in to make themselves a hot chocolate, not knowing whether they would need it for another night or not. I am at once jealous and full of admiration at that, and pledge to drink my pasta water at the first opportunity. Tonight, though, it's steak and *pisco* sours all round. Well, almost all round. Your national drink tastes awful, sorry Chile. I drink beer.

Moving on to the most southerly yacht club in the world, on board a decommissioned navy vessel in the harbour, we have a few more drinks then call it a night. Neither of us want to wake up on a yacht in the morning halfway to God knows where.

My lasting memory of Puerto Williams? As we head out of town for the last time we spot Fussy, in a brand new collar, chowing down on a huge bowl of pasta. Maybe he was a vegetarian?

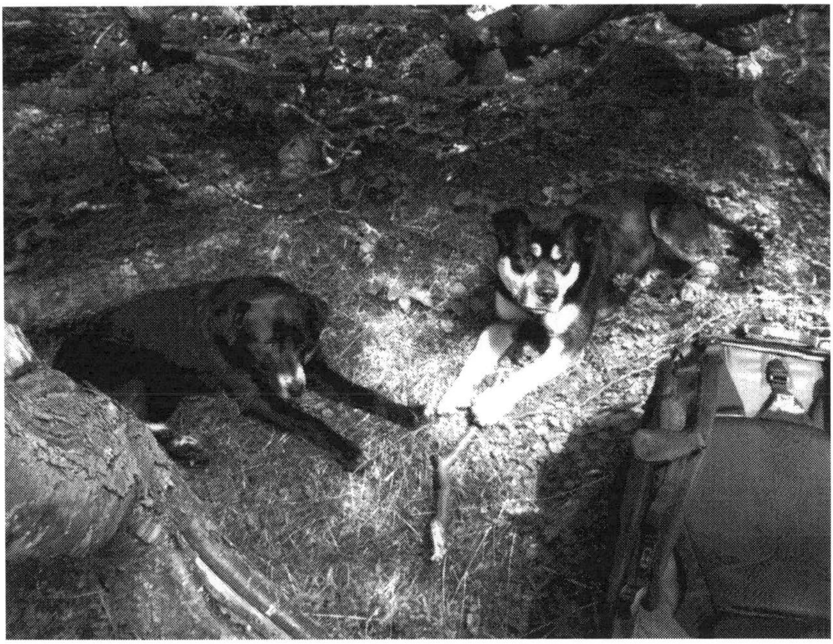

4- A stark contrast

Next stop, Torres Del Paine National Park...but first we have to get there. Michael and Jo, and Annie, join us for the first leg of the journey. This is a 30 hour trip on a grotty old car ferry that the locals of Puerto Williams use to connect to Punta Arenas, on the Chilean mainland. The scenery is nothing short of spectacular as we motor along the Beagle channel. We spend hours out on deck in freezing conditions as we pass glacier after glacier...after glacier; me in my puffer jacket, shorts, socks and jandals, and Jo, my sole competition for fashion icon of the trip, in her sleeping bag. As night falls we turn north into the Magellan Straight, eventually arriving in Punta Arenas midway through the next afternoon.

Michael, Jo and Annie are pressing on to Puerto Natales, the hub for Torres Del Paine [TDP], on the next bus. Our schedule isn't as tight so we're spending the night in Punta Arenas, and we say our goodbyes. By the time we've worked out that Punta Arenas is a bit of a dump it's too late; the last bus has gone so we have no option but to follow through with our plan. We end up staying in "Granny's house," a *hospedaje* run by two ladies in their seventies, at least. They are very welcoming and the house is packed with cheap, quirky antique items they've collected over the years, but it's quite plain to see these *grande dames* are just too old to clean. It's a bed for the night though and, come morning, we're on the first bus out of town.

We've had a taster now so we can't wait to hit the trail again, and once in Puerto Natales, we head straight for the supermarket. Inspired by our friends on the Dientes trek we buy cheese. But we don't stop there. Dried tomatoes, gherkins, peas, olives and three different kinds of meat are also added to the menu. This is a ten day trek, or so says the best-known (and probably the most widely consulted) travel guide going, so we'll need a few creature comforts. Screw the extra weight. Well, actually, we intend to eat it.

The Paine circuit; day 1

Arriving at the entrance to the national park –arguably the most famous attraction in Chile– we are pleasantly surprised to find that ours is the only busload of people there. The fun begins. First up, there's an entry fee to pay. Secondly, we're asked to sign a waiver, acknowledging that we're aware of the park rules and intend to obey them. Next, there's a safety video! For God's sake, are they intending to chaperone us around the trails as well?? My misery is complete when I walk outside after completing the requirements and am greeted by another nine busloads of people. I have a feeling this is not going to be the wilderness experience we were hoping for.

Shunning the shuttle bus option straight to the start of the track proper, we consult the map and decide to head off down a little used trail, in an effort to distance ourselves from the crowd. It's a slightly longer trail, not quite as scenic, but it's flat, and we're alone.

"There's a Puma!" I yell.

"Oh, no it's not." Me, again.

Ten minutes pass...

"There's a Puma!"

"Oh, no it isn't."

And so on. Eventually Amanda starts humouring me. The next time I yell there's a Puma, she growls like one. Pleased she's playing, I increase my "sightings." Amanda, knowing how easily amused I am, continues growling all the way through the four hour, 12km trek to camp. (And continues to do so over the course of the trek, and over the next month of travel before the joke finally wears thin...for her.)

At Campamento Seron we find three things of note. The first is a scale set up to weigh your backpack. With ten days' worth of food I decide against this; I don't want to be demoralised from the start. The second thing is a LOT of tents, which means a lot of people. And they keep rolling in well past dusk- the people that is, not the tents, although the tents are part of the deal of course. And the third? One dirty, smelly toilet...to share between approximately 100 people. I go and hide in the tent, hoping it's all a bad dream.

Eventually, feeling the need for food, I emerge to cook dinner. Outside is chaos. Tents absolutely everywhere and late arrivals with no regard for anyone else, taking over established campsites. One incident in particular annoys the crap out of me as a picnic table that an Australian couple have camped beside, and therefore claimed (Tony's Camping Etiquette 101) is taken over by a large group of late arrivals who drink and talk well into the early hours of the morning. I can't wait to get out of here.

Day 2

The Australians strike back! Driven from their table the night before, they're up at dawn to make breakfast. The table has mysteriously moved during the night but rather than move it back and quietly go about preparing the morning's meal, in the spirit of true vengeance, they leave it where it is and proceed to be as loud as humanly possible. I am fondly reminded of my old boss, Mike, who would mow the lawn at 6am if his neighbours or son had a party the night before. I only wish I had a lawnmower to lend these Aussie battlers.

After commending the Australians on their performance we hit the trail, keen to distance ourselves from the hordes. It doesn't take us long to catch up with a couple who refer to themselves as "The Wrinklies;" an elderly husband and wife team from the UK who are doing the ten day circuit with a hired tent. We won't meet them again on this trek but enjoy listening to their stories over a glass of wine later in our travels. I especially like their "motivation tactics" for the younger people on the trail:

"We see people in the distance who are moving slowly, and resting a lot," Mr Wrinkly says. "But when we catch them up they seem to acquire huge motivation not to be passed by us, and start to move quicker than they probably ever have. We find it highly amusing."

I hope I'm still that active 25 years from now.

It's a perfect morning for a walk and the trail has become increasingly scenic after a pretty ordinary first day. Beautiful mountain scenery, and off in the distance, what appears to be a glacier. But as the morning rolls on, clouds start to appear and all of a sudden it's a race. Amanda (and therefore me) versus the clouds that threaten to spoil her photo opportunity of the glacier at Lago Dickson. And it's a race we win, knocking off 19 kilometres in just over four hours. That's pretty good going with about 20 kilos of extra weight. We reward ourselves with a leisurely lunch of salami, olive and cheese wraps (a vast improvement from the dehydrated food of our previous trek) against the backdrop of a glacier that runs into a fantastically blue lake, complete with icebergs.

After lunch, with only nine kilometres to the next campsite, we decide to press on. It's a decision that we'll later come to regret. Campamento Dickson is in a stunning location and although I'm sure it gets super busy, there's plenty of space to distance yourself from the crowd if you want to.

The campsite we decide to head for instead, Campamento Los Perros, pales in comparison. It's a damp site, under some trees, with some building work going on. With the weather due to take a turn for the worse, we set up camp very close to the trail. We've been told that sometimes you're not allowed to cross the pass (which is on tomorrow's agenda) if the weather is bad. We make plans to wake up before the rangers so they don't have the opportunity to stop us.

It's already cold. This becomes more concerning when Amanda goes to wash the dishes and comes back five minutes later, almost in tears, unfinished, but already unable to feel her hands. I finish up then join her in the tent with my fingers also on the verge of frostbite. After a 28 kilometre day I drift off to sleep easily, serenaded by the sound of hammering and the occasional screech of a circular saw, for which they switch the generator on especially. Heaven...

Day 3

Our early start pays off as we most certainly get the best conditions the day has to offer. This amounts to light drizzle as we start off on the 680m ascent to the highest point on the Paine circuit, Paso John Gardner, sitting proudly at 1241 meters above sea level. Unfortunately the higher we trudge, the less we can see as we encounter increasingly heavy snow. By the time we reach the top, it's a complete white out and only the footsteps of an even earlier riser are there to guide us. We follow the footprints, hoping the owner of them hasn't walked over a cliff. There's no doubt that the late starters are really going to struggle today as the snow starts to pile up around us.

On our way down it dawns on us that we are travelling right beside a huge glacier, one we haven't been able to see because of the bad weather. Glacier Grey certainly looks impressive on the map; if only we could see it so clearly in real life. With only 12 kilometres in the bag today, and after a knee-jarringly steep descent, we decide to call it a day at Campamento Paso. As soon as we stop, the cold hits us pretty hard; we retire to our sleeping bags quickly.

When we arise three hours later we are greeted by glorious sunshine and a perfectly clear day. And boy can we see the glacier now! It's MASSIVE. And we are sleeping less than 100 metres from it. We spend the rest of the day basking in the sun, sprawled out on a rock looking down on this awesome feat of nature. Going by position alone, this is the best campsite we've stayed in. Most people walk straight past it as well…which makes it even better!

Day 4

Today we hit what is referred to as the W. This is by far the most popular part of the trail. There are five star lodges, boats to ferry people to different parts of the trail and a massive variety of different kinds of trekkers. From hard-core mud-splashed trekkers like us, there to embrace whatever nature has to offer, to day walkers, carrying nothing but plastic shopping bags, who run for cover every time they see a menacing cloud; and everything in between.

Once again we start out early in an effort to avoid the crowds but that's simply not possible on this part of the trail. There are people everywhere. It's raining so we forego the next two campsites, deciding it's far better to be walking in the rain than sitting in it. The campsites are also quite expensive and are situated beside very flash looking *refugios*, or mountain huts. Walking through one of the campsites I am stunned to see the poor quality of some of the tents on display. Several look like they were purchased at toy stores to give kids something to play in. Have these people not heard of the famous Patagonian tent shredding winds?

Other than the toy tents, the rain most of the day, and the low cloud that accompanies it, the only thing we really see on this 30 kilometre stretch is the remains of a massive fire that destroyed 48 acres of the park in late 2011. It's quite a depressing sight. We roll into Campamento Italiano in a leisurely eight hours.

Sitting down for a cup of tea once we're set up, we can't help but stare at the party setting up camp beside us. A couple have turned up, carrying all their gear in shopping bags. As the large tent goes up and the tarpaulin is draped over it, we have a bit of a giggle. But when they bring out the king sized air mattress complete with hand pump, pillows, sheets and duvet, we both near wet ourselves. The astonishing thing is that this isn't out of the ordinary here.

Suddenly a blast from the recent past appears in the form of our French Canadian solo trekking friend, Annie. Considering we'd given her a day's head start she is very surprised to see us. We are secretly stoked to have caught up with the trekking terminator.

> Amanda- Let's be honest, it wasn't *exactly* a surprise to see her. We deliberately walked past two campsites to catch up to her so we'd be as legendary as she is!

While we catch up with her and someone else she's met on the trail, I pluck up the courage to do something I've wanted to do for the last three days. Say the word puma in front of other people.

"Have you seen any puma?" I enquire of Annie and her friend.

"Raaaorghhhhhhhhhh," Amanda adds.

Blank looks follow. We offer no explanation.

> Amanda- I KNEW Tony was going to do this at some stage. I also knew it would be really humiliating but the thought of his disappointment if I didn't take the bait was too much to bear so I lay my dignity on the line.

Day 5

After our victory against the clouds on day two, it's their turn today. From Campamento Italiano, there's the option of an 11 kilometre return trip up the Valle De Frances to Campamento Britanico and back. European travel in TDP. Donning the day packs, we get another early start, following a raging river heading up the valley. On the way up we're lucky to see some chunks of ice separate from the mountains they cling to and crash onto the rocks below. It's an awesome spectacle.

We also enter a trekking duel. Having passed them on day three and not expecting to see them again, we are passed by a Canadian couple in their 60s. We pass them again. They pass us again. And so it continues...all the way up the valley to the viewpoint. Unfortunately the stunningly diverse valley is not revealing its full self. Other than the occasional glimpse of a mountain peak, the best view we get is of cloud. Rather than hang around at the view point getting cold and hoping the weather will clear, we head out of the valley, out of the clouds and back into the sun, kicking the Canadians' arses in the race down.

Campamento Italiano is surrounded by trees- and completely sodden after a few days of rain. It makes no sense to us to be hanging around a damp, cold campsite when we could be walking in the sunshine so we pack up and head off. Annie, having done the valley yesterday, is making her way to Campamento Chileno so we decide to go there as well. It doesn't look that far on the map. The trek duelling Canadian team break camp before us, heading for the same place. Fully expecting to catch up, we farewell them with the usual line:

"See you on the trail."

We don't.

It's a beautiful day for a walk. Rather less beautiful are the heavy packs on our backs, and the 80-odd kilometres in our legs from the four previous days; the walk beside another stunning lake should've been a lot more enjoyable than it was. It's a hard slog.

We wind up a long day with a rewarding, but extortionately priced, beer at Refugio Chileno. Until they kick us out because we're not paying guests. This seems strange to us because they certainly didn't give us this beer for free. We're both immensely pissed off with this but, too tired to argue, we walk back out into the cold.

For the first time ever we then put up a tent on a wooden platform. The ground is so uneven around here that it seems to be the only way to get a level site. While this situation may be ideal for some tents, it's not for ours. More frustration follows but we finally get it up, sort of. We're confident that as soon as we're in it, it won't blow away. The gold-plated (spray painted) pneumatic nail gun my work gave me as a going away gift would've helped no end and I rue its missed opportunity. Just an air compressor and a very long extension lead short of the perfect solution.

We catch up with Annie, who's already been up to see the famous towers for which the park is named. We decide to get another early start in the morning, pop up the trail and have a look for ourselves, and then all walk out of the park together. If we can keep up...

Day 6

Up bright and early we start heading up the trail to take a peek at the Torres Del Paine. It's clear from the start that it's not clear at all! In fact it becomes so clear that we are not going to see anything, we turn back when we hit the final steep scramble to the actual view point. Amanda's knee is giving her grief and neither of us has the desire or the energy for another climb- especially to see nothing. I find a walking stick to help Amanda down the trail and before long her shoulder is also an issue. It was quite a big stick I guess.

> Amanda- It wasn't a flipping stick, it was a whole goddamn tree!

At least it takes her mind off her knee. We're back and breaking camp within 15 minutes and at the end of the trail, waiting for a shuttle bus out, in another hour. A smidgen less than 120 kilometres knocked off in five days and three hours.

We have completely overdone it and are totally knackered but that doesn't stop us marvelling at the guided tour groups we watch leaving the US$500-a-night, four star hotel we're waiting beside. For a start they're going to see what we saw for free today: nothing. Secondly, why the hell would you need a guide here? Even on the far less populated back part of the circuit, the trails are well marked and maintained. Quite frankly, a blindfolded llama could walk this trail. Backwards.

While we're waiting at the shuttle bus stop, chomping down on the most hideous looking, artificially enhanced hotdogs (that taste great!), our two Canadian friends turn up...and wave as they stride by. No shuttle bus for their 14 kilometre trip back to the park entrance. Our shuttle bus eventually arrives at the park entrance just as they do and we commend them on their super trekking abilities. It turns out they've knocked the circuit off in four days. We make a silent commitment to select our duelling partners better in the future.

Back in Puerto Natales, we meet up with Annie for dinner. It's my birthday and in an awesome gesture, both Amanda and Annie give me the fat off their massive Chilean steaks as a present. I am touched. We get to talking about the trail over dinner. The scenery is great (when the sun's out), but the park is overcrowded and suffering because of it. With premium price tags on every aspect of the trail, it's hard not to believe that profit rules above all else.

So, powers that be, your apparent disregard for this wilderness area is duly noted...but keep that money machine rolling.

5- The Fitzroy range beckons

After six days trekking in Torres Del Paine we're up for a bit of a change so decide to head to El Chalten in Argentina... for a little bit more trekking! On the way we decide to check out Perito Moreno glacier.

Perito Moreno is one of the only glaciers in the world that is still advancing, apparently. What a spectacular sight it is too. Our introduction to this natural wonder couldn't have been more perfect. As we walk through the trees obscuring the view I became more and more excited as I listen to chunks of ice fall and hit the water below. We emerge from the trees just in time to see a HUGE chunk of ice come away from the face and plunge down. The resulting sound is deafening. Its sheer monstrosity is a fantastic sight; I haven't even had time to take out my camera.

For the next three hours we stare longingly at chunks we think are ready to drop, only to hear a splash in the water to our left, or right. It's quite frustrating- until we hit pay dirt. Both of us hear an ominous cracking sound, turn our cameras in that direction, and see a block of ice the size of a skyscraper peel itself off the shelf and completely smash the lake below. Fantastic times a thousand!

Amanda, happy that that'll be the best of the action for the day, then curls up on a bench and goes to sleep. I take up a solo vigil, but Amanda's got the right idea.

We eventually jump back on the bus and head back to El Calafate. From there it's a short bus ride to the supposed trekking capital of Argentina.

Picture perfect Fitzroy

El Chalten, Argentina, is a town that was built in 1985 because of a border conflict with Chile. Nothing says Patagonia like a craggy, snow-capped mountain, and this place has plenty. We've pencilled in a three day trek around the Fitzroy range. As our bus rolls into town, the weather is absolutely perfect so we quickly amend our trek plans. Cerro Torre, one of the craggiest of the craggy peaks in the area is notoriously difficult to spot, by all accounts, due to constant cloud covering. Not today though, so we dump our gear in our newest home and head out to take a look.

Our quick actions bring terrific rewards. Cerro Torre. Standing 3102m high, and there's not a single cloud to impede our view. The four and a half hour trek has been well worth the effort.

On the way home I am rewarded some more with my first ever sighting of a non- cartoon woodpecker (two actually). I will develop a strange affection for these crazy little critters over the duration of our trip: their Spanish name is the same as my (former) profession, *carpintero*, which is Spanish for carpenter.

Perusing our newly acquired maps over a huge plate of Argentinean meat later in the evening, we realise that we've already done almost half of our planned route. Not bad for four and a half hours work. A chance meeting with Michael and Jo in El Calafate brought about a session involving a few bottles of Argentina's finest export, and some top tips. Travelling a bit faster than we are, Michael and Jo have *been there, done that*. They told us about a lovely little camp site at Lago Capri so, without further ado, we decide to trek out to the lake the following morning and set up base camp there for some more day walks.

With our packs full to the brim, since we only need to carry them for about two hours, we head off after a leisurely breakfast. The day couldn't be more perfect; again, not a cloud in the sky. Even forgetting the salami and the cheese, both mandatory trek items now, and making a two kilometre dash to retrieve them from the hostel fridge, doesn't put a dent in our mood.

After about two hours of hard slog we reach the lake. And what a campsite! Perfectly situated, it overlooks Lago Capri with a view towards the stunningly picturesque Mt Fitzroy.

And no one else is camping here. Perfectly dry weather seals the deal, especially after more than our fair share of soggy days in Torres Del Paine. Plenty of time to get the tent up, relax and take it all in.

The tent

A Vaude Taurus Ultralite. The best four season's lightweight tent we can afford. Weight: 2.4kg. Value: about NZ$800. Times erected, 12, including twice in the lounge at home; once, for making sure it was in working order, the second, for our going away photo shoot. Erecting it should be no problem, right? Wrong. After about an hour and a half we still don't have a place to stay for the night. For some reason the tent doesn't seem to go up the way it's supposed to. Both Amanda and I go over and over things, looking for something we may've missed. Surely we're not that dumb?!? Two hours pass and we finally rule out user error. There's no doubt about it, the tent has shrunk...or the poles have grown...Either way, we're less than impressed: *major* gear failure in the heart of Patagonia. Anger and brute force take over as we risk breakage getting things into place but finally we have a home in the wilderness. My perfect day is ruined. We think back to the Dientes trek where Amanda was taking the piss out of Michael and Jo's tent. Is this our punishment? Yes Michael, the Karma gods have struck. Luckily it's not fatal.

Day 2

We're hoping to wake to a view of the snow covered peaks of the mighty Fitzroy, sparkling in the sunrise, but clouds prevail. They soon part however, and we breakfast by the lake, taking in the magnificence of the view once again. Yesterday's tent episode has receded into memory somewhat, but it's unlikely we'll forget it; our fight with the manufacturers went on for more than six months after the event. Still, our plan for this trek was to stay put for three days, so I'm happy the offending tent is vaguely functional and we can get on with enjoying what we're here for.

Day two's excursion is a climb to the Mt Fitzroy view point at Laguna De Los Tres. With the weather holding, we eagerly set off, very happy with the lighter weight of our day packs. We're really starting to notice our increasing fitness levels now and the climb to the lake is knocked off pretty quickly. Unfortunately the clouds have rolled over by the time we get there so we don't get to see the mountain close up in its full splendour. It's still pretty good though and we bask in the solitude for a good 45 minutes before other people show up and we continue on our way.

Next on the agenda for the day is a lunch stop at a hidden glacier. It's flat, easy going until we hit a turn-off, then it becomes a rock-hopping exercise which gets harder and harder as the rocks get bigger and bigger. We actually go under some. It's particularly frustrating for Amanda with her shorter stride, but we eventually reach our destination and are able to sprawl out in the sun at a lake, complete with icebergs. The glacier isn't the best we've seen but the solitude of the place makes up for that.

"Shall we go for a swim?" I joke.

"Why don't you swim out to that iceberg and lay on it pretending to be a walrus so I can take a photo?" Amanda suggests.

As I'm contemplating this challenge, the iceberg flips over before our very eyes. That's as good an excuse as any to wimp out. But the seed is sow and to save face I announce I'll be going for a swim in the lake beside camp.

After a two hour "lunch" we decide to head back to base. It's turned into another glorious day and the two hour trek back to camp is the perfect warm up for my planned swim. We approach the lake and I'm down to my undies in a flash. After a quick look around to make sure no one's about, I wade out, and before the cold changes my mind, dive in. There's no ice in this lake but parts of my anatomy tell me it's still damn cold. After I surface and turn around to head back to shore I happen to glance past a bluff to the next beach along...where a tour group of about twenty people is looking at me and pointing!

Not enjoying the attention I'm out quick smart and re-clothed, happy I didn't opt for a skinny dip- I imagine they're happy about this as well. As we walk past them on the way back to camp some old ladies ask me to do it again so they can take photos. I pretend not to speak English. We reach the safety of camp and I go and hide in the tent.

Day 3

In the morning with the weather still clear, we're reluctant to leave. A perfectly dry camp site is a pleasure we've never experienced, thanks to the ever-present, heavy dew of the New Zealand bush. After the absolute soaking we got at Torres Del Paine we're happy just to be in the wilderness and dry for a change. With the ground we covered whilst carrying only day packs, we've done all the walking we planned for the area so we decide to hang out at camp, comfy on our Fitzroy viewing platform. Amanda reads and I, my book finished, am on Puma Patrol. I'll spot one yet...but maybe not this time. I start to wonder if my technique is a little sub-standard: lying in the sun, getting up every half hour to half-heartedly scan the wilderness.

During the day a ranger stops to admire our tent. Walking over to introduce himself, he then asks if we want to sell it. We tell him of our drama trying to put it up two days earlier and, strangely, he's still interested. We're curious as to why and, when we press him on it, we find out that it's near impossible to get a quality tent in Argentina. This news brings the realisation that a replacement could be out of the question for a very long time so, as much as I want to get rid of the piece of shit, it looks like we're stuck with it. Reluctantly we decline his offer.

The next day, since we've brought only enough food for four days, we pack up camp and head back to town. Straight home for a shower? No; we spot a bakery on the way so we pop in for a couple of pastries and a hot chocolate. Music by Kiwi band The Black Seeds plays in the background; a reminder of home in the heart of Patagonia.

After freshening up back at the hostel, we hit town for the obligatory large plate of protein and a few beers, dropping our clothes at the laundromat on the way. Its name: The Maori Laundry. I kid you not.

After a few more days in this chilled out little town, it's time to press on. The question is, do we take a 24 hour-plus bus ride to Bariloche like most travellers seem to do from here? Too easy! This is how *we* roll...

The bus
First up is an uneventful 40 kilometre bus ride down a gravel road to Lago Del Desierto. And it sure is desierto...ed! You can count the buildings here on one hand.

The boat
Generally when we're doing multi-day treks, we store gear at our hostel base to make our packs a bit lighter. Not so with this journey. It's one way. Everything we own in this part of the world is on our backs, plus food. That is why we opt for the ferry ride to the end of the lake rather than the twelve kilometre trek beside it.

We make ourselves known at the ferry "terminal," a small shack beside the lake.

"When does the boat leave?" Amanda asks in her best Spanish.

The answer is vague; I can see that by the guy's body language. Unsure of what's happening, we sit down to wait. Amanda passes the time taking on a local child in a game of football. I watch over them to make sure there are no "hand of God" incidents in this England V Argentina game.

Eventually tiring of football, Amanda makes the mistake of showing her new football buddy a game on her iPhone. With half the battery gone and no idea when she'll be able to charge it again, she manages to pry it out of his reluctant hands a couple of hours later, just as the boat captain turns up.

Captain Reluctant takes us out onto the jetty and points up the lake to our destination. Ah yes, water spouts. It doesn't look like we'll be going anywhere just yet! The Patagonian wind is finally introducing itself to us, after about a month of relative calm. We decide to check out "town" and the local camp site. Town consists of a grumpy old man selling hot dogs. As I walk into the campsite and past him to check out if it's a good sheltered place to camp, I get what sounds like a complete bollocking... in Spanish. Backtracking, I realise I've inadvertently started walking down a trail leading to a glacier and this man's demanding money for it. Not likely pal.

With town done we decide to buy a hot dog off Mr Grumpy and are charged 50 pesos. A bit on the steep side but hey, there isn't much competition around here. We pay up and eat up. While we're eating, Amanda gets chatting to a couple of Argentinean tourists on a day trip from El Chalten, and finds out they got charged 30 pesos. It's then that we decide there's no way we're camping at Mr Grumpy Thieving Bastard's campsite and we head off to look for a friendlier, less legal site in the surrounding bush.

With one or two sites earmarked we head back to the jetty. It's started raining now and Captain Reluctant says we can go and wait on the boat out of the rain if we want. Not long after that, the first guy we talked to (who turns out to be the first mate, and a very nice guy) gives us the news that we were pretty sure was coming all along. The boat isn't going today. Lacking sea legs, or in this case lake legs, I look down to the next water spout forming and am quite relieved. Amanda tells First Matey about Mr Grumpy Thieving Bastard's overpriced hot dogs and our reluctance to go and camp there.

"You can camp behind my house if you want," First Matey offers. "You can even walk on a trail from the back of the house to go and see the glacier he tried to charge you for! Or, you could sleep on the boat."

With the wind howling and the rain falling it's a no brainer. We opt for the boat. Private room with ensuite and totally lake front with a view to the snow capped mountains. How much? Free! There's a down side though. The lake is rough and the boat's resting loudly on its mooring. And there are no curtains. All the same, we feel we've chosen the best option and head to bed, hoping that this delay is only going to be one day. The border closes in six days for winter and it's a long backtrack.

We wake up to another glorious day in Patagonia; the wind has miraculously dropped and there's no doubt we'll be on our way today. Sure enough First Matey comes out to share the good news. In recognition of his kindness (and on behalf of our backs) we decide to give him half our food. We're in such a remote place, things must be hard to come by out here, and we briefly entertain the notion that he may've never even seen half the stuff we give him...until we find out he's from Buenos Aires.

Finally the boat is off. Half way across the lake we sneak a peek back at where we've come from and are rewarded with a crystal clear view of the north face of Mt Fitzroy. It's awesome to be saying goodbye to this majestic mountain without interference from the cloud cover of the last three or four days.

The trek

With border formalities out of the way, we ask the friendly officials which way it is to Chile and they show us the start of the trail. As I said earlier, the town of El Chalten was created in 1985 as a result of a border dispute with Chile. To strengthen their claim Argentina decided to populate the area. Chile may well have had the same idea but first they had to build a road. If it was anything like the road building I've seen, one person would've worked and four would have watched the worker. It's probably no surprise that they fell short of their goal. Today's border is situated where the road ends.

First though, there's six kilometres of uphill trail to walk. Even after a good rest this turns out to be by far the toughest part of the trail for us, our legs and backs complaining at every step. The extra weight on our backs is entirely responsible. Maybe not so much the actual weight (-they're probably only five kilograms heavier than usual), but the knowledge of that weight. Mind games.

> Amanda- Yes, although my pack was only about a third of my body weight it felt almost as heavy as I was!

Approaching the border we come across our first signs of the continuing military presence in the area. A crack squad of Argentinean Commandos? No. A group of soldiers who have walked out to the border for a bit of sightseeing. They offer a cheery hello before returning to their photo shoot. A little later we are passed by two Chilean soldiers coming back from a recon mission into enemy territory... Or, a few beers with the Argentinean border guards.

Finally reaching the border, we drop the packs and sit down for a bit of lunch, deciding to eat in Argentina. After lunch there's one more thing to do...I jump to Chile...then back to Argentina...

"Chile! Argentina! Chile! Argentina!" I shout as I jump from country to country for the next five minutes.

"How old are you?" Amanda asks.

Waving goodbye to Argentina we finally commit to the Chilean side, and to the 14 kilometres of gravel road between us and our destination, Candelario Mansilla. It's downhill, so it's welcome relief for our legs. Not our backs though.

As we walk through this historical place, I try to keep my mind occupied by imagining the military activity that must have gone on here in the early eighties. What are those large clearings beside the road every so often? Obviously tank bays! We come across an abandoned Chilean airfield and I temporarily forget the weight of my pack and pretend I'm an Argentinean plane dive bombing the enemy. It's my coping mechanism for pain I think, being stupid. Coping with me being stupid is Amanda's coping mechanism, whether she wants it to be or not.

Halfway to our destination we are passed by a Chilean all terrain troop carrier. Or to be more precise, a tour company doing some recce work, in a crazy little six-wheeled vehicle, for a trip they plan to advertise. Unfortunately there isn't room for us in their ATV and they continue on their way. Not much further along, we come across three mysterious sacks in the middle of the road and realise these must've fallen off the back of the truck, so to speak. We're loaded enough already to pick these up as well so we're forced to leave them where they are. But we do the math and quicken our pace: with three less sacks on the ATV, there could now be room for us, or at least for our packs.

Unfortunately, when they realise they're missing some gear, the ATV crew decide to send one guy back to look for it. We meet him along the way, and the ATV half an hour further along, waiting. How one guy is supposed to carry three sacks is anyone's guess. After we tell them we saw their errant sacks, they obviously realise this as well and turn around reluctantly to follow him. We see them for the last time as they tear past us again; there's still no room for us- or our packs. Our helpfulness hasn't been rewarded.

Approximately four kilometres from our destination a 4X4 stops. An Argentinean family have hired a local driver to pick them up at the border rather than attempt the walk with two small children and all their luggage. A sensible decision. Sadly there is no room for us in this vehicle either, but they do offer to take our packs to the immigration building. Amanda has her pack off and in the car in a shot! I'm a little more reluctant; will this be cheating? I started with my pack and that's how I want to finish; there's not that far to go now. But, before my brain can finish processing these very thoughts, my pack is also off and mysteriously finds itself in the vehicle as well. After the initial guilt it's like Christmas! The remaining four kilometres are by far the most enjoyable part of the day.

Once we're done with border formalities, the friendly 4X4 driver asks if we'd like him to take our bags to his place. We've done a bit of research on this one and already know that this tiny array of buildings populated by one family is the only accommodation option available so it's another no brainer, and we set off at a leisurely pace for the final two kilometre walk. With recent memories of the shrunken tent still weighing heavily on our minds we decide to take a dorm room rather than camp. We are then invited to share the warmth and the facilities of the house that the Argentinean family have rented. Luckily they speak English and we chat long into the night. When Amanda decides to bring up my border jumping antics:

"He did that too!" The woman laughs, pointing at her husband.

It must be a man thing.

We have some time to look around the place in the morning before the ferry leaves. Only one family lives here permanently. When the border closes for winter the population plummets from 14 to six. It's a self-sufficient and surely tough life here, especially in winter. They slaughter their own meat, get their power from a small stream with a water wheel and grow what veggies they can. Therefore I am somewhat surprised when I help the old woman carry supplies up from the wharf, to find that their only purchase from what could be classified as civilisation around here is four two-litre bottles of Coca Cola! Oh, and they still have cable TV. When there's power.

Another boat and bus

Split up the middle by the border, this lake is Lago O Higgins on the Chilean side and Lago San Martin in Argentina. It's the same lake for God's sake, is it really necessary to confuse the issue? During summer a ferry takes day-trippers out to view the O Higgins glacier at the end of the lake. This ferry is our ride to Villa O Higgins. It's a weird little boat that looks strangely ineffective as it motors through rough conditions. I start wondering if there is a way I can walk there.

By 5pm when it's our turn, conditions have thankfully improved and we settle in for the four hour journey. Along the way, we stop only to pick up four dogs, two goats, a camera crew and what appear to be a couple of actors. As ya do. We manage to get some onscreen time ourselves as the cameras keep rolling once everyone/thing is aboard. Much to the actors' disgust, the goats seem to be the star of this show.

At 9pm we dock and chaos erupts. All sorts of different vehicles have arrived to take people seven kilometres up the road to Villa O Higgins. We end up in a ten seater minivan.

"I can take you anywhere you want to go in town," the driver says. "But I can highly recommend the eco-camp just outside town because I am the owner."

What the hell, we haven't camped for a while so, with darkness already upon us and rain setting in, we agree to go and check it out. It's a nice set-up and we decide to stay, having temporarily forgotten our shrunken tent. There's only one thing worse than putting up a shrunken tent: putting up a shrunken tent in the dark, while it's raining. I go to bed grumpy again.

6- The Carretera Austral

The Carretera Austral is a road built on the orders of infamous Chilean dictator Augusto Pinochet in an effort to show a presence in the area during the Beagle border conflict with Argentina. The road itself is a clever way to connect and unite previously cut off communities to the rest of Chile. The last 100 kilometres to Villa O Higgins were completed in the year 2000, long after the conflicts were resolved and Pinochet was history. There are plans to go further but at this stage Villa O Higgins remains the end of the road.

Rumour has it 1000 people live in Villa O Higgins, our starting point for the journey up this remote road. I would dispute that, especially seeing as it's the end of the tourist season. We see maybe ten people who look like locals. Restaurants we breakfast at beg us to come back for lunch and we have to knock on the door of the shops to get them to open. The shops offer packets of biscuits and other assorted highly-processed food...and the odd half-rotten tomato. Here begins our long search for Brian. More on Brian later.

Cycling the Carretera Austral is the thing to do it seems. Our rustic eco camp, situated just outside town in a lovely bush setting, is populated almost exclusively by cyclists. Two French guys we meet tell us of the trials of cycle-touring over an absolutely fantastic gourmet pizza they've cooked for everyone. Their stories pale in comparison to the solo female unicyclist. Yes, you read that right; she is unicycling from Ushuaia, Argentina to Santiago, Chile. *Unicycling.*

> Amanda- Solo, no support crew...carrying all her gear, tent included.

All three cycled the border crossing we walked. Cycling through wonderful scenery, freedom camping in remote Patagonia at the end of the day? I can certainly see the appeal.

The first leg of our journey is a bit of a side trip, veering off the Carretera Austral to Caleta Tortel, a tiny village only connected to the outside world by road in 2003. The bus ride there is spectacular as well as thrilling. The narrow gravel road winds its way high above lakes and rivers, and as the driver attacks the next blind bend with complete disregard for his own -or our- safety, I start to wonder why life jackets aren't "under the seat in front of you" on this bus. I'm sitting "cliff side" with a view to the water and rocks below, not for the faint hearted. I get some great views...straight down at times.

Our bus ticket clearly states, Villa O Higgins to Caleta Tortel but it comes as no surprise to us when we're delivered to the turn off, twenty two kilometres from town. We've done our homework and this is normal; it's no longer financially viable for buses to travel to Caleta Tortel directly from Villa O Higgins. Or maybe they just think it's fun dropping gringos off in the middle of nowhere then watching them wondering what the hell to do next.

We've never hitchhiked before and this obviously isn't the place to be starting. In the five hour bus ride to get to where we are now; I didn't spot a single vehicle on the road. And it's raining. Rather than sit around in the rain waiting for a vehicle that may or may not come, we do what we do best, and start walking. It's a wonderfully desolate part of the world to be walking through but once again our full to the brim packs make us pray for transport.

One and a half hours later, "hitchhiking" is no longer fun.

"I hope this place is worth it," Amanda grumbles.

"*I* hope there's a bus out of here!" I respond.

15 minutes later, a vehicle! He waves on his way past. Five minutes later, another vehicle. Rush hour! This one stops and we finally become real hitchhikers, sitting on the back of a ute in the pissing rain with only our packs for comfort.

> Amanda- ...As we're shaken half to death on a rocky gravel road with a driver who thinks he's on the motorway!

With only a brief stop to remove a dead dog from the road, the last 13 kilometres are knocked off in good time.

Caleta Tortel

Caleta Tortel is the weirdest town I've ever seen. There's a large wooden walkway built around the waterfront, made out of the local export, the Cypress tree. Then there are a whole lot of smaller walkways heading into the hills, where people who didn't arrive here in time to secure waterfront living now reside. The only road stops at the edge of town.

This town exists for timber milling. It seems like nearly everyone has their own portable mill. Even the local playground is made entirely out of timber. Unsurprisingly, the slide doesn't seem to have been used...ever.

Receiving an estimated seven metres of rainfall per year, Caleta Tortel isn't really somewhere you'd want to stay too long. We walk a few trails in the area and hang out at the local plazas, seeing how many people we can actually get to stop and enjoy them: there definitely seems to be more plazas here than there are people. After three weeks we finally procure the tools we need to perform a bit of surgery on our shrunken tent, sawing fifty millimetres off one of the poles so everything fits; time will tell if it retains its integrity. Tent surgery completed, it's time to press on. Unfortunately when we eventually find an open sign on the shop selling bus tickets, the next bus out of town is sold out. We secure tickets for the one after, two days away.

When we leave, we almost feel like locals, having stayed twice as long as other, more organised outsiders have done. We wave at Unicycle Girl as we bus off in the other direction; she is only five kilometres shy of town and a bed for the night. After four days on the road she's probably too knackered to notice.

Three more hours of gravel bring us to the thriving metropolis of Cochrane, population 3000. Unfortunately for us we've arrived on the Thursday before Easter. The place is a ghost town and getting information for potential treks in the area, a nightmare. Not wanting to hang around a place with very little appeal any longer than we have to, we book the first bus north, pinning our trek hopes on a tiny little town, three hours up the gravel road. Cochrane's redeeming feature? A regular bus service out of town!

Trekking the Patagonian ice fields...nearly!

Within ten minutes of arriving in Puerto Rio Tranquilo, our packs are stored and we're off on a boat trip on the lake, heading to the star attraction in this area, the marble caves. The caves are interesting but the really striking feature of this area is the mountains. We're also a hop, skip and jump away from the Northern Patagonian ice fields. And we can't wait to get back to town to start researching.

Said town is a small place and it doesn't take us long to track down the man we're looking for. But he doesn't give us the news we wanted. Being the end of the season, demand for tours has waned considerably. We take photos of his maps with the thought of going it alone, and spend the evening at a lake-front restaurant, mulling over our options.

Without the right gear for full-on glacier travel, the first decision is a no brainer. We need the tour guy's gear- and also his experience. The second decision takes a lot longer. At US$500 a day for a minimum of eight days, we'd have to fork out a whopping $4000. Ok, so it doesn't take that much longer: we can travel for well over a month on that kind of money; seems a bit of a waste to throw it all away on eight days.

Trek plans dashed we decide to press on. There's no bus station in town so we simply walk out to the main road early the next morning and wait for buses to materialise. The first one does: it's full. The second one is also full, as is the third. Fourth time lucky? No. By this time there are eight of us gringos waiting to escape this place, including one Canadian guy who has been trying unsuccessfully for the last two days now. It's Easter Monday and it seems the whole of Chile is going home, via Puerto Rio Tranquilo. Except for the local who's just spotted a cash cow.

"I have a ten seater minivan, I charge 9000 pesos per seat to take you to Coyhaique" Mr Entrepreneur says.

"There's only eight of us," someone points out.

"Then you pay for other two seats and we go now," Mr Entrepreneur states.

"We're not going to Coyhaique. How much to Villa Cerro Castillo?" Amanda asks.

"9000 pesos."

"But it's only halfway to Coyhaique!"

"9000 pesos, you pay for two more seats, we go now."

Mr Entrepreneur just got a name change. We decline Mr Greedy's offer and apologise to the six others waiting, knowing they have to either find four more travellers or pay for four more seats now. After four hours of waiting for a bus we head back to the hostel and book another night.

The least we can do now is go out and see the glacier we would've been climbing on the first day of our trek. The $500-a-day guide rents bikes for considerably less so we decide to ride the 12 kilometres out to the glacier. Our first bike ride in six months is even harder for me, recovering from a cold. I'm so knackered I don't even make it to the lake- according to the map, a mere six kilometres from town. In fact, I barely make it up a hill to *see* the lake. I calculate that to get to it I'll have to go down again, which means up on the way back. I decide we have a better view of the lake from the top of this hill. It's a good snooze spot and downhill most the way home.

Walking home after dropping the bikes off, we bump into Mr Greedy again. He doesn't seem to be our friend anymore, not surprising since we probably just cost him 90 000 pesos. That'll teach him.

There are two seats on the first bus we wave down the next morning and we're soon on our way to Villa Cerro Castillo for a bit of trekking, at a lot less than $500 a day.

Our first impressions of Villa Cerro Castillo are not good. The majority of the buildings look like they're held together by gaffer tape and there look to be more dogs than humans. The recommended accommodation in the latest edition of our go-to travel guide turns out to have been closed for over a year and there isn't much else to choose from. We end up choosing a hostel on what could loosely be described as the main drag. It's a bit of a dive and is filled with road workers, which is an excellent incentive to get organised and get out into the wilderness.

Incentivised, we get an early start. The road workers started earlier so I help myself to the breakfast they left on the table, deciding they should have cleaned up after themselves if they didn't want something like that to happen. As an afterthought, I leave them a bottle of beer I've been carrying.

Cerro Castillo trek; day 1

Our goal for day one is to visit Campamento NeoZelandes, a mere 16 kilometres away. It's a Kiwi pilgrimage. Heavily laden and map-less, we wander out of town. Unfortunately our plan hits a bit of a hiccup when the refugio a kilometre out of town is closed for the season and we can't store our excess gear there. It's a long trudge back to town to find storage.

Fearing the wrath of the road workers who probably have a very good idea who ate their breakfast, we decide to go and check out the other place in town. They are more than happy to take our excess luggage off us after we commit to a night's stay upon our return.

A couple of extra kilometres under our belts already, we stop off and buy a two-litre bottle of coke. While we're drinking this outside the visitor's centre (which closed in February) I notice a pane of glass missing in one of the windows. Amanda could fit through there easily. We still don't have a map and really have no idea where we're going. I move in for a closer look. Much to Amanda's relief there's nothing in there worth slipping in for, unless we want to take a chair and a desk with us. We resign ourselves to the fact that we'll be map-less, finish the coke and set out once again.

As we're leaving, something catches my eye. Why on earth I stop to look at a crumpled up piece of paper in the gutter is a complete mystery, but my curiosity is rewarded. I have just found a map! A very crude one on the back of a pamphlet welcoming you to Villa Cerro Castillo, but beggars can't be choosers. We stride off with a new found confidence, now more sure of our direction.

The first eight kilometres down a gravel road are thankfully flat and before ya know it, we've found the start of the trail. We turn off the road, heading into the mountains. Before long we start the steep climb and are soon struggling. It's a hot day, and in a cruel twist of fate, the river that the map said we'd be walking beside is at the bottom of a very deep gorge. Amanda's also feeling a bit under the weather and can feel another cold coming on. A tough day just got tougher.

After a very hot and dry two hours, we're finally low enough to have access to the river as the trail crosses it. I dip my bottle in and drink my fill not even bothering to filter it. The awesome taste of water from a cold mountain stream renews my energy and I'm ready for the final push to Campamento NeoZelandes, four kilometres away. Instead, we cross the river, walk up the bank and find an unexpected bonus.

A cool little campsite right by the river –complete with picnic table- makes it an easy decision to drop our packs and set up camp. Not marked on our map, this unexpected site is a godsend for Amanda who's fading fast. But like a true Kiwi (resident), she won't let anything stop her making the pilgrimage four kilometres further up the trail to our original destination. We set out after lunch and, with only our day packs, it's a whole lot easier.

We are well into the trees now and the stunning colours of a Patagonian autumn are everywhere. It spurs us on and keeps the cameras clicking, all the way to a piece of New Zealand history, in Chile.

Campamento NeoZelandes is named for a small mountaineering party from New Zealand that established a base camp here in 1976, and proceeded to make several first ascents of some of the surrounding mountains. And speaking of mountain climbing, Cerro Castillo looks pretty doable from here, with scree slopes three quarters of the way to the summit. We've done enough climbing for the day though, and are content to wander this beautifully lush valley for a few hours, immersed once again in pristine wilderness.

With darkness approaching we make short work of the four kilometres downhill back to our base camp, cook up a huge feed, then hit the sack early.

Day 2
With no vegetables to lend a helping hand, Amanda's immune system is losing the battle and cold number five digs its claws in. While revising our options over breakfast, I hear a twig snap and turn to see three girls walking out of the forest, not actually on any trail I've been able to find. The leader sees me, gives a huge smile and waves. Her pace quickens, the others are hot on her tail. Suddenly she slips, and falls heavily. I look away, unable to

suppress that awful instinct to laugh at another's misfortune. But there's no stopping her, she's on a mission, back on her feet in a flash.

"PEOPLE!" She screams as she approaches.

It's a Yoshi moment: these three Israeli girls haven't seen another person for five days- and have failed to find a single established campsite on the entire trek, camping wild every night. They tell us the camp we're heading to doesn't exist. We bask in their delight for a while before they set off again, after we've pointed them in the right direction.

Although I find it highly unlikely that "our next campsite doesn't exist", this new information, coupled with Amanda's ill health, is enough to warrant a change of plans and we decide to stay put. Not one to sit around feeling sorry for herself, Amanda suggests we do the steep climb up to the glacial lake at the base of Cerro Castillo. We're thinking that day packs will make the climb easier. They don't.

> Amanda- Wow, did I suggest that? I'm pretty damn hard core aren't I!

This is one tough climb, on a track more suited to goat than human. Amanda is struggling for breath and stopping often. I don't even have a cold as an excuse as I struggle to keep up with her demon pace between rests; she appears to have retained her usual hill climbing theory of "its best to get it out of the way quickly." Every step we take confirms what an excellent decision it was to leave the big packs behind.

Climbing out of the trees onto a rocky plateau we rejoice, thinking we've made it to the top. But no, the increasingly difficult-to-follow poled route goes straight up the side of a large rocky moraine- a pile of material transported to its present spot by past glacial movement. We trudge on, picking our way around massive boulders.

Finally we reach another plateau, and the end of an incredibly difficult 1000 metre climb. (We later find out that the trail rating changes from medium to difficult if you don't travel in the accepted direction, like us.) Is it worth it? Hell yes. We're no longer in the mountains; we're *ON* the mountains. Only Cerro Castillo soars higher than us. It's a beautifully clear day and we can see all the way to Argentina from our vantage point.

A short walk across the plateau brings us to what we came here to see. And we're not disappointed.

We sit down for lunch, and a well earned rest, overlooking an absolutely stunning glacial lake which is fed by the glacier clinging to the side of Cerro Castillo. A perfect outlook.

In fact, it's so perfect we don't want to leave after lunch. Not wanting to miss this golden opportunity, glacier or no glacier, I whip my shirt off for a spot of sunbathing. Amanda once again thinks she's married a crazy.

As we're leaving we spot two guys way off in the distance, at the bottom of the gully, heading in the direction of our camp. Thinking they may have missed a marker pole, we yell and yell but they are too far away to hear us. As we walk along, I realise that they're following a poled route as well. I wonder if it's the old trail someone warned us about. Or were *we* on the old trail? What the hell; we decide to head back down the same way we came up and, although still a difficult trail to follow at times, it's awesome to be going downhill. We are back to camp in half the time it took us for the outward journey. I reward myself with a swim in the ice cold river.

About an hour later, two Israeli guys we met as we got off the bus in Villa Cerro Castillo walk into camp. As we all share a packet of biscuits around the picnic table they show us the video of their descent; we clearly chose the best track down. Theirs is a very scary looking scree run, not dissimilar in gradient to day four on the Dientes track. Even though it's a fast descent, we still beat them by a full hour. The rest of the trail must've been truly awful.

Israeli Guys have done the full trail (and found ALL the campsites) which we didn't do for logistical reasons. When we met them the first time, we were getting off the bus and they were trying to get on, unsuccessfully. The last we saw of them, they were trying to thumb a lift to the start of the trail, some 40km away. With the park's office, and trek information, a further 25km, the trail isn't really designed for people travelling north. Israeli Guys' weather window was closing and, with a day's head start, they figured they'd just beat the bad weather to town. We wouldn't have. That's as good an excuse as any!

Israeli Guys eventually head off to spend the night at Campamento NeoZelandes and we settle in for our last night in the bush, Amanda heading to bed at 6.30pm after a torrid day; me, sitting at the picnic table in the dark, listening to the sounds of nature...and hoping that sound behind me wasn't a puma...

| Amanda- Raaaorghhhhhhhhh! |

Day 3

Our trek out the next day is memorable for two reasons. The first is that it's all downhill. The second is that not long after we hit the road, we're offered a lift by the farmer's son, a happy chap named Washington. Another godsend. The wind's picking up and the rain is close behind. Although I would've liked to see how fast we could knock off a wind-assisted 8km along the road back to town, getting soaked to the skin doing it is *not* part of the plan. We'll be happy to have a roof over our heads tonight. Washington drops us off at the hostel and we are reunited with our stored gear...and shown to our room.

Whilst there's a roof -of sorts- over our head, the windows in our room are 'interesting', to say the least. Rather than a window that opens the usual way a window opens, the frames on these ones have been nailed into place (although just with a single nail each side). If you want to open the window, you just push the bottom of the frame and it tilts. The Patagonian wind is howling through the half inch gap between the wall and the frame. This causes our door to flutter in the wind- perhaps because our door is a shower curtain.

While the owners bravely attempt to supply us with something they're not altogether familiar with, a hot shower, we learn that CONAF, the park's administration outfit, refuses to supply Villa Cerro Castillo with trek information, since it wants people to start from the other end, and so pay the entry fee. Fair enough I suppose. We later find out from Israeli Guys, who've also made their way here, that the pay booth, like everything else in Patagonia outside January or February, is shut.

Finally showered, after a two hour effort by the owners to give us lukewarm water, it's time to head over to the local bus restaurant for the mandatory post trek protein boost. We dig into two plates of what is widely regarded as Chile's national dish, *chorriana*. Fried meat, eggs, onions and chips, covered in gravy. Heart attack material. Later, we can actually feel our muscles repairing themselves. And our hearts working overtime to pump the fat around our bodies.

Back in our room, we decide to hit the sack early. Amanda, fully enclosed in puffer jacket and sleeping bag, jumps into a bed made up with every blanket we have. I jump in too, but forego the sleeping bag. As we lie in bed listening to the wind howl, the shower curtain flutter and a door (someone else's) squeak, we realise we'd rather be in the bloody tent...shrunken or not!

> Amanda-I'd like it noted for the record that the shower curtain was doing more than flutter!

Coyhaique

Bright and early the next day we board a bus to Chilean Patagonia's major settlement, Coyhaique. One hundred metres down the road, a surprise. After a touch over 400 hundred kilometres of gravel road and eight hours of bus travel on it, we hit paved road! It is bliss, and a sure sign that we're heading towards something that resembles civilisation.

Sure enough, we roll into town and get off the bus in the pouring rain. We seek shelter in a cafe. Yes, a cafe! It sells hot chocolate and has wifi! We have no problems staying there until the rain stops and we can search out some accommodation. The rain lasts hours; we were prepared to wait days.

Our next surprise is the supermarket. It is big! It has fresh produce! A rare occurrence in this part of the world. Civilisation, a supermarket, fresh produce...could almost be described as a religious experience. Our long search for Brian is over.

We have just found broccoli! Patagonia has a severe vegetable shortage and we're sure the lack of fresh greens has been responsible for our poor health since we got here. Amanda especially has been craving broccoli. She buys the biggest broccoli she can find, I pack it into my bag and we hit the road, needing to press on, having fallen well behind schedule. We decide to name our latest travel acquisition Brian...at least until we can find a kitchen worthy of his presence.

A medical emergency

Arriving early to the Coyhaique bus station we sit down and wait, watching bus after bus load up and leave. And they're big buses, at least 30-seaters. It'll be great to get back on a bigger bus after the series of minivans and 4X4s we've experienced so far. My mind envisions the extra leg room happily.

Our bus finally arrives and it's a bloody ten-seater. How cruel. The loading process is, as usual, long and drawn out as the driver tries to fit eight passengers, and all their gear. Amanda and I are travelling light, a backpack each. The locals aren't.

After a lot of effort, stacking bags around the passengers who grabbed their seats early, the driver motions for us to get in. We slot into the seats just beside the door and we think we've got lucky with a spare seat beside us. We think wrong; two late arrivals see to that. The driver squeezes their luggage in, the lady squeezes into the back seat and an old guy barely manages to climb into the van and sit beside me. He looks about 108.

"He'll be lucky to survive the trip," I whisper to Amanda.

She hits me; ok, maybe it wasn't a whisper...But I feel safe in the knowledge that there are no English speakers amongst this lot. They don't even speak Spanish down here; they speak a weird Patagonian dialect loosely based on Spanish! No locals that we've met have even known where New Zealand is, let alone possess the ability to interpret a Kiwi accent. I'd bet that half these people have never even heard of Santiago, their own capital city.

With a fully laden vehicle, and zero room to move, we settle in as best we can for the six-hour journey. At least we're still on tar seal. This small comfort lasts about an hour whereupon the seal suddenly stops and is replaced by, without doubt, the *worst* piece of road in Chile. We're almost swallowed whole by some of the pot holes.

About four hours into the journey, everyone except the driver, Amanda, and I, is asleep. Amanda and I are engrossed in our mp3 players as we look at the scenery out the window, when Old Guy beside me decides to start encroaching on my space. I've had this little tussle before, on planes mainly. Yep, I'm the guy who puts his arm on an arm rest and won't move it for the duration of the flight, so you don't even get a look in. Me, sitting beside someone like me, can make for an interesting tussle, each of us constantly looking for an opening to win back said arm rest. I'm very good at this game Old Guy; it pays not to mess with me.

But Old Guy isn't the pushover I anticipated. After ten minutes, I find myself on the back foot of this little tussle and break game rule number one, making eye contact. I'm completely shocked by what I see: Old Guy seems to be dying right there before me, having some kind of fit. Not speaking a word of Spanish, I franticly tap the man in front of me on the shoulder until he wakes up, and point. The driver pulls over and the entire bus swings into action.

His daughter informs us that Old Guy is a diabetic and has travelled all the way to Coyhaique to seek treatment, only to be turned away because nothing can be done for him. We hand over our juice to a woman who's identified herself as a nurse and she shoves it down his throat. Old Guy doesn't respond so the decision's made to high tail it to the nearest town, still an hour's drive away, to seek medical treatment. The road is still heavily potholed so 'high tailing it' is actually only going about 5kph faster than before. His daughter massages him and talks to him continuously, trying to keep him conscious. Being at ground zero I decide to get in on the action too.

"Hang in there bro," I say, giving him a squeeze on the leg.

I'm pretty sure it's because of this that he makes it.

The road improves slightly and the driver guns it, managing to reach the town of Puyuhuapi in half the expected time. He's phoned ahead of course, but the police are still trying to track a doctor down as we arrive at the still-closed local hospital. Everyone piles out of the vehicle to wait and the nurse rushes off to a neighbour's house to borrow a cup of sugar. Blocked in by Old Guy we have no other option but to stay in the vehicle.

Finally the local medic arrives and opens up the hospital. He fetches a wheelchair, the other passengers help Old Guy to it, and we are finally free. He looks slightly better as he's wheeled into the hospital but that's where today's journey ends for him and his daughter. Did he make it home? I can't answer that, but his odds weren't good...

After about an hour we're back on the road and, with no further incidents, we finally reach our destination, La Junta. Everyone else is continuing on so, having bonded with these people through a very unpleasant situation, I wave as we walk off, offering a friendly *buenos dias (*good morning/hello*)*. No, my Spanish hasn't improved at all.

The arse end of nowhere

Being the only ones to get off the bus should've been the first warning. La Junta is, for lack of a better word, shut. Not lacking a few better words, it is a shit hole! Our initial plan was to find a bus out to the remote coastal village of Raul Marin Balmaceda. But that's a tough ask when you can't find the bus station, or a single helpful person.

"Where do we buy bus tickets?" Amanda asks the local mechanic, in the only place in town that seems to be open.

"Why are you here? It is April," the mechanic replies rudely.

The visitor's centre here closed at the end of February. Obviously that doesn't account for this dickhead's behaviour, but I think I know what does. There was a statue of Augusto Pinochet in this town until recently. Half the population voted to get rid of it; I'm guessing we just met the other half.

For two days we sit in our room watching movies on TV, while the rain pours down outside. Rather than boil Brian up on our little gas cooker, we eat the reasonably priced meals provided by the hostel owner. We are the only guests after all, and probably her only source of income at this time of year. We make a pact to stir fry Brian in a real wok at the first opportunity we have. It's what he would've wanted.

When the rain finally stops we hit the town and find some stores that are actually open. We find another tourist information centre with a phone number to ring after hours. Amanda calls the number excitedly, hoping maybe we can actually do what we came here to do. Someone answers.

"Hello! We were wondering if you could come down and open your store so we can have a look at the tours you offer."

"I'm sorry," the voice says. "I live in Santiago and only open the store in January and February"

Patagonian summer has thwarted us again. We begin to wonder if we will ever get out of this town.

One of the four businesses we find open a day later is a restaurant so we decide to head out for dinner rather than eat at the hostel. It's fate. Here we meet by far the happiest and friendliest man in town. Not only does he tell us there is a bus leaving tomorrow, he phones the company and tells us we are his family and are entitled to "local" seats. We'd heard rumours that sometimes locals are prioritised on buses and, as we've found out, buses are few and far between. As an added bonus he tells us where the "bus station" is. As we head back to the hostel we keep our eyes peeled and, by some miracle, spot a sign about the size of a piece of A4 paper taped inside the window of a house. Fancy not spotting that...

Finally, a bus out of this arse-end-of-nowhere. It's a 6am departure so Amanda sets the alarm on the phone. What we're about to find out is that the Chilean Government has changed the date of daylight savings and has yet to inform the internet...

We catch an early night, blissfully unaware...

Nek minute...

"SHIIIIT!" Amanda screams. *"GET UP TONY, ITS TEN TO SIX!!"*

All hell breaks loose. There is no way we are missing this bus. It's taken three days to find it and God only knows when the next one out of town is. Problem one: thinking we'd have plenty of time to pack in the morning, we've left our stuff lying around the room. What follows is a record-breaking speed pack.

"Have we forgotten anything?"

"I don't know!" Amanda replies, and with that, she's out the door running.

Not me. Unlike the rest of my body, my bladder has decided to wake up so I'm a quick toilet stop and a quicker room check behind her for the 400 metre dash to the bus station.

Heavy pack bouncing on my back I close in on Amanda as she starts to tire.

"You go on," she gasps as I draw up beside her.

"OK."

Three steps later I'm completely knackered as well and also slow to a walk. The last 100 metres is more of a shuffle. You try waking up, packing, buckling on a heavy pack and running 400 metres in ten minutes.

It's bang on six when we turn the corner and spot the bus. We made it! And it's a big bus too, at least a 30-seater! Approaching it, we see another vehicle parked beside the bus. It's a six-seater 4X4 with five people already in it and, surprise surprise, it turns out that this is our transport. Right now, neither of us cares; we're just relieved to finally be escaping La Junta. It was close.

Amanda's pack fits in the boot but Amanda doesn't quite fit in the back seat. She will be spending the duration of the 90 minute journey on a fellow backpacker's knee. I, on the other hand, get the front seat all to myself. Well, apart from my pack. I don't know who's got it worse, but I can't feel my legs after 40 minutes.

Villa Santa Lucia, where we are dropped off, is the end of the Carretera Austral for us. We're turning east now and heading for Futaleufu on the border with Argentina. It's also a one-horse town, a fitting place to end an at times frustrating journey up this road. Travelling out of season on public transport wasn't exactly ideal but it got the job done in the end. As we settle in for the six hour wait for the bus to Futaleufu, a dog strolls up and pisses on my backpack. It is the final indignity.

We've been carrying Brian for almost a week now and he's starting to go a bit yellow. Luckily in our hostel in Futaleufu, we have not only a kitchen, but a wok as well. This is where Brian's journey ends, in a wok filled with salami, carrot, onion and soy sauce. We are able to continue because of his sacrifice.

7- To pole or not to pole?

Cerro Hielo Azul, El Bolson

After catching a ride over the border into Argentina with North American Nate the hostel owner (who's taking his dog to the vet in Esquel), we find ourselves in the hippy town of El Bolson. It's famous for its micro breweries and handicrafts market, but we'll get to that later. It's also famous for its trekking and that's why we are here.

To pole or not to pole? That is the question.

After hearing Annie rave about them, Amanda has decided she wants trekking poles, hoping that these will help with her recurring knee problems. I'm not entirely sold on the idea but with a 1000 metre climb on the first day of our trek, I'm willing to give it a go.

Day 1

With gear stored and backpacks at their 'trekking weight' we make our way down to the hire store to check out pole options. After about 30 minutes of waiting for it to open, we decide we should probably read the sign on the door again. Yep: "Open at 10am." It's 10.15 now and Latinos aren't known for their punctuality.

"I wonder if this owner lives in Santiago," I joke, thinking back to La Junta, Chile.

Amanda gets nervous, reads the shop sign again, and discovers that winter opening hours are from 4.30pm until 6pm. Short day! Off to a great start, again. We flag down the next taxi to take us to the trail head...pole-less.

Mr Taxi Driver drops us off, with some precise and expert direction:

"Go over that swing bridge and turn right."

We're on our way.

As we approach the swing bridge I survey its condition with some trepidation. It's in a pretty bad state of repair, but I've seen worse. Actually, no I haven't. Crossing it's like playing a game of hopscotch, needing to land on boards that'll actually support your weight rather than on one of the rotting ones. Except that we're playing with full packs on, 20 metres above a river.

Happy to make it across alive, we follow the trail right, walking along the river's edge.

20 minutes later we come to a "private property" sign. Something's obviously not right here. Consulting our rather rudimentary map for the first time, I realise we're on the wrong side of the river and have no option but to backtrack. With an estimated seven hour trek to the first camp, on top of our late start, we can't afford another mistake like this. I curse myself for listening to a taxi driver who's probably never set foot on these trails.

Finally on the right side of the river, we start making good progress and things start falling into place on the map. Our only delay comes when I spot a bamboo grove and nature provides us with a couple of trekking poles each. Time to see what the fuss is all about.

Eventually we come to another swing bridge, according to the map the right one this time. And it makes the one we crossed earlier look incredibly safe. After debating whether to just rock hop across the river, we decide a rotting swing bridge is the lesser of two evils here, and another game of fully-laden aerial hopscotch ensues.

Almost straight after the bridge the trail turns away from the river and we start our climb. For four hours we tramp through strangely silent forest, the silence broken only rarely by the occasional...cow. We arrive at the refugio late afternoon, just in time for beer o'clock.

El Bolson is a big hops growing area. All the refugios here brew their own beer. It's one of the things that fascinated us about this place when we read about it and we had to come and see it for ourselves. One bottle of home brew is enough though; we depart the refugio for the nearby campground before we get too comfortable. I've carried the damn tent all the way up here so I intend to use it. We grab an early night; tomorrow we become mountain climbers.

The poles pass the *Day One: Uphill* test. Are they responsible for our quicker pace and the fact that we seem less fatigued? Or are we just getting fitter? Amanda is already a convert; I'm still on the fence.

Day 2

The main attraction in the area is the local glacier, a short climb from the camp ground. There's also a trail that continues to the summit of 2150m high Barda Negra which is supposed to give you views clear into Chile on a good day.

Last night we decided to climb this mountain if the weather was good. Exactly eight minutes after that decision was made, the heavens opened and the rain didn't stop for 12 hours. During the night I didn't feel well and, unable to sleep, I eventually moved to the cooking shelter so as not to disturb Amanda with my misery. There, I brewed some tea and listened to the rain pouring down outside, and I knew that all chances of climbing our first peak in South America were gone.

By 10am the sun's back out and hope returns. We leave camp, crossing a river that wasn't there yesterday, and head off in the direction of the glacier. They proved their worth yesterday but today, the poles turn out to be more of a hindrance on the steep rock-hop to the glacier. As far as glaciers go, this one turns out to be pretty shit anyway. It's a beautiful clear day in Argentina but Chile is covered with cloud and because of that, and gale force winds up here, we decide not to climb Barda Negra. The poles seem even less helpful on the downhill leg back to camp.

After lunch we break camp and hit the trail to the next refugio, an estimated five hours away. It's great to be surrounded by the colours of autumn on a beautiful sunny day in Patagonia. But we're both feeling pretty tired as we finally reach the top of another small climb. As luck would have it, we spot a perfectly placed refugio and decide to pop in for a quick home brew before knocking off the last three hours to our intended campsite.

Half an hour later, we finish our beer and hit the trail. Well, not quite. We manage to walk about 100 metres from the refugio before putting up the tent and calling it a day...and then heading back for another beer. After a month in Chile, Amanda is thrilled to be talking to an Argentinean, whose Spanish she can actually understand; her and the hut warden talk up a storm. She learns he's from Buenos Aires and lives in this refugio for six months of the year, brewing beer and winding down from big city life. She also discovers that we're the first Kiwis to ever visit the place...since he's been living here anyway.

Eventually, we retire to the tent and, as we settle back into nature, we realise what an awesome little place we've discovered on this unscheduled stop. Surrounded by mountains, with Cerro Hielo Azul standing the proudest of them all, and overlooking a lake with beautiful rusty coloured autumn leaves on the trees all around.

Without doubt the second best campsite (after Lago Capri, El Chalten) so far, made even better by the fact that ours is the only tent for miles. Oh, and we can pop back to the refugio for a home brew if we want. Our decision has left us with a bit to do though...seven hours to the road tomorrow, then around 15km back to El Bolson, hopefully by bus.

Day 3

Deciding against another beer before we set off, we hit the trail early knowing we have a big day ahead of us. It is this day that the poles come into their own. The two-hour, very steep descent to a river leaves us with a relatively flat 12km walk out to the road. Well, that's what the description in the travel guide says anyway.

Based on that information I suggest a time trial. Two hours out to the road, an average speed of 6kph. Amanda accepts the challenge and races off, setting a cracking pace. Bamboo poles fly as I race to catch up. And we go at it like that...all the way to the first hill. No worries, we've read there's only one and race up it barely skipping a beat. I tuck my poles under my arms pretending I'm a downhill skier as we fly down the other side. Then we get to another hill. OK, wasn't expecting this... but we make short work of it anyway. By the sixth and largest climb of the day I am *highly* pissed off and am swearing at the travel guide for the misinformation. Throughout our travels, this travel guide, well-used and known the world over, will become a nemesis of sorts.

At the top of this hill we finally see a sign: *"THE END"*. Another game of aerial hopscotch over the worst swing bridge yet, then another climb, and we actually reach the end, knocking off the undulating 12km in a rage-driven two-and-a-quarter hours.

Neither of us can be bothered waiting for a bus so we call a taxi from the local camp ground. As is tradition, we leave our trusty bamboo poles at the start of the trail so someone else can make use of them.

I've totally toasted myself, as usual, so the next two days are spent in bed getting over cold number four. With Brian the broccoli a distant memory we have resorted to vitamin tablets to supplement our deficiencies. It's all a bit late for me, though I do manage to get in a few raspberry flavoured beers before we leave.

According to Amanda, the handicraft market was a bit shit.

Nahuel Huapi, Bariloche

Three hours down the road is Bariloche. My continuing cold hasn't stopped us from planning another trek here. Besides, it's nothing a good strenuous walk and some fresh air won't sort out, I'm sure. Bariloche is similar to Queenstown, New Zealand in many ways. It's built beside a lake, has mountains all around, and if you're looking for adventure sport, you'll find it here...somewhere.

So, there must be a place that hires trekking poles right? Wrong! After a frustrating search Amanda has had enough. She decides to buy some, and off we go shopping. Eventually she settles on some bottom of the range Lekis. I take a look at the price. What the hell, they're cheap as chips, I may as well get some too. Until I discover the plastic handles. I am cursed with notoriously sweaty hands, so I doubt these will work for me. But I've more or less committed to purchasing; I can't back out.

"How much are the next best ones?" I ask.

"We don't have any in stock, but we do have the range above that one," replies the shop owner, the master of the up-sell.

Suddenly, after being on the fence, I am potentially about to buy poles that are twice as expensive as Amanda's. I don't want to make that kind of commitment and now I'm wishing I could forget the whole thing.

"Just buy them!" Amanda commands, sensing my reluctance. "You'll need better ones anyway because you're so heavy," she adds.

Offence replaces reluctance, but it has the desired effect and we finally leave the store with our poles.

When we head to the park office the next day, we find that part of the five day circuit is closed due to heavy snow. This reduces our trek to three days. Not ideal but we'll take what we can get.

Day 1

We get yet another of our poor starts. Checking out of the hotel, we head down to the bus stop for our ride to the start of the trail. An hour later we're still waiting, blissfully unaware that the bus is now running on the winter timetable while we've been looking at the summer one. We have come to realise that the locals really only talk about two seasons in Patagonia: January and February are summer; the rest of the year is winter.

Eventually we realise our mistake and recheck the schedule. OK, there's a bus due in ten minutes. It is at that moment that I find I still have the hotel room key in my pocket. And off I sprint. Luckily the bus is late and I arrive back in time to catch it.

On the bus we catch up with Steve and Katrijn, a Belgian couple we met briefly, way back in Caleta Tortel, Chile. Michael from the Dientes trek coined the term 'treek,' or trekking geek, to describe people like us. Well, in Steve and Katrijn, we have more than met our match. Much more organised than us, complete with specially ordered maps for the regions they want to explore, there is almost no part of Patagonia that they haven't seen. They even have a pack raft in case they fancy taking to the water. Super treeks. True adventurers. 'Nutters' is also apt. We may be starting in the same place as they are today but that's where the similarities end. They're heading off the established route on an eight day through-trek to El Bolson. Most people take the bus.

As we clamber out of the bus we can't help but look up at the ridgeline we'll be walking along soon, a mere 1500m climb away. No time like the present; off we go, striding purposefully, towards the chair lift. To our utter dismay, it's closed. Still not 100% fit after my cold, I now face the proposition of the largest climb we've done to date. In my state it could kill me. But super treek Steve comes up with a plan featuring a gondola and I am saved!

The gondola drops us off 200 metres below the ridgeline and with the help of our new poles we make light work of the remaining climb. We bid farewell to the Belgians, who have decided to stop for lunch, and walk off along the ridge, taking in the glorious panorama on a beautiful sunny day.

It isn't long before we leave the safety of the ski fields behind and head back into untamed wilderness.

"There's no way that's the way," says Amanda when I point out the direction we're heading.

Much to her horror, it is. Traversing a trail with a sheer 600m drop to one side is replaced with two hours of rock-hopping as we climb and descend, avoiding impassable bluffs along the way. For Amanda, this kind of trekking is right up there with her other pet hate, mud. Like mud, I love this shit! It's slow going though.

Amanda has put her Lekis away to climb but, having paid twice as much for mine, I aim to get value for money. And that ploy pays off when I discover their main advantage over bamboo poles; wrist straps. I can let go of the poles completely and have them dangle from my wrists as I climb. Bonus.

Eventually, we come to a t-junction. To our left, about an hour's walk away, is a refugio. To the right, about three hours away, a "closed" campsite. How do you close a campsite? We've reached a point in our Patagonian trekking lives where we've decided to completely disregard the various rules laid out by the park authorities here. We're sensible, environmentally conscious humans after all. And it doesn't appear that any of the locals follow the rules. Our decision at this t-junction takes us left towards the refugio. We're both short on water and there's a lake on the way.

After a short descent we drink our fill at the lake, and then continue on our way. Following the trail towards a large drop-off, we gaze down into the valley below, spotting the refugio in the distance.

"Bugger that! Let's camp here," I suggest, realising we'd face an extensive uphill battle in the morning just to get back to where we are now, in order to continue on the circuit.

Amanda agrees wholeheartedly and we set about putting up the tent in a spot with a readymade defensive wall, at the base of Cerro Catedral. Someone else has had the same idea before us.

The sun goes down very early here and, surrounded by rock walls at nearly 2000m in elevation, that means cold. We're tucked up warmly in the tent by 6pm, wondering what tomorrow will throw at us.

Day 2

Heading back to the t-junction on the ridge we continue on down the main trail. It's not long until we start our descent into the next valley.

"There's no way *that's* the way," says Amanda in a moment of déjà vu; I'm pointing pretty much straight down a rock face this time.

"It is."

"Oh, shit."

An hour and a kilometre later, we reach the valley floor, happy that we'll be able to get some actual walking done as we head up it.

It's not long until we pass the "closed" campsite, reluctantly. It looks like a great little spot.

At the head of the valley there's just the matter of one more steep ascent and we'll be as good as at Refugio Jacob. This one really has me struggling though, still not having fully shaken that lingering cold. But I get there in the end. We sit down for a rest and a bit of lunch at the top, and work out our plan of attack. Should we skip the refugio? We've heard there's a very good wild camping site down the next valley. If we go for this option, the bonus is that it'll make tomorrow's walk out shorter. It's early in the day and I'm going to feel shit whether I'm walking or sitting around in a refugio. A short day tomorrow, and a warm comfy hotel at the end of it sounds pretty good to me!

Without further ado, after another steep descent, we're down in the next valley. After two hours we're regretting the decision as we still haven't made camp. But luck is on our side, in the form of the refugio warden, on his way back from town.

"We're looking for a place to camp," says Amanda.

"There's a nice little spot by the river, about half an hour's walk more," the warden replies.

Apparently even the wardens disregard park rules.

"Look! There's a La-Z- Boy!" I exclaim as we approach the site.

Sure enough, some bright spark has built a reclining chair, less the cushioning and leather of the commercial model. I promptly slump in it, totally spent after a hard day. Amanda sets up camp while I take in the idyllic surroundings, in a more supervisory role.

Once camp's set up, Amanda, deciding to attend to the call of nature, wanders off into the surrounding bush. Not long afterwards I also need what I commonly refer to as a "bush poo" and wander off into the trees myself. Finding a nice, secluded little spot, I start digging a hole and find myself practically on top of a very fresh looking deposit. It seems Amanda and I have chosen the exact same place. I recover, re-cover, and walk off to find "the men's". I don't tell Amanda until three days later. She is horrified.

Day 3

An uninspiring 10km walk to the main road, where we wait ten minutes for a bus, and we're back at the hotel by 12.30pm. We pop into the park office to let them know we're back safe and they start asking questions about our route.

"Is there snow up there?"

"No."

"Was the refugio warden at Jacob?"

"No, we walked past that refugio intending to camp illegally further down the valley. We did meet the warden on the way down the trail though and he told us a great place to wild camp."

We didn't actually say that. But it's clear that the park office relies heavily on people like us for their information, people who've bothered to actually get out there. We wonder now if the original trail we wanted to do was really snowed in, or whether someone saw a little bit of snow and reported it to the park officials, who closed the trail from the safety of their office. I guess we'll never know. But I do know one thing: I'm a pole convert, and proud of it.

8- Adventures in Pucon

Having had a taste of adventure, Argentinean style, we decide to see what's on offer on the Chilean side. Our bus brings us to Puerto Varas, which, apparently, is going to be "the next Pucon" (Chile's adventure capital). It still looks a long way off and we simply don't have the time so we decide to head to the current Pucon the next day.

Pucon, the current version, is even more like Queenstown than Bariloche was. Apart from the active volcano that is. Within minutes of arriving at Hostel Elementos we've signed up for the number one attraction in the area, climbing the 2850m Volcano Villarrica. That's in two day's time so we can fit in a bit of a warm up. Maybe a bike ride or some white water rafting. You know, something not too strenuous to get the blood flowing...

We rather surprise ourselves, then, when we find ourselves starting out on a trek the very next day, a trek that includes a 1000m climb to a lookout point. But, we don't want to tire ourselves out for our upcoming summit attempt so we turn back about an hour from the lookout.

At a barbeque the hostel puts on for its guests that night, it becomes apparent that, probably for the first time on our travels, we're in a hostel with people more our own ages. Well, Amanda's age anyway. We meet Elsa from Belgium. No surprise really, we've met her five times before. Amanda even sat on her knee on the ride out of La Junta. We wonder who is following who.

We meet Danny and Karen from the UK. Karen has us in hysterics as she tells us all about her sister who works for a piles call centre. Also, having travelled from the north, in less developed countries, they tell us how they came to rely on an international fast food chain for a few creature comforts: using the McWifi, while sitting in the McAircon, after having a McShit; this became their standard practise. After a long conversation with Danny I'm almost convinced to do the Inca trail in a tour group. He brushes aside my concerns about being teamed up with ignorant, arrogant and annoying people and says they had a good group and could go at their own pace.

We will see...

Johnny and Sarah from Australia are a wee bit younger but up for a bit of an adventure, so we forgive them their youth. In fact, their story about the Torres Del Paine circuit trek completely wins the night, narrowly edging out that of the piles hotline.

They'd never trekked before they decided to do the ten day TDP circuit, so they took part in an induction course put on by a tour company on the ins and outs of trekking. There was one thing this course didn't cover though.

"We'd never so much as farted in front of each other," Sarah tells us, setting the scene.

It is obviously a new relationship.

"Neither of us realised you were supposed to boil the water on the trail and, by day three, we were both very ill," she continues. "Suddenly, from not even farting in front of one another, we were squatting by the trail, side by side, with each other and our backpacks for support, experiencing explosive diarrhoea. A real relationship builder."

I pick myself up off the ground; having fallen off my seat laughing. Johnny just sits there, smiling.

We also chat to various people who've already done the climb. Difficult is the word most often used to describe it. Amanda does a bit of research online:

"Two people died on our climb," one review says.

"Group was too large, very unsafe practises," says another.

"Our tour company took us up in shocking weather rather than refund our money, very dangerous."

And so on.

Luckily an extensive online search fails to find any bad reviews for the company we've signed up with. Pablo the guide, who's made himself known to us, assures us we're in a small group and the weather looks good for the morning. He is confident we will not die.

I am also confident we will not die but, as we join the group in the morning, I'm not so confident I won't need to kill someone. Enter stage right *the* most annoying person I have ever met. Being completely full of herself and loving the sound of her own voice are this woman's most apparent qualities. It's only been 12 hours since

Danny attempted to persuade me that a guided trek was a good thing. One complete moron on my first ever guided trek has put paid to that, in the space of five minutes.

Our first decision of the day is whether to take the chairlift or not. We have to pay for this privilege, of course, but it will put us 400 metres higher than we are now- and it looks quite a boring walk. It could also mean the difference between summiting or not if we're to believe what others have said about the difficulty of this climb. At this point, the group will split up so it's a simple decision in the end: we'll do whatever Annoying Woman *doesn't*. She decides to walk; we can't get to the chairlift quick enough. Pablo, the lead guide has the same idea, leaving his 2IC with the talker.

At the top of the chairlift Pablo announces:

"Congratulations, you have now made it further than most Brazilians who attempt this climb."

He goes on to tell us that some don't even make it to the start of the chairlift, even after paying between 30 000 and 40 000 pesos to make the attempt.

There are no more easy rides from here though and Pablo sets off up the volcano with our group of five close behind. It's not long until Amanda asks him to pick up his dreadfully slow pace, and with the agreement of the group, he does. With four seasoned trekkers in tow, plus one guy who's determined to keep up rather than lose face, Pablo tells us it's good to be going at a decent pace for a change.

I suppose climbing this mountain every day, at the pace of the slowest person in the group, could lose its shine somewhat. And after hearing about the Brazilians (lack of) effort, I can only imagine how dreadfully slow that is. But it's clear that Pablo loves it up here, regardless of the pace. We pause for a time to admire a condor soaring before pressing on towards the glacier.

Glacier travel. I've done it once in health-and-safety-conscious New Zealand, where ropes and ladders are used to traverse the most dangerous areas. But this is South America. After travelling here for more than three months, I'm pretty sure there aren't any words for health-and-safety in Spanish.

Walking poles away, crampons on, and ice axes at the ready, we're taken through the "self-arrest technique" at the start of the glacier. If we fall, this technique will be all that stands between us and possible death, or at the very least, serious injury. We all agree it's a good idea to spend a bit of time on it. Ten minutes later we continue on up the glacier. The main thing we have learnt? Don't fall.

> Amanda- It's worth noting here that this part of the ascent is where most deaths on this mountain occur, with people losing their footing on the ice and sliding over a sheer 600m drop...

After only 2 ½ hours, we don't quite believe it when we hit the summit. We've found this 1000m climb incredibly easy. We walk to the edge of, then peer into, the steaming crater...where three people fell to their deaths after the snow gave way on a winter climb. Their bodies were never recovered. Then we have lunch on a cliff edge where Pablo saw two people blown over the edge by the wind only two months ago. They did recover those ones. Needless to say, we stay well away from edges...preferring to watch members of the larger groups jockey for positions there, putting themselves at risk for the sake of a photo. I don't know the circumstances in which people died up here, but from what I can see, there are some pretty stupid people in the world.

Coming down is a lot quicker, and much more fun! Strapping on our bum protectors we head for the snow slides, a series of chutes in the snow. The first couple are pretty tame and Pablo shows us how to control our speed and how to stop with our ice axes. The final slide is the big daddy. It's not long before I'm tearing down it, completely out of control. It's AWESOME fun! But there's still the small matter of stopping that needs to be addressed. I am the bowling ball, the two people that have gone before me are the seven ten split...and true to form I pass straight through the middle of them, eventually coming to a halt about ten metres on. I've used all my strength to finally stop myself; my arm feels like it's about to fall off.

"You need to work on your technique," Pablo says, smiling.

I'm not the only one. A thoroughly pissed off Amanda walks down the final chute. She's not been able to get any speed going whatsoever, resorting to rowing with her ice axe on the first two slides. On the third, and steepest, of the slides, she couldn't move at all.

"It's ok for you," she says, as she finally makes it down. "You're heavy."

> Amanda- the truth is my arse was just too wide!

The second reference to my excess weight in a week? I let it...slide.

We clear the snow fields without further incident; we clear the glacier without incident; and after a very fast scree run all the way to the car park, we can finally call ourselves volcano conquerors. All this in less than four hours. Thank God for that: Amanda can finally go to the toilet. It's a busy mountain with not a lot of privacy...

The next day the heavens open and the volcano disappears from sight. This puts paid to the four day trek we planned to do in the area but we're not done adventuring here yet; there's much more defying of death to come.

What do you do in the pouring rain? Go white water rafting of course...on a river in flood. Along with Amanda and me, Danny, Karen, Johnny, Sarah and Elsa all sign up. There's too many of us for one raft so the numbers are made up by friends and family of the guides, and two boats hit the river.

Inexplicably, the Spanish speaking guide joins Danny, Karen, Elsa, Amanda and I in one raft. Elsa speaks a little Spanish, Amanda is still struggling with the Chilean pronunciation and the rest of us are, well, deficient. The other boat, with the English speaking guide, carries mostly family and friends of the guides, i.e., Spanish speakers. Johnny and Sara are the exception. We wonder if a bribe has changed hands.

No worries; it's pissing with rain and the river's in flood; what could possibly go wrong? We've been given a comprehensive safety briefing, after all. Not! The first few minor rapids pass without incident as the guide, already thoroughly enjoying himself, steers us sideways and backwards through them. We quickly realise he's all about the fun. Good, that's what we're here for. But the next rapid is a biggie, grade four plus; now it's really down to business.

We hit the rapid and just like that, we're all out of the raft and trying to swim in 100 metres of churning water. All except Amanda that is; as the raft overturns, she climbs it like a monkey, clings on for dear life and manages to stay in once it rights itself. As does the guide, who is now laughing his head off. All I've managed is rearranging Danny's nose on my way out.

> Amanda-No way was I going in freezing cold glacier fed river water in the middle of winter!

    The guide ascertains that a grade four rapid is not the safest place to be taking a swim and sets to work, with the help of his able assistant Amanda. Having managed to grab the side of the raft, I am the first one ready to get back in so he gives me a helping hand. Meanwhile Amanda's holding onto Karen and Elsa who've also made it back to the raft. Danny seems to have almost got himself back in, but he can't quite make up his mind, and clings on, half in, half out. Then he appears to make a decision and goes in for another dip. Photographic evidence later shows that Elsa is responsible for that "decision;" her efforts to get in the boat actually drag Danny back out. We're still in the rapid. I'm lying flat, trying not to fall out again, while the guide's pulling Karen back in. Danny gives her a helping push and separates himself from the boat in doing so.

He goes down quite a large drop unaided, disappearing from sight briefly, but eventually makes it back to the boat where Amanda and the guide grab him again. I'm at the other end of the boat and make a grab for Elsa.

Try as I might I just can't get her into the boat on my own. With no other options I simply cling onto her and wait for help to come. It finally does and the whole crew are reunited back in the boat...just as the rapid ends. About 90 seconds have passed.

We carry on, paddling hard just to keep warm after our unscheduled swim. As we approach the next big rapid the guide gives us a new instruction. Until now it's been (paddle) forward, back...stop. Now he introduces "*piso*." Apparently, this is Spanish for floor. When he yells "*piso*," we are to crouch on the floor of the raft and hang on.

We approach the big rapid.

"*PISO!*"

After our first experience in the rapids, we're all on the floor before the guide spits out the last syllable. All except Amanda that is...she stands to get a better view, wondering what all the fuss is about, looking down on us thoroughly drenched mere mortals.

> Amanda- We hadn't even reached the real rapid and you were all cowering in the bottom of the raft like a bunch of babies!

Happily, we come through this one intact.

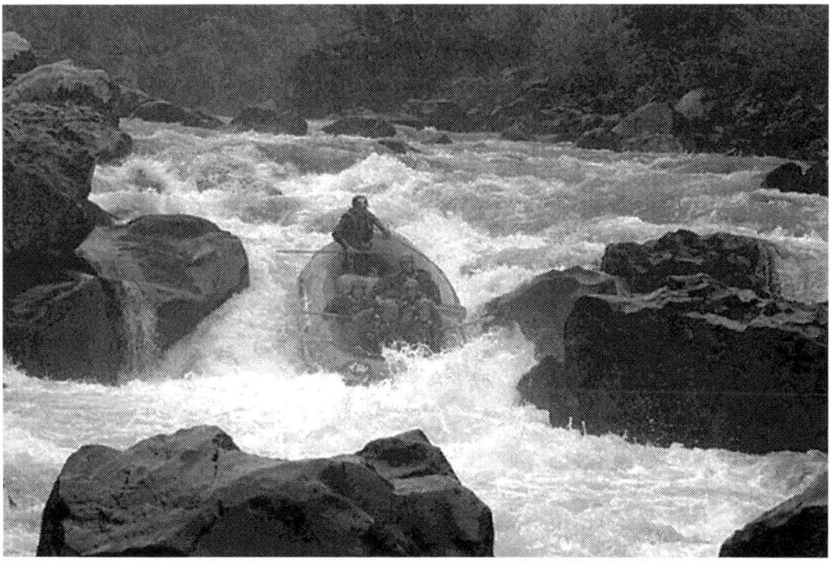

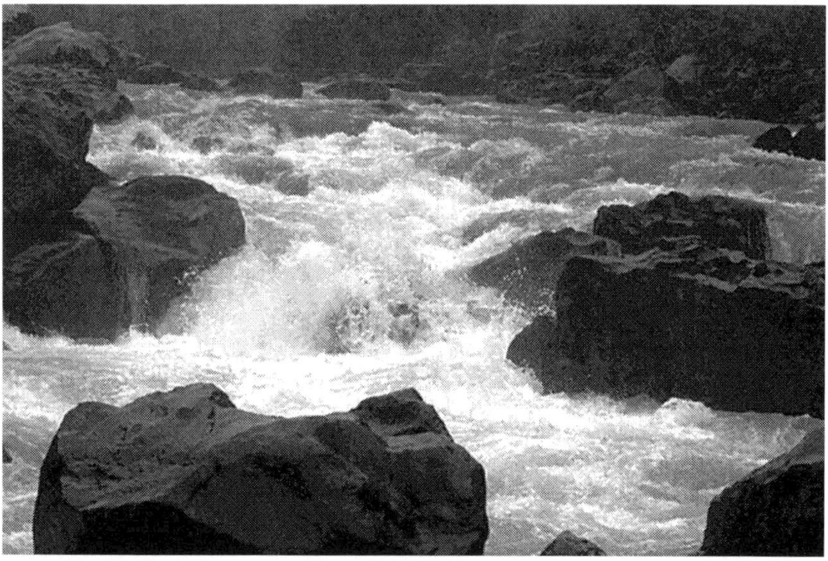

"Why the fuck no *piso* last time?" I demand of the guide.

The bastard understands me and starts laughing hysterically, again. Everyone else agrees I have a valid point.

Next up, a grade six rapid. Amanda is keen to run it but the company is not so keen to take a bunch of novices through. The guide tells us he'll take the raft down himself while we walk around. As I'm walking, I take a sneak peek through the trees and see the guide walking beside the river with a rope tied to the empty boat. It doesn't look that bad. We walk through the bush for a few 100 metres more, then head back out to the river...where we witness one of the kayakers who are with us run the rapid. What I couldn't see from the bush is the five metre waterfall the kayaker shoots over. Impressive! I'm pretty happy not to be swimming through that one.

Our rafts are parked just on the other side of the pool at the base of the waterfall. I wonder how on earth we're going to get to them. The English speaking guide apparently reads my mind:

"You jump from here and swim."

Without further ado I walk to the ledge and hurl myself off the three metre drop into the freezing water below. Everyone else follows suit; half of us have already been swimming once today anyway; we can't really get any wetter than we already are. Amanda hesitates- she's still more or less dry. Plus, she's never done a jump this high into a river before. But it's only a slight hesitation; with a crowd looking on, there's no way she's going to be the only one not to do this. She takes the plunge, and resurfaces with a smile a mile wide. Later, she tells me it was actually a grimace.

> Amanda- Yeah! I couldn't breathe the water was sooo cold. It was horrific!

Elsa takes a lot longer, dreading the thought of being in the river again, but is finally coaxed over the edge and we're once again back in the rafts and on our way.

With one more major rapid to go, we "*piso*" pretty damn quickly and make it through without incident. Suddenly the guide yells "*piso*" again. I'm on the floor in a flash, wondering why. Everyone starts waving. What the hell is going on? It turns out he yelled picture.

Through the last minor rapids the guide reverts to his form of fun again, aiming for and hitting rocks; going down rapids sideways and backwards; and doing 360 degree spins for no apparent reason. Is he trying to tip us out again? I wouldn't be surprised. He tells us it's his third time down the river today. I tell him his driving hasn't improved much. More hysterical laughter follows...

9- The lone cactus

Argentina just got cheaper. Having recently discovered there is a black market for US$ (or blue market as the official website calls it) we stock up in Santiago, Chile and jump on a bus across the border to Argentina's wine capital, Mendoza. Having made the decision not to head back to Buenos Aires, we decide to change enough money for our remaining time in Argentina. And off we go looking for the money changers. We walk a while and wait for the inevitable...

"*Cambio.*" The magic word, whispered by an innocuous looking pedestrian.

Amanda the negotiator swings into action.

"We want to change $US1000, what's your best rate?"

"8.8 pesos."

We've been officially getting around 4.2 for our New Zealand dollar, making it around 5.5 for a US dollar. It sounds like a great deal, but we've done our homework, checking the "blue" rates on the website.

"9.5," Amanda counters.

She settles on 9.3.

There are five cops standing in close proximity to the negotiations that have just taken place. Do you think that concerns the blue market guy? Not a bit. It's clear the cops don't care either.

We're more concerned with bringing out $US1000 in full view of Joe Public. Luckily Mr Blue Market has an "office" which just happens to be the first cafe he spots. After a quick word with the owner he ushers us to a vacant table. Once seated we swap wads of notes, and I take my time looking through 93 hundred peso notes for counterfeits. With no idea what I'm looking for, all I'm doing is handing back the occasional random bill and asking for a replacement. Amanda judges his reaction carefully. Mr Blue Market seems above board and we have given the impression we're streetwise. Transaction completed, we all shake hands and walk out of the office.

"That must be what a drug deal is like," Amanda says once we're back out on the street. "It was awesome!"

With pesos acquired for the remainder of our time in Argentina, and after sampling a bottle or two of Mendoza's famous wine, we leave town, heading north in search of a warm up trek before our next major undertaking.

Cerro Wank, a mountain beside the tiny pedestrian-only town of La Cumbrecita, sounds like it fits the bill perfectly. What red-blooded kiwi male would come all the way to South America and *not* climb it? One showing slightly more maturity than me I guess, but the potential for innuendo is just too good an opportunity to miss.

La Cumbrecita, nestled in the hills and with no traffic noise, is the perfect place to chill out for a few days. Which is just as well, Amanda is fighting off cold number six.

With her bed-ridden, it's up to me to acquire food for our upcoming expedition. My shopping trip is going well until I find that the eggs are kept out back and I actually have to ask for them. I try an English/Spanish combination, asking the shopkeeper for... eggs *por favor*... That doesn't work. I wait for the shop to clear out a bit and start making clucking noises. He just looks at me strangely. In a last ditch attempt, I go with a full-on chicken dance. He walks out the back, gets my eggs...and is still laughing when I leave the shop. Win! Who needs Spanish when you can speak chicken?

> Amanda- I was embarrassed and I wasn't even there!

After a couple of rest days, Amanda is feeling a lot better and we're ready for our summit attempt. Already at quite a high altitude, it's only actually a 300m altitude gain...so more of a hill really. We start off slowly, working up to a steady pace. Amanda is still a bit crook so I give her a helping hand. As we approach the climax, our excitement builds. After 45 minutes we are at the top, standing erect, breathless, but fully satisfied. Cerro Wank; what did you expect?

> Amanda-I can't believe you've included this! Luckily mum won't get it...

Nevado De Cachi

The four hour journey from Salta to Cachi, on quite possibly the worst bus in Argentina, a place known for its excellent buses, is nothing short of spectacular! It's an adrenalin-filled, scenery-overloaded climb up and over a 3400m pass. The bus driver even stops on the top of the pass for the only gringos on the bus to get out and take some photos. Well worth the 20 peso fare- and the hat that Amanda left on the bus.

Cachi is like a movie set of the Wild West, with whitewashed buildings and more horses than cars. The only thing missing is tumbleweed rolling down a deserted street. At 2470m, it's the perfect place for us to acclimatise for our first ever trek at altitude.

The trail proper takes us up a valley over a 5800m pass, with the option of conquering one of the easiest 6000m peaks on earth, then down into the next valley and out. As great as that sounds we are realists; the highest we've ever been on a trek is the 2850m of Volcano Villarrica in Pucon. We simply don't know how our bodies will adjust to walking and sleeping at altitude, so our watered down plan for this one is to stay in the valley rather than cross the high pass- and going higher if we're feeling ok. If the abundant, but not entirely factual, information on the internet is to be believed, if we go too high too quickly our brains will explode. Armed with that information we both get an excellent night's sleep, after writing our families an email reassuring them not to panic. Unless they don't hear from us within six days... In which case, panicking would be a perfectly valid option.

Day 1

When his axle is in serious danger of breaking in two, the taxi driver finally decides it's time to drop us off. We arrange for a pick up on Sunday at 2pm, four days from now. Our back up option is a 16km walk back to Cachi...or maybe one of the locals in Las Pailas, the closest town, will lend us a horse. The altimeter reads 3000m.

Setting off up the valley we are immediately aware of two things. The first is our shortness of breath. Full packs at this height certainly get the lungs working overtime. We go slowly. The second is another excellent reason to go slowly. I've never been anywhere, or seen anything, like this before; cacti as far as the eye can see. There's nothing even remotely like this in New Zealand. It's wicked!

But boy is it tough going. After two hours and five kilometres we've had enough for the day and set up camp. Without a doubt the best campsite we have had to date: We're completely alone at 3321 metres in elevation, with cacti in every direction. Rest and recovery is the plan for the remainder of the day. That, and coping with a throbbing headache as our brains ready themselves to explode.

Day 2
Starts off a bit nippy! With Amanda on sleeping arrangement duty, my job is cooking, and brewing cups of tea, particularly important on cold mornings when she's struggling to get out of her toasty warm sleeping bag. I walk down to the stream to get some water and discover it has almost completely frozen over. Undeterred, I smash some ice away and fill up our two water bottles. By the time I've walked back to camp, about 150m, and prepared the cooking gear, both bottles have frozen over. Suddenly I feel a lot colder.

Surrounded by mountains, the sun seems to take forever to show itself but it's a welcome relief when it does. Frozen to the bone, with the altitude still slowing us down considerably, we take quite a while to get going, finally departing this awesome campsite just after midday.

Not much further up the valley we leave the last cactus behind. At 3397m, I look left and right and it almost looks like there is a line the cacti will not cross. Without them, this place seems desolate. We decide to drop the packs and head further up the valley, exploring for a campsite on par with the one we've left behind.

Our initial goal is an established campsite I have GPS coordinates for, 5km further up the valley and sitting at 4200m. Already struggling at 3300m, I'm pretty sure we shouldn't be going that high this early. My brain may be threatening to explode but it still seems to be making sensible decisions.

Our scouting trip further up the valley takes us to 3600m. Even with the sun out, it's considerably colder at this altitude and we can't find a good campsite with access to water. It's a no brainer...we turn around and head back to the best campsite ever. Really, we'd made the decision not to eross the pass before we

even started out; returning to camp is kind of inevitable. It's a good inevitable though.
Day 3
Comfortable in our surroundings we decide not to move camp. But it's time to climb a mountain all the same. From the dozens we're surrounded by, I pick the one that looks the easiest. How hard can it be? I saw a cow halfway up it yesterday.

Amanda is struggling with the altitude a bit more than I am and sets the pace, as is customary. It's my kind of pace for a change, the slow kind. We work our way through leg-shredding scrub for about an hour then, sensing the top is within reach, Amanda's second wind kicks in. With great effort I manage to keep up, and we're at the summit in 90 minutes. 3771 metres; a new altitude record. Brains intact.

I'm sure that no human has ever been on top of this insignificant peak so I decide that gives us naming rights. There is a large cow pat on the summit, but everyone knows cows can't name mountains. We name the peak Cerro Lone Cactus, in homage to the cactus we passed on the way up, at 3498m, a full 101 metres higher than any other in the valley. Downhill is much faster, but even more leg shredding.

Back at camp for the mandatory R&R, the harsh reality of camping in a desert full of cacti hits home. No sitting around on rocks resting for me... today it's full horizontal. Consequently, an hour later I'm picking spines out of the clothes I used to lie on... and Amanda is picking them out of my back and arse. Lesson learned.

Day 4
We are very reluctant to leave our lovely little campsite. Although we haven't done much, nowhere on our travels so far have I felt more content. Alas, we have a taxi to catch. As we break camp and start heading back towards civilisation, we walk past the first people we've seen in four days: a climbing party who are looking to climb Nevado de Cachi. They ask us for trail information.

"How did you find the climb?" one asks.

"Easy as mate."

(Amanda tells the truth.)

Our leisurely stroll down to the settlement of Las Pailas takes in a part of the valley that we didn't see previously (the last time we came this way, we were hanging on for dear life as the taxi driver did his rally driver impersonation.) Mud bricks dry in the sun, getting ready for that next house extension. Red peppers are laid out on the ground, also drying in the sun, and bringing even more colour to this kaleidoscopic rural scene.

Capping it all off, this profound, if out of place, graffiti, written on one of the shacks:

"He who works the land owns the land."

Unfortunately for us, our taxi driver doesn't own any land around here! By 2.30pm we are resigned to the fact that the arsehole isn't working today, the land or anything else, and we start walking, implementing plan B. What started off as a leisurely 5km stroll down the valley has now become 21km of hard slog.

It's a beautiful day, and a beautiful valley to be walking down but heavy packs have us yearning for the chance to hitch a ride for only the third time in our travels. We would actually have to see a car for that to happen though. With its two-car-rush-hour, the road to Caleta Tortel, Chile, was busy compared to this.

It's not long before I run out of water and, with the river inaccessible, I can feel my energy draining away with each step. Luckily we come across what looks like an irrigation ditch, carrying murky brown water to the maize fields. Amanda looks on in disgust as I fill my water bottle up. Desperate times call for desperate measures: the filter will be working extra hard today. Our saving grace is the fact that it's all downhill and we finally walk into town, 2½ hours after we set out.

You'd think the first order of the day would be to track down the taxi driver and give him a right old bollocking, but no, we decide on beer instead. We are thirsty and drinking will achieve more. As we're about to enter the bar I spot something familiar.

"Is that guy wearing an Otago cycle shirt?" I ask Amanda.

Otago is a province in the South Island of New Zealand.

Before she can answer I hear a familiar accent behind me.

"Are you guys Kiwis?"

The next thing we know we're at the table drinking beer with 15 Kiwis on a high Andes cycle tour. They're being driven to the top of high passes and get to bike down the other side. Sounds like fun! Almost done in Argentina, they have Bolivia and Peru still to do...all in the space of 30 days.

"We've been camping in the mountains," Amanda tells them when they ask what we're doing here.

"Bloody Kiwis eh! Doesn't matter if you're in the arse end of nowhere, you'll always meet them, usually walking out of the mountains," one quips.

It's good to be speaking Kiwi again after four months on the road. A few beers later we part ways as they continue on their journey and we return to the hostel for a much needed shower. After a couple more days of R&R we head back to Salta.

> Amanda- I can't believe you failed to mention the bed bug incident! It's true folks, Cachi was everything he said it was but it also involved being attacked by bed bugs on our first night there and you telling me I had "mind bugs" from my first episode four months ago...until you squashed one of the bastards that was biting you! I had 20 bites by that point...

Hitting a restaurant back in Salta, we decide to order the local speciality, a *parillada*. It doesn't take long for a huge dish of meat to arrive. I spot what looks like a mushroom so I chuck it in my mouth; I love mushrooms. It's *WAY* to chewy to be a mushroom though. Meanwhile, Amanda has her own problems identifying what she's tentatively nibbling on, refusing to fully commit to the unknown. More easily identifiable are kidneys and black pudding.

"You'll be eating all that," she informs me.

Finally, curiosity gets the better of us and we call the waiter over. Amanda asks him what my mystery meat is first of all:

"*Intestino*," the waiter replies.

Well, that sounds a lot like intestine, so that's that mystery solved.

She then asks what her unidentifiable meat is and he churns out something indecipherable in Spanish. When blank looks follow he reverts to probably the only two English words he knows:

"*Cow teet.*"

Amanda eats the chips.

10- A tale of two valleys

The bus ride from Salta, over the border to San Pedro de Atacama in Chile, is completely drama free. Unless you count being stuck in a bus on a 4800m pass in the Andes for four hours when traffic grinds to a halt. Howling winds are blowing snow over the road, making conditions too treacherous for driving; ok, so maybe not *entirely* drama free. We hear whispers of cars being blown off the road ahead. Some idiot jumps off the bus because he needs a smoke, some other idiot (me) gets off for no apparent reason!

Eventually we make it to "the driest place on earth." It hasn't rained in San Pedro De Atacama for 400 years, according to Wikipedia. Or five days, if you believe the local Amanda chatted to on the bus from Salta. Or maybe three months, if you believe the local accommodation tout whose offer we take up. So many options...

San Pedro is a quaint little town, but some of its quaintness is diminished by its heavy orientation towards tourism. There are travel agencies on nearly every street, selling tours of every description. The question is do we want to spend Our Special Day visiting the sights with a bunch of strangers? Hell no. We decide to hire bikes.

This Special Day is our tenth wedding anniversary. And to celebrate it, I've seen a 42km mountain bike route online (complete with GPS waypoints) that'll take us through two of the major attractions in the area, The Valley of the Dead, and The Valley of the Moon. Surprisingly this suggestion is met with very little opposition from Amanda...possibly due to the outrageous prices the organised tours go for around here.

We hire our bikes and set off early, giving ourselves nine and a half hours (until the shop closes) to complete the circuit...and take in some attractions along the way. After taking a wrong turn only 200m out of town, and wasting precious energy going up a small hill, we realise there's a better than average chance we're going to need every minute of it.

We already have a long day ahead so it seems like a great idea to completely divert from our plan. On an impulse we decide to visit the ancient ruin, Pucara de Quitor. It dates back to the twelfth century and has been recommended by a friend. Just like that, our 42km bike ride has become 48km.

This stone fortress, built by the Atacameño people to defend themselves from other towns in the area, turns out to be a bit disappointing. Half the site is now, albeit probably rightly, blocked off to preserve the ruins. Had the walls been lined with 300 heads, detached from the bodies of the residents defeated by the Spanish many years later, it may've been worth the extra six kilometres.

We stock up on more water at the visitors centre and continue on our way...

...Into the Valley of the Dead. Only then do we realise our gross error in judgement. We are at 2400m elevation. OK, we knew that. It's bloody hot. Yep, we knew that too- hence the four litres of water we are carrying...*each*. What did we forget then?

Deserts tend to have more than their fair share of sand!

OK if you're at the beach, not so good when you're on a cheap, heavy mountain bike, with four litres of water, plus food, on your back. We now experience the desert equivalent to our swing bridge aerial hopscotch in Argentina. Hop off the bike and push, clear the sand, hop on it again. And so on. Until we get to a sand dune...

This is when we realise why this area is named The Valley of the Dead. It is named for all the idiots who have tried to cycle through it and haven't had the sense to turn back upon reaching this dune. Two other cyclists do just that after seeing us halfway up it, pushing our bikes. The Hill of the Dead seems apt.

After a long hard slog we make it to the top, and collapse into the only shade we've seen for an hour. As we sit back and take in the view, I once again find myself thinking I've never been anywhere quite like this before. The valley itself, full of interesting, craggy rock formations; and in the distance, dozens of completely symmetrical snow-capped volcanos permeate our view.

A little bit more riding and a lot more sand and we're finally back on tarmac. A double blessing of 6km downhill, no pedalling required, *and* a cool breeze to freshen us up a bit. It's not long until we're back in the desert though, turning off the main road and heading for the back entrance of The Valley of the Moon. We come to a cross roads. I hop off my bike and get busy working out where we are in relation to where we should be.

"Oh my God, look, a mine field!" Amanda says as she spots a warning sign.

"Cool" I reply, busily trying to decipher the GPS and confirm the direction we're supposed to be heading.

Success: "OK, it's this way. Let's go!"

"TONY!!!! DON'T CUT ACROSS THERE!!! STAY ON THE ROAD!!!"

"What for?"

"BECAUSE IT'S A FUCKING MINEFIELD!!!"

"Oh, is it? Cool! OK."

"You NEVER listen!"

Limbs intact, we continue on towards The Valley of the Moon.

It's not long until we arrive at the back entrance. Closed, the sign reads.

There's a large steel barrier blocking our way and 'No Entry' signs all around- in Spanish. Luckily the barrier isn't good enough to keep a bike out, and we can't read Spanish; and we *certainly* don't fancy back-tracking from here. Throwing our bikes over the barrier we continue into the park on foot, pushing our bikes up a hill on a salt road. The salt is hard and makes a far better cycling surface than sand does, but we are knackered.

When we reach the top of the hill, the Valley of the Moon opens out before us. My first thought? *Is the moon this salty?* Not according to someone's ratings on Trip Advisor.

"Not moon-like at all!" the review reads.

How many people have actually been to the moon and are in a position to compare? Is the reviewer Neil Armstrong? Is he a Trip Advisor member? So many questions left unanswered, including who on earth cares if it's not moon-like? The Valley of the Dead was not dead-like. They're still pretty awesome. And best of all for cyclists...this moon is flat.

With time to kill until sunset we decide to cycle to an old salt mine over the bumpiest road I've ever cycled on. It's a salt mine... and it's salty. I lick a few walls in an attempt to ease my cramping legs.

Amanda- Disgusting! God only knows how many people licked that wall before you...

The highlight of any trip anyone takes to The Valley of the Moon is watching the sunset from the top of the grand dune. Every man and his dog seem to have turned up for this one. Tour companies bus them in, others have cycled from town, and still others are here with their own transport. It is a crowded dune but we're looking for a little more privacy for our viewing. With plenty of time before the sun goes down we walk off down a ridge and away from the crowds. Then we sit down and wait.

And well worth the wait it is too. As the sun disappears below the horizon, the surrounding mountains change colour from brown, to red, then to purple, before they are finally swallowed up by darkness. All that's missing from this fantastic anniversary moment is a bottle of wine.

With 15km to go to complete our circuit, and already suffering from dehydration, we've probably done ourselves a favour *not* bringing one.

Just after sunset we spot a park ranger walking out along the ridge towards us. We've come in the back way and haven't paid the entrance fee. Briefly I consider evasive manoeuvres, but with almost a sheer drop on either side of the ridge, escape options are limited.

Amanda goes with the easier option, as he approaches us and speaks.

"I'm sorry, we don't speak Spanish."

"The park closes in eight minutes," the ranger replies in perfect English.

Happily, we haven't been busted... but I am left wondering how you close an area the size of this. Minefields maybe?

20 minutes later, after we've had a chat and asked him to take some pictures of us, the ranger walks off towards another group who don't look like they have any intention of leaving. With the sun gone, it's suddenly very cold so we decide it's time for us to get going too. It's a surprisingly good feeling to be cold again after toasting ourselves nicely in the desert all day.

Arriving back at the bikes, we find a group of French cyclists about to leave. It's cold so, unbeknown to them, we decide to race them. We're neck 'n' neck as we hit the only road out of here. Time for our secret weapons... We flick on our top of the range mountain bike lights and night becomes day as we race away from the French pack, easily avoiding MOST of the sand traps on the road. The ones we hit do cause a few hair-raising moments as we hurtle down the hill. The French, on the other hand, have hired lights. Or more appropriately, "darks."

Finally we hit the tarmac of the main road and sneak a peek behind us. Unsurprisingly the French are nowhere to be seen so we enjoy a 10km cruise back to town, claiming victory and arriving a full two hours before the hire shop shuts.

Three days later, after we've recovered from our mammoth desert ride, we sign up for the tour we actually came here for. It's a three-day 4X4 trip across the *altiplano* (high plains), and over the salt flats to Uyuni, Bolivia. We've been reluctant to join the overpriced outings in the Atacama area because we've heard such good things about this trip. We have high expectations.

On the morning of departure we walk to the tour operator's office and are dead on time for our 7.45am pickup. Our ride picks us up at eight thirty, and drives us about 400m to Chilean customs. We check out of Chile for the final time, and then stand around for an hour for no apparent reason. Our expectations have lowered dramatically...already.

Eventually there's movement from all the other tour companies and yes, we are off too... on our way to Bolivia at last.

11- Bolivia tried to kill us

4X4 to Uyuni: day 1
Immigration in Bolivia is a shack in the middle of nowhere.

> Amanda- A shack surrounded by snow sitting at at least 4000m. No fancy equipment, just 2 men, 2 chairs a desk and an immigration stamp.

The procedure is as uncomplicated as the building would suggest and we are quickly on our way. Our tour's already better than some of the ones we've read about: our Bolivian driver doesn't turn up drunk!

We are joined on this trip by two Peruvians, two Chileans, four Brits, an American and a German, in a pair of rough and ready 4X4s. Much to Amanda's delight we end up in the predominantly Spanish-speaking crew. She is especially thrilled to be trying to understand Chileans once more after a few "gringo" days in San Pedro de Atacama. Luckily for me these guys also speak a bit of English.

I manage to acquire the front seat which makes a prime photo and video shooting position. Our driver is a speed demon; luckily, he's also an excellent driver. From every seat in the vehicle it's plain to see the magic in this place. Snow-capped mountains, looming large, even up here at 4000m; crystal clear and brightly coloured lakes; geysers; and even some hot pools, which end up being very hard to get out of. The scenery and the cold mountain air see to that.

A couple of the more incredible sights we see involve humans though. We see two trekkers, complete with full backpacks, trudging along what passes for a road in these parts. These guys are only trumped in lunacy by two cyclists pushing their bikes through unrideable sand, panniers full to the brim. As much as I like a bit of endurance sport, these guys take it to the next level and I'm very happy to have chosen a quicker mode of transport. The pained expressions on their faces suggest they would be more than happy to trade places. Not today thanks. Not tomorrow either.

Nearing twilight we arrive at our first night's accommodation. Situated at an altitude of 4300 metres. Rumour has it that the temperature will drop to as low as -18°C (0°F) outside. Luckily we're not staying outside. Unluckily, there is no heating. Running out of clothes to put on before climbing into her sleeping bag, Amanda also manages to wear her backpack. An interesting pyjama option.

Day 2

With more chance of being crushed to death by the sheer weight of clothes, blankets, backpacks and sleeping bags we wore to bed than developing hypothermia, we survive the night.

What can day two throw at us? As much as day one? More. More mountains, more lakes. Add in some picturesque deserts, smoking volcanoes and thousands of flamingos, and day one's scenery is almost entirely eclipsed.

In less than 48 hours, Bolivia has become Amanda's favourite country- and I have taken almost 1000 photos. They won't be winning any competitions (I end up deleting most of them) but I somehow got a bit carried away, caught up in the Bolivian moment.

Day two's sightseeing ends with a well earned beer at our next night's accommodation, a private room in a salt hotel. Salt blocks for the walls and granules for the floor. It's like getting out of bed in your very own salt shaker. This salt shaker's pretty flash. It has flushing toilets, although it must be said that they don't actually work.

We have a meal of fried llama and share a couple of bottles of wine with the group in honour of our last night together. Then it's off to bed for an early night in preparation for tomorrow's 4am start, necessary to get to the salt flats for sunrise.

Day 3

Unfortunately the other group occupying the hotel decides to stay up until 3am playing drinking games. I am blissfully unaware of proceedings as I've worn ear plugs to bed and don't hear a thing. I seem to be the only one though. And it certainly doesn't mean I'm not more than happy to take part in the morning's vengeance.

Our pattern of revenge is the tried and true method championed by the Aussie battlers on the TDP circuit in Chile, and others before them no doubt.

Knowing that the drinkers have had little more than an hour's sleep, our entire group prepares to leave at 4am, loudly. Shouts echo through the hotel and conversations become louder and louder as people gain confidence. Never a shrinking violet, Amanda rallies the troops with a military-like roll call.

"YOU GUYS READY?" she yells.

"YES!" a chorus of voices replies.

"ARE YOU SURE?"

"YES!!!"

"OK, LET'S GO!"

Then it's my turn to contribute, slamming the truck door again...and again; the damn thing just won't close properly! Luckily it latches shut just as we leave. With a long day ahead of them (they're heading in the other direction), travelling at over 5000 metres in altitude, our partying friends are likely in for a pretty rough day- if they manage to drag themselves out of bed in time for it, that is. Our job here is done.

Unfortunately my day is about to take a turn for the worse too. So far, I've worn shorts for the entirety of our four months travel. Today I will learn my lesson. We're setting out so early, the sun isn't up. I'm sitting in the passenger seat and I'm noticing the cold on my bare legs for the first time. With a deadline to keep to and my warmer trousers packed away, I have no alternative but to tough it out, and hope that as soon as the sun comes out I'll warm up quickly. But damn is it cold!

> Amanda- Meanwhile in the back seat I'm wearing NZ's finest merino wear, super thick fleece trousers and my 30 below sleeping bag...and I'm still cold!

Stopping in the middle of the salt flats just before sunrise gives me the opportunity to get out and get moving to warm up. But alas, I'm so cold I can hardly even move: my legs have become so cold that running on the spot is way more of a chore than it should be. The sunrise, however, is breathtaking. The ensuing battle over who will take their gloves off to actually get the sunrise shot on Amanda's phone is enough to keep my mind occupied for the time being. No, touch screens don't work when you're wearing gloves, not the ones we have anyway.

Once the sun's up, we pile back into the vehicles, destination: a cactus island in the middle of the salt flats. As others explore, the bulk of my time on the island is spent sitting in the sun trying to warm up.

Back at the car park I manage to steal the warmth of a fire made by one of about 20 other groups that have converged on Cactus Island, and feeling is partially restored to my limbs. Sadly, they will continue to make their displeasure known for days to come.

The final leg of the three day journey is a long drive across the salt flats, with a quick stop for some crazy photos. The whiteness of the area provides for photo magic: I am able to "lift our vehicle and hold it up with one hand" and Amanda manages to finally get me where she wants me...in the palm of her hand.

It's all good fun, but to be honest, the lack of change in the salt flats scenery pales in comparison to our two previous days of scenery overload.

And then there's Uyuni, the end of the line.

With rubbish blowing around as far as the eye can see, it seems we've reached the real Bolivia. After three days in pristine wilderness, it's something of an anti-climax. In the time we've been here, Bolivia has already done its best to freeze me to death. The Bolivian Near-Death Experiences table sees me take a one-nil lead. But it doesn't take Amanda long to equalise.

Our friends from the salt flat tour booked ahead and managed to secure themselves rooms in (reputedly) the best hostel in Uyuni. Unfortunately, we didn't, so we search out the next best option and end up at a cheap hotel. I think our room is probably the closest thing to a Siberian gulag that I will ever experience. Situated on the shaded side of the building, and with no heating, the temperature in the room is below freezing. Oh, and there's no hot water. Undeterred, and feeling smelly after three days without facilities, Amanda decides to have a shower anyway.

> Amanda- I was highly deterred...but I smelt bad!

After hearing her screams and seeing the look on her face as she runs out of the bathroom and dives into her sleeping bag I decide to stay smelly. She doesn't move for a very long time. I check for a pulse every now and then. Tony, 1, Amanda, 1.

Back to school!
Not until we reach the city of Sucre does Bolivia make another attempt on our lives. We've signed up at the local Spanish school for a month's worth of lessons. Once I would've considered going back to school a fate worse than death, but on my first day, although nervous, I have to admit I'm a little excited.

It is at this point that I learn that with a Bolivian behind the wheel of a car, anything can happen. Sucre, whilst a very picturesque "white city," where white washed churches and colonial buildings dominate the city centre, has narrow streets, very narrow pavements...and a serious traffic problem. Particularly if you're a pedestrian. Walking to school on my very first day I'm almost crushed between two vehicles as one backs out of a driveway without looking, into an already gridlocked street. It's only my quick reactions that save me. More aware now, I am surprised when the exact same thing nearly happens again only five minutes later. Tony, 2; Amanda, 1.

But Amanda's not done yet...

Revelling in the abundance of cheap, plentiful street food after expensive Chile is about to take its toll. After less than a week in Bolivia, Amanda comes down with a case of food poisoning. It's not a pretty sight...and she's feeling so bad she actually misses some days of her first week back at school. Amanda is so conscientious, she probably even knows how to spell it, and this is most unlike her.

Over the next two weeks, bouts of illness come and go until finally, things come to a head. Amanda decides it's time to go to the doctor- a terrifying enough proposition in a foreign country, let alone a developing one. We enlist the help of her Spanish teacher, Carla, in an effort to allay our fears.

After a series of taxis, one in which the driver drives with one hand, holds an infant with the other *and* still manages to talk on a mobile phone (a third hand perhaps?), we pull up to the hospital. Carla knows the doctor so she pulls a few strings and Amanda is seen almost immediately. And it's a quick diagnosis. He prods her stomach a bit then proclaims...

"You have salmonella."

Apparently no tests required.

"Oh. Where do you think I've picked that up?" Amanda asks

"Probably in Uyuni, it's a dirty place."

I wonder if he ever visits the local market. One lady was selling meat there that sat uncovered in the sun, on a cloth on the pavement...complete with flies buzzing around, and random dogs sniffing. They may have been salivating too. The genius doctor prescribes a course of antibiotics. It's two all.

With Amanda now reluctant to eat at the local places we opt for the "gringo" eateries in town, when we need wifi, or cooking for ourselves otherwise. One particular night it's my speciality, chilli. After cutting up the chilli peppers I feel the need for a quick toilet visit. ALWAYS wash your hands after chopping up chilli's *before* you go for a wee folks. I can't really blame Bolivia for that one can I?

As we settle into Sucre life, living with Maria, one of the teachers at the Spanish school, we decide on a night out or two...very uncharacteristic for the both of us. But in Bolivia the price is right and the company is good. Maria, Aussie flatmate Victoria, Amanda and I hit the town. Sitting in the bar of the local gringo hangout we're joined by North American Billy. Together we rid the world of about seven bottles of wine and 12 pints of beer for the total cost of around 440 Bolivianos. Binge drinking at its finest. We will pay for this very cheap night out in other ways. Out of our group of five, one will sensibly go home early, one will vomit and one will fall over and knock out some teeth. Perhaps unsurprisingly, a majority vote on detailing exactly who did what has been omitted to protect all parties. We never see Billy again...

A few weeks later we have a new flatmate, James, a twenty-something from the UK. He joins in the fun one night and completely puts us oldies to shame. Not content to wind it up at closing time on "Mojito night," he kicks on, joining the friendly drunken Bolivians that give us a ride home, at a local karaoke bar. Amanda and I join Victoria back in retirement. James -and our weeklong hangovers after the first night- have shown us this is a young person's game. No near deaths...unless you count a few million brain cells?

By now I'm enjoying Spanish school less and less. The constant barrage of Spanish grammar my teacher forces on me daily finally overwhelms me.

"FUCK THIS SHIT!!!" I scream as I throw my book across the room.

Unsurprisingly, teacher Guisell looks scared. I'm normally a pretty laid-back bloke, not usually given to displays of such explosive force, and this outburst has come from nowhere. Luckily it's nearing the end of the day and we can both go home and gather our thoughts.

Unbeknown to me Guisell confides in Amanda's teacher Carla... Amanda hears all about my little temper tantrum the next day, and fills me in on part of the conversation.

"What do I do?" Guisell asks the much more experienced Carla.

"You should probably stop teaching him grammar." Carla replies. Clearly Carla is a very intelligent woman.

Lessons become a lot more fun after that...even when Guisell leaves the school a week later. I hasten to add this is completely unrelated. I hope. Word has obviously got around and the grammar-less fun continues when Erica takes over. Unfortunately I still don't learn very much, even as a month of lessons extends to six weeks. Maybe grammar's a little more important than I thought... Clearly, languages are just not my thing...

Death by chocolate?

Our next destination Santa Cruz is a mere 500km away, but it's still a whopping 15 hour bus ride. We stock up on food and board the bus. Pleasantly surprised by the quality of the roads between Uyuni and Sucre, we are about to get a rude awakening...

About an hour down the bumpiest road I've ever been on, a little girl two seats in front of us spews. Amanda's lightning-quick reflexes save me from following suit; she has the window seat and winds down the window swiftly, the fresh air and dust clearing the smell from my nostrils. Not the best scenario on a full bus, poor old mum cleans up after her vomit-drenched child as best she can. A little further down the line we pick up some more passengers. With no seats to sit in they promptly lie down in the aisles and go to sleep, one managing to lie right in the pile of vomit, much to my amusement.

As the road worsens and we cling on for dear life, Amanda makes Bolivian bus passenger mistake number one...and looks out the window.

"Shit!" she exclaims. "Our back wheel just went over the edge of the cliff!"

This goes some way towards explaining why she suddenly attached herself to my thigh with a vice-like grip. I'm in an aisle seat, happily oblivious- and preferring to stay that way.

"Why do you need to tell me things like that? Stop looking out the window."

About midnight Amanda calls for the 400g bar of nut chocolate that I've been carrying in my pocket. Unfortunately it has melted but I hand it to her anyway.

"How the hell I'm I supposed to eat that?"

"I don't know."

I'm just happy to be rid of it.

Hoping it will set, so she can eat it more easily later, she puts it down the side of her seat, well away from any body heat.

Two hours later something amazing happens...Amanda actually manages to go to sleep. But her acute sense of smell doesn't allow her to sleep long.

> Amanda- It was more like I was dreaming about chocolate then had a sinking feeling as consciousness returned...

She is woken after ten minutes by the strong smell of chocolate. Still happily oblivious despite being shaken half to death, I'm engrossed in my MP3 player and have failed to notice anything amiss.

"Oh. My. God." Amanda whispers, as she reaches down to investigate, and sits back up, her hand pretty well coated with a dripping smear of sticky brown stuff. And a peanut or two.

The giant bag of liquid chocolate has dislodged itself from its strategic placement over the course of this very bumpy ride, and somehow worked its way under Amanda's bum...where it has exploded in spectacular fashion, covering her back and arse with liquid chocolate. What a mess!

With very few options available, Amanda goes to work cleaning the chocolate off her seat the best she can. I hold the torch, trying not to laugh too much. She then strips down to her bra and undies and gets to work on her clothes. In what may well be my wisest move ever, I decide not to put down the torch and pick up the camera. She is not seeing the funny side, well, not yet anyway. It's a long cleanup process, and I'm pretty sure that Amanda can now say she's the only traveller in Bolivia to have travelled for two hours on a public bus dressed in only her undies and a bra. Not a near death experience, but very traumatic all the same- for one of us anyway.

Finally we arrive in Santa Cruz, happy to be at sea level once again. And to change out of chocolate covered clothing. It's 6am, 5°C (41°F) and foggy. Not quite the weather we were expecting in the Amazon Basin. Santa Cruz is a big city with not a lot to offer us. The wealthiest city in Bolivia should be able to provide a better medical service than Sucre though, something Amanda desperately needs, as she continues to struggle with a recurring bout of food poisoning. First stop: the doctor.

> Amanda- So far, almost half my time in Bolivia has been spent in the toilet and clean toilets are not Bolivia's strong suit!

After watching Miss Transvestite Bolivia on the waiting room TV for two hours (Bolivian men make VERY ugly women) the doctor finally arrives at work. There was an emergency apparently; one his receptionist was also strangely involved in. To his credit, this guy actually orders tests done and the next day Amanda goes back on her own (I am retrieving a cash card an atm swallowed) for the verdict.

"You have an unknown bug," the doctor reports, after arriving two hours late again following another "emergency." Or perhaps the same one?

He prescribes another course of antibiotics. Tony, 2; Amanda, 3.

Without really trying, Bolivia has now done its best to kill us five times. However, in Santa Cruz we meet Aussie Albert and his nameless friend who are clearly in a lot more mortal danger: young lads, taking drugs and partying hard. Neither of them speaks a word of Spanish. Albert tells us of their latest attempt to score some weed.

"We walked into the dodgiest part of town, looked for a dude with dreadlocks and asked him where we could score. Before you know it we're in this tranny's flat, smoking a joint. My mate disappears out to the toilet and while he's gone this tranny tries to feel me up. Not wanting me cobber to miss out on the experience, I decide to go to the toilet when he gets back. When I return he says "dude, fuck the dope, let's get out of here! He just touched my dick!"

How these guys are still alive amazes me. At the very least, you'd think they'd have been robbed! Recounting this story still amuses me no end. It's not the last encounter with Albert...but for now, he's off to La Paz. We've decided to take another road. Road? Loosely speaking...

The road less travelled

The first leg of our epic bus journey is a ten hour overnighter to Trinidad. Surprisingly, we're travelling a fully paved road in a bus with comfy reclining seats. From Trinidad we delve a little more into the unknown. The route to Rurrenabaque is impassable during the wet season apparently. Even in dry season a bus travelling this road is a rare occurrence. Luckily there's an airport in Trinidad so, if all else fails, we have the option of flying.

But that's an option we don't have time to consider as we hop off our overnight bus and are immediately accosted by touts selling bus tickets to Rurre. Too easy. This is where the real adventure begins...

Our bus pulls up. Five star comfort, air con, entertainment system, and toilet...well, that's what the sign on the door says. The reality is spectacularly different. The bus is in a shocking state of repair, even for Bolivia. The seats are as hard as rock, the windows don't close and the windscreen is smashed. Worse still, we are in what I have (not so) affectionately dubbed "the death seats." Situated right behind the driver, these seats offer little peace of mind as Bolivian drivers dice with death on a regular basis, passing slow moving traffic at will, and showing little concern for oncoming traffic. Or corners. Or anything else for that matter.

An hour out of town we catch the car ferry across the Rio Mamore. Or put more precisely, we catch a floating platform with a motor.

It's a rather interesting process to watch as we file off the bus and watch it being loaded onto the "ferry." What follows on the other side of the river is eight hours of complete torture. Once again, we're shaken half to death on another bad road, wishing we could actually close the windows, rather than breathe in the dust generated in such dry, sandy conditions. Some travellers would say it's character building. I would say bullshit.

After inhaling the equivalent of our body weights in dust, we arrive in the small town of San Borja. The bus is unloaded, people and luggage both, and travellers stand around wondering what the hell is going on. Eventually we realise we're being transferred to ten-seater minivans for the remaining six hours of the journey to Rurre. Our new ride is more comfortable than the last bus...but not by much.

As we drive into the crossroads town of Yucumo, the driver speaks for the first time:

"Get out, I need to go and do something."

We follow the lead of the Bolivians in the van and file out of the vehicle onto the street. With that, the driver, the vehicle, and all our bags, are gone. We are left standing on a street corner in a rural Bolivian town, in the dark.

"Is he coming back?" Amanda asks one of the other passengers, feeling a bit silly for asking.

They shrug. It's not such a silly question after all.

Eventually, after a nervous hour's wait, our van returns and we're back on our way. As an added bonus, our bags are still on board. Four hours later we roll into Rurrenabaque and fall into the first hostel we see. After 35 hours on (or waiting for) buses, on some of the worst roads in existence, we're both completely shattered.

Evacuation from the Amazon

Without a doubt, one of the things I've been most looking forward to in South America is an Amazon jungle expedition. The trouble is that there are so many different tours and tour companies in Rurre, we have no idea where to begin. Having spent nearly three months in Bolivia we've also become quite thrifty and we baulk at some of the prices. And it's clear that some companies are a lot less ethical than others. We read review after review online describing "rack em and stack em" tours, whose guides attract wildlife by feeding it.

Foregoing a trek in the Amazon jungle proper, we instead opt for a three day pampas tour and book with the company that there's been the least complaints about. According to the online reviews, this boat trip up an Amazon River tributary will give us the best chance at spotting the most wildlife. The accommodation for three days in the jungle is described as "rustic."

That's also how you could describe the road to the river. A bumpy, dusty, three-hour ride is made only slightly more comfortable by the first vehicle with air conditioning we've encountered in Bolivia. In a country where 'air con' generally means 'no windows,' this is a rare treat indeed and we savour our time in the vehicle. It's also a rare treat to be slightly less concerned about the state of the road, and Bolivian driving, than usual.

After stopping for lunch, it's only a short drive to the river to meet our boat. It's a three hour boat journey downriver to the lodge, and a wild life extravaganza right from the start. In the water we see alligators, caimans and turtles. On the river bank we spot capybaras. Imagine what the offspring of a guinea pig and Brian the dog from Family Guy would look like. That's a capybara. In the trees we see monkeys, at least three different kinds; and many different species of birds. My tablet goes mad, becoming a real camera for a while.

It's hot in the Amazon Basin so when our guide, Lewis, spots some pink river dolphins and asks if anyone wants to swim with them, I don't need a second invitation. I'm not really paying much attention to what the other boat-load of gringos are doing (piranha fishing), or to the fact that this is still the same river in which we've just been watching alligators and caimans.

You might wonder what it's like, to swim with pink river dolphins... I don't really know. I never get close enough to cross "swimming with pink river dolphins" off my bucket list. The closest I get is "being avoided by pink river dolphins." After about ten minutes of frustration I decide it's time to get out, a decision helped considerably by the fact that something bites me! It suddenly dawns on me that I am in a murky brown river with absolutely no idea what's around me in the water. The guide said it was OK to swim here, it must be safe right?

I make for the boat quick smart when I remember I'm in a country where the concept of Health & Safety doesn't exist. In the process of pulling myself onto the boat, I slip on the slimy mud river bottom and something stings me: excellent motivation for me to vault into the boat unaided. My toes are numb for about four hours.

With me safely back on board, the boat continues downriver to our accommodation; a lodge right on the river bank. We're shown to our rooms. I have a bit of a lie down before we're scheduled to head off to "the sunset place," From my prone position, I admire the wasps' nest above my bed, which itself is by far the most uncomfortable I have ever laid on. Yep, rustic.

Apparently a long standing Amazonian tradition, "the sunset place" is where all the local villagers get together for a beer and a game of football. Sounds good. Unfortunately this particular sunset place is on the agenda of every single tour company on the river. It strongly resembles a party hostel, replete with the young crowd that frequents party hostels, and we've purposely avoided them throughout our travels. We grin and bear it just long enough to have a beer and enjoy the sunset before escaping the madness and heading back to the lodge for dinner.

About an hour after dinner things start turning to custard.

I am allergic to honey. I've had several severe reactions since discovering this allergy, where all my airways have closed up. I now carry an Epipen, which is a shot of adrenalin for emergency use. Obviously, I tend to avoid honey. But that's not always possible.

Lying in bed I start feeling a bit off. Thinking I recognise the symptoms of an allergic reaction, I go back over the day's food intake. Were those honey glazed bananas I had for lunch I wonder? I haven't had an allergic reaction for well over a year now so I brush it off. It just seems too much effort to grab an antihistamine and an asthma inhaler now that I'm cocooned in my mosquito net-draped bed. I haven't even brought my Epipen with me. Besides, the generator is off and I have no idea where my torch is. Instead of being sensible, getting up and getting everything I need, annoying everyone in the dorm in the process, I close my eyes and wait for sleep to envelop me.

It doesn't. The sounds of the jungle get me through the night. Alligators diving into the river; bats flying around in the room; and the occasional larger bug trying to bash its way through my mosquito net, all kind of cool. It's a shame I'm not in the frame of mind to fully appreciate it.

By morning I have a splitting headache and am running a fever. I stick with my original self-diagnosis and throw in heat stroke to explain away the other symptoms. Amanda and the rest of the group are going searching for an anaconda. This involves three hours walking around in a marsh. I can't even summon the energy to get out of bed, so a walk in the heat of the day is totally out of the question. The chances of actually finding an anaconda are apparently very slim anyway. I comfort myself by believing I've just avoided a pointless three hour walk in gumboots. According to Murphy's Law, they actually find one. Now I feel just a little bit gutted.

Kidding myself that I feel vaguely better, and with no walking planned, I decide to join the afternoon's excursion. As soon as I'm on the boat with a cool breeze on me I begin to perk up a bit. The purpose of this outing is to explore further downriver and stop somewhere for a spot of piranha fishing. I do love a good spot of fishing.

The six gringos in the boat then proceed to feed the fish for the next 45 minutes, whilst Lewis the guide seems to catch fish almost at will. Finally after nearly an hour of complete fish-less frustration, I manage to land one and a plan for revenge on flesh-eating fish starts forming in my mind.

With enough piranhas on board to feed the group (-ten for Lewis; two for everyone else) we make our way back to base, stopping en route to check more wildlife off our "seen" list. We spot a sloth at the top of a tree and in a sudden brainstorm my photographic genius kicks in with an idea to take a photo of someone else's photo. Actually, it's a rubbish idea. Hence no photo insert here...

Back at base, I'm fading fast, feeling worse than I did this morning. Positive that it was a cheeky little piranha that bit me when I was swimming, I feel suitably avenged as all the fish are cooked up for dinner. I force down a bite, fair's fair, before I turn in for the night. Prepared this time I take a couple of painkillers and a sleeping pill, make sure my torch is close at hand and settle down once again on the uncomfortable bed.

Waking up at five the next morning feeling even worse, I decide that my diagnosis might be a bit off and consult Nurse Amanda. She takes my temperature and it reads 39.6°C (103°F), nearly three degrees hotter than normal. She orders me into the shower quick smart to get my temperature down. An hour later I've mustered up the energy to do as I'm told. I stand under the shower watching the trickle of water evaporate pretty much as soon as it hits my forehead. It's been a tough twenty steps to the shower block and I return happily to my bed.

Amanda is not so happy though. She recruits Lewis onto the medical staff. He takes one look at me and agrees it's time to leave. NO WAY am I going to be *"that guy"* –the one that totally ruins the trip for everyone else– and I argue as strongly as I can. With a dangerously high temperature however, that's not very strongly. I'm hugely outnumbered when Amanda and Lewis discuss this with the rest of the group and they all agree it's hospital time. As much as I hate that we're going early because of me, I'm relieved I'll be out of the jungle soon.

My relief is short-lived. After a short wait at the local hospital in the small town of Santa Rosa I get to see the doctor on duty. She asks my name, measures my height, notes my weight then offers up her miracle cure: a course of antibiotics. I'm pretty sure you could walk into a hospital in Bolivia with your head cut off and a doctor would prescribe a course of antibiotics. Lewis is astounded at this misdiagnosis; it's clearly not food poisoning.

"If you're not better tomorrow, I can recommend a really good witch doctor."

I'm too sick the next day to take him up on his kind offer...luckily. Flu is suspected; real flu, not the man variety. It's three all.

For three days I lay in bed, only venturing out for cold showers and food. Finally we make a decision to escape the suffocating heat that seems to be hindering my recovery, and fly to La Paz. Struggling out to dinner on our final night in Rurre we bump into Aussie Albert at the restaurant. His nameless friend is absent.

We tell him what we've been up to since we last met, and what our plans are next.

"We signed up for a Pampas trip too." he tells us. "Halfway out to the river I saw this wheel fly past the vehicle we were in. It didn't take me long to realise it was our wheel. We were stuck by the side of the road for six hours waiting to be rescued. Luckily the driver had some weed."

"So, you're off to La Paz tomorrow? La Paz is Awesome! We asked around and found cocaine cafes, got wasted, and let fireworks off in our mouths."

Can't wait.

"Where's your mate?" I ask him.

"Oh, he just found out he has $18 left in his bank account; he's eating in."

The death road

There's only one thing worse than having the flu in the heat of the Amazon Basin. Namely, flying into La Paz (4000m above sea level) when you already have the flu, and then trying to adjust to the lack of oxygen at the higher altitude. Our first inner sprung mattress in four months makes for a slightly more comfortable sick bed.

Another attraction we've been looking forward to, with only slight trepidation, is the "world's most dangerous road" mountain bike ride just outside La Paz. Having barely managed to get out of bed for the last week with this horror flu, I am forced to sit this one out. I'm just well enough to walk with Amanda to the tour office and support her through the emotional turmoil at the mere thought of doing this. As she's signing waivers and gathering information, I helpfully point out photos showing crosses on the side of the road, and a thank you letter from the parents of a boy who died "doing what he loved." It's not called The Death Road for nothing. Amanda reads the fine print of our travel insurance over dinner to see if she is covered. She is not.

At 8am the next day my long wait begins when Amanda leaves. She's not due back until 7pm. Still feeling pretty poorly, I don't need a road to feel like death so I keep occupied by staying in bed until lunchtime.

Upon rising, I head out to experience a few personal Bolivian firsts. My first first is stomach related: I head out to a restaurant to ease my hunger pains...WITHOUT HAND SANITISER (a mandatory item when eating out in Bolivia). In my second first, my chosen restaurant displays a sign: "no dogs allowed." The third first? There are no dogs! Lunch was chicken, definitely not a first.

My next adventure is a lone trip to a Bolivian cash machine. I've heard stories about friends of friends being robbed whilst withdrawing cash, so we've been careful never to withdraw cash after dark and always do it as a team, Amanda watching my back and warding people off with a menacing look.

Eying up my first machine going solo, I approach cautiously; making sure no one is in close proximity. I withdraw my cash quickly and walk away from the machine purposefully. Deciding to put a busy road between me and any would-be muggers, I spot a gap in traffic and make my way safely to the traffic island in the centre of the duel carriage-way. It is here, when I take a step out onto the road that I'm almost run over by a motorcade carrying none other than Bolivian president Evo Morales. I didn't cycle the death road but I've certainly had my fair share of dangers for the day.

Amanda walks in the door at 9pm, a worrying two hours later than scheduled.

"Easy as," she assures me, regarding the death ride.

Apparently the toilet stop before it was harder.

Paying her money and walking towards the "toilet," Amanda is horrified to discover that it's nothing more than a hole in the ground...a hole in the ground that is currently overflowing. Not knowing whether she'd get another opportunity before her ride, she waded through the sewage, squatted down and went about her business, taking great care not to dangle her clothes in the muck.

It is in this precarious position that she realises the toilet door is one of those saloon types, and now, mid-squat, she has a clear view of the outside world. And they of her! Thankfully, the coast is clear for the moment.

Things take a dramatic and sudden turn for the worse when she loses balance and begins to fall towards the excrement-covered floor. Quick reactions save her from a fate worse than death as she thrusts her hands against the side walls and manages to steady herself...only to find that the walls are also covered in shit.

Quickly finishing up before her dilemma is witnessed, she goes to the sink to wash her hands. Well, it's not a sink, it's a bucket of stagnant water with flies and other unidentified stuff floating in it, posing as a sink. Nothing is posing as a bar of soap.

Back on the bus she is safely reunited with her bottle of hand sanitiser, but the damage is done. The world's most dangerous toilet has scarred her for life. This episode seals victory for Amanda, she wins the "Bolivia tried to kill us" series 4-3.

My lasting memory of Bolivia is the man I saw on the Isla del Sol, an island on the highest navigable lake in the world, Lake Titicaca. He is carrying a fridge/freezer unit on his back, nearly twice his height, up the steep trail from the jetty to the town. We walked up with full backpacks on and it nearly killed the both of us. Imagine carrying a fridge/freezer on your back up a steep incline at over 4000m in altitude. They breed 'em tough here. They need to.

12- Drama in Colca Canyon

    Across the border to Peru. After a brief stopover in Puno to visit the floating islands of Uros on Lake Titicaca, we find ourselves in yet another "white city," Arequipa. We are welcomed to big city Peru with a terrifying taxi ride into the city centre. This ride introduces us to the Peruvian intersection rule of tooting to let people know you are coming, and then accelerating regardless. Amazingly, we arrive at our hostel.
    We have come here to catch a bus into the Colca Canyon, where we plan to venture out on our first trek since the Nevado De Cachi in Argentina, nearly four months ago. Unfortunately, fellow travellers on the famous floating reed islands tell us that a recent earthquake has damaged the trails, and continuing rock falls have made the trek dangerous. It's time to go undercover...
    There are plenty of tour companies offering trekking in the canyon so, posing as interested parties, we start our investigations. Happily we find that not all the trails are closed; tour companies are running an overnight trip down to "the oasis," the tourist haunt at the bottom of the canyon. It doesn't sound like what we had in mind though.
    "What if we wanted to go for longer?" Amanda asks casually.
    "There's another trail to the west that still allows you to do a three day loop. It avoids the damaged main trail." Mr Tour Guy informs us. "That's all the information we have received on trail conditions in the area."
    "OK, thank you. You've been very helpful. We'll be back if we decide to do it," Amanda lies.
    Our intel mission has armed us with a few options so we board the bus for the four hour journey to Cabanaconde, deep in the canyon. A bus change in Chivey, the canyon's main hub, gives us the chance to get out and get a decent look at this place for the first time. Indigenous women in brightly coloured costumes dominate

the scenery, closely followed by the awesome spectacle that is terraced farming, in which paddocks line the steep sides of the canyon for as far as the eye can see. It's a 1000 year old practice that has endured into the present day.

As we continue on to Cabanaconde, the earthquake damage becomes apparent and we skirt around rockfalls on the road, getting precariously close to the 600 metre drop to the river below. Luckily darkness engulfs us and, as per Bolivian Bus Travel rule number one, we can remain oblivious. The Bolivian Bus Guide could've been written for Peru; it works as well here: out of sight, out of mind...

A couple of hours later we've survived another bus trip and check into our hostel. In our room we discover the best pillows we've seen in eight months! This is no small thing; Amanda is ecstatic and wants to go to sleep straight away. Instead, we retire to the bar and start grilling the hostel owner for trek information...whilst eating gourmet alpaca pizza.

Trek; day 1

With the information provided by the hostel owner pretty similar to what we learned from a tour operator in Arequipa, we decide to walk a three day loop, heading west, rather than the eastbound trip recommended in our travel guide. The distances don't look great so we also decide to travel light and do it in two days. But first we have condors to see.

Cruz del Condor is a short bus ride from Cabanaconde. From the uppermost point of the viewing platforms, the cliffs plunge 1200m to the bottom of the canyon, enabling the Andean condor to glide around on the resulting updraft, almost within touching distance. Being among the first people to arrive this morning, we stand around bored for a while; there's a few condors in the distance but none really venture too close. This is a bit shit. We amuse ourselves pretending to be condors and taking photos of each other hanging out over the 1200 metre drop.

Aware that we have a long day of walking ahead of us, we're just about to pack it in and catch the next bus back to town when the condors arrive. And what an entrance! For the next hour or so we are entranced by up to a dozen condors, gliding within metres of us. We completely forget about the long day ahead; this is truly spectacular. It also gets very busy. Bus loads of people arriving on tours from Arequipa (a VERY early start for them) who also take full advantage of the local market that springs up here every morning. I'm not surprised; I'd stay all day for this.

Eventually though, Amanda drags me away from the viewing platform and onto a passing bus taking us back to Cabanaconde. We hastily throw together some last minute supplies and are back walking again after a lengthy lay off. But it wouldn't be the start of a trek without some kind of stuff up...

Heading west, we arrive at another viewing platform with no idea which way to go next. My brilliant navigational skills come into play:

"The woman in front of us went this way...let's follow her."

Brilliant. It's easier to trust a complete stranger's judgement than to actually navigate; I've relied on this throughout my orienteering/adventure racing career. Judging by my success rate in the latter, perhaps it hasn't served me so well...

We catch up with the solo trekker just as the trail we've been following ends. Fantastic; we're in a paddock. Jen from Australia is as stumped as we are; she didn't see an alternative trail either. We spend the next ten minutes either being yelled at, or being helped, by a local farmer...it's hard to know which: the language is completely indecipherable. She could be gesturing for us to get off her fields; on the other hand, she could be telling us which way the trail heads. We decide it's the latter, walk across her fields, jump a fence or two and are reunited with one very distinct trail. How on earth did we all miss that?

Soon we're snaking our way down an arid cliff side in the 1200m descent to the river below. Sheltered from the breeze that helped cool us as we traversed the rim of the canyon, it's noticeably hotter the further down we get, but with our trusty walking poles to help us on the steep, gravelly surface, we soon leave Jen behind. She's no slouch though, and we end up trek duelling all the way to the bridge at the bottom, where we stop for lunch. From there, we decide to walk together.

It's around this time that I realise we have a water problem. We've brought a litre and a half each, intending to fill our filter bottles in the canyon river. We've also brought purification tablets as a backup. But even with filter bottles and purification tablets I'm not sure I would drink the river water- it looks absolutely disgusting. There's also thermal activity upstream- and all the nasties that brings. It's all quite irrelevant anyway; the river's inaccessible from the trail. Water plan A, fail.

No worries. Consulting our rudimentary map, we revert to plan B and pin our hopes on a village we'll be walking through, having been assured by the hostel owner we'd have no problem buying water from the locals. Bidding farewell to Jen, who's staying the night at a hostel further downriver, we begin the long climb out the other side of the canyon. It's not much longer until we get to the village indicated on our map.

"I thought a village was supposed to have people," Amanda comments.

Try as we might we're unable to find any signs of life. And it's a long way to the next village. Water plan B, fail. This is where we should have turned back.

Instead, we move onto water plan C, ration. Not that we have a lot left to ration: I'm empty, and Amanda, knowing how I struggle with the heat, is sharing her last half litre with me. We've only done about half of the 1000m climb and I'm really starting to struggle. Lacking refreshment I get slower and slower.as dehydration rears its ugly head. Amanda does her best to motivate me but I'm struggling *and* stubborn, and I have to stop and rest every five minutes. I can see the *mirador* (lookout point) in the distance but the damn thing doesn't seem to be getting any closer. Eventually we come to the first piece of shade for the day and I decide to lie down, happy to be out of the sun.

"Just five minutes," I say.

Five turns to ten...then 15. Amanda gets angry. Although she's given me most of her water and is obviously dehydrated as well, she is coherent enough to have seen the urgency of the situation. I couldn't give a fuck about the situation; I just want to lie in the shade.

> Amanda-I'm totally freaking out by this point. Tony's not thinking rationally at all; his brain has melted in the heat! I'm worried that his slow pace and all the rests are making the situation worse but no amount of cajoling seems to convince him that we need to keep moving. I'm calculating in my mind if I can run for help if he loses consciousness but I've given him all my water and I'm not even sure *I* would make it.

"We're turning around," she threatens.

I hate backtracking with a vengeance and her threat hits the spot nicely, the perfect motivation to get me moving. It's now further back to the hostel where Jen is than it is to the next village. We are committed.

"I'll be ok as soon as I get to the top," I mumble.

Amanda then empties out my day pack and fills up her own and we set off on the final push to the elusive *mirador*.

After what feels like an eternity, we reach the top and the trail levels out. We don't even bother going to the viewing platform; the scenery hasn't changed for the entire day so we don't see the point. Besides, it's an extra 30m uphill: it could well kill me. With at least six kilometres still to walk, Amanda walks on with no less urgency than before and I struggle along behind her, up to 100m behind at times. Even on the flat I can go no faster. But, I am moving.

"If a guy can cut his own arm off and walk out of a canyon in Utah, then I can bloody well do this," I say to myself, in a morbid attempt at self-motivation.

And I do. An hour after leaving the *mirador* behind, we arrive in the small village of Milata...and it's populated! Not only is it populated, the first thing we see is *a lady selling drinks!* A two litre bottle of coke and a two litre bottle of water later, we are saved. It's cost us 25 sols but quite frankly I would have paid anything. I'm just glad I didn't have to give my right arm. We sit back savouring the feeling of liquid lubricating dry throats, watching our rescuer (the store owner) weave, her toes the loom. As the sun dips below the mountains and the cool air restores us, we reflect on the day's events. It's not much of a reflection really. We've been complete idiots, committed rookie errors, and, on balance, we're bloody lucky we came out with nothing more than heat stroke. I'd hate to think how two of me would've coped. Without Amanda's dogged determination things could've been much worse...

Darkness is approaching and we need a place to stay.

"Where's the hostel?" Amanda asks the shop keeper.

"In the next village."

"Oh bollocks," I mutter.

Luckily, the next village is less than a kilometre away and, fully hydrated in the cool evening breeze, we knock it off in no time. After seven hours on our feet, we walk into the only hostel in town and are shown to our room, carefully negotiating a very rickety staircase on the way. The floor is more "hole" than actual floor, the roof is only half completed and, by the sounds of it, we're sleeping on top of a chicken coop. Happily, the bed looks pretty good.

"Dinner's at eight," our friendly hostel owner tells us.

Idly, I wonder why it's so late. When I pop out for a shower I notice the cooking shelter. Everything is being cooked on an open fire. Cool. This is the main reason we decided to stay at a lesser known village rather than the very touristy oasis at the bottom of the canyon. Here, we get to immerse ourselves in the local way of life; something that doesn't look like it's changed much for hundreds of years.

Tea is fish, obviously caught from the river below. Blocking the image in my mind of how disgustingly polluted that river was, I eat the fish, heads and all. My body needs the protein after a tough day. After dinner, we join the family watching Cable TV, apparently something of a tradition here. Less traditional is the movie, "Tron Legacy;" even in another language, it's crap.

Day 2

At about 3am, our suspicions the night before are confirmed: we *are* sleeping above a chicken coop, and one of the roosters has decided everyone's had enough sleep.

> Amanda- About 3am?? The bloody thing crowed all night! *You* maybe slept!

For five minutes he is in full voice, and then all goes quiet. Fifteen minutes later he starts up again. Five minutes later, silence. Just as we're nodding off back to sleep, he starts up again... This continues until 5am when we finally decide we've had enough, get up and hit the trail.

In my dazed and confused state yesterday, I rather unfortunately failed to notice I was developing huge blisters. I curse the Bolivian "clogs" I had to purchase in La Paz after leaving my trusty trail running shoes in the Amazon jungle (in another dazed and confused state!) Lacking medical supplies, I have no option but to grin and bear it.

Spurred on by the thought of a better breakfast than the Snickers bar we've brought with us, we're closing in on the oasis within an hour. Crossing the river into camp, I am once again glad I didn't –or wouldn't- drink the river water. It is *filthy*. Some things are worse than dehydration.

Arriving at the array of buildings offering accommodation, we are struck once again by the distinct lack of people. We eventually find some- and some food. Over breakfast we notice a change in the weather. It's overcast today, so nowhere near as hot as yesterday, which will make the tough climb out of the canyon a little more bearable. It's the strengthening wind that's a more immediate concern. We have to hold onto our breakfast plates so they don't blow away and can hear rocks bouncing their way down the canyon walls. We discuss the dangers with two other people making their way out today. They're not sure if they want to try the steep climb in high winds. We, on the other hand, are completely sure we'll tackle this climb regardless; nothing could be worse than yesterday. As I climb the steps out of the restaurant one of my blisters pops. Bugger.

Amanda has her homing legs on. I am in a more-than-usual slow and steady mood, yesterday's dramas having almost completely done me in. Once again Amanda scouts the terrain in front of us. It's not long before she realises I'm still struggling and takes the unprecedented step of allowing me to overtake. Normally a front runner, claiming the psychological advantage, she's just made the ultimate sacrifice; I dig deep into my reserves to try and up the pace. It works! The psychological advantage is all the motivation I need, and the going gets easier.

What isn't easier is the constant stream of dust and grit being blown in our eyes. The path is a well-trodden one and there's no real danger of falling in the high winds, the major concern is things falling on us. Everywhere we turn, small stones are working loose and showering us. Then we hear thunder. I look to the sky; it's overcast but the clouds don't look that menacing and there's no accompanying lightning.

As we turn onto the next switchback we realise what we actually heard. A huge boulder has dislodged itself and "thundered" onto the trail. Luckily, it's gone no further. Two men, who must've narrowly avoided death by boulder, are trying to move it so they can get their donkeys through. I'd lend them a hand, but I'm a realist...we have no chance of moving that monster. My slow pace may well have stopped us from being crushed to death! There's an upside to dehydration after all...

In just under three hours we're back in Cabanaconde. The climb out wasn't exactly easy, but it was a lot easier than what we endured going in. After a shower and a bit of a lie down, we find our way back to the bar, and some more gourmet pizza. We meet up with Jen, who conquered two 1000m-plus climbs on her second day on the trail to also break free of the canyons clutches. We tell her of our misadventures...

"There was a lady selling water about 200 metres further down the trail you turned off," she tells us.

Typical.

After living with Victoria in Bolivia for six weeks, we've missed having an Aussie around. We find we have a lot in common with Jen, as well as similar trek plans so it's an easy decision to name her "Replacement Australian."

Dehydration, heat stroke, blisters, roosters and falling boulders. Was it worth it? Yes. If only to say...

"I've been to the bottom of the second deepest canyon on earth and survived...just."

13- Scenery, archaeology and techno

Amanda, Jen and I are easy prey for the unscrupulous taxi drivers that stalk South American bus stations (well, South America in general really), looking for tired travellers getting off overnight buses to take advantage of. Too knackered to care, Amanda and I pay up about triple the going rate... after we're dropped off at our hostel less than a kilometre up the road. Jen's staying closer to the city centre so at least gets slightly better bang for her buck.

Over the next few days we hang out in the tourist mecca that is Cusco, eating the first decent Western food we've come across in quite some time; taking in some sights (those Incas were quite good builders); relentlessly being asked to buy paintings and other crafts; and researching trekking options.

Eventually we make a decision and it's a big one: an organised tour and trek along the Salcantay trail to Machu Picchu. Normally preferring to trek independently, we're breaking routine in a big way but with food, accommodation, entry to Machu Picchu and the train back to Cusco all included in the cost, we simply can't say no. For US$220pp, this five day trip is pretty unbeatable value. After a series of questions are answered to our satisfaction, we sign up and delve into the unknown.

Salcantay trail; day 1

For a pleasant change in trekking routine, our first action doesn't involve getting lost. Arising at 4:36am for a 4:30am pickup, it's still a less than perfect start to the day. Luckily Peruvians like a bit of a sleep-in as well; our ride arrives at 5:15. We are delivered to a waiting bus and introduced to our two guides- and to the other 15 people that make up our party. I guess you get that with the cheap options.

After a few hours on the bus we arrive in the tiny town of Mollepata, where the trail begins. Over breakfast we get the first indication that our tour company has simply told us what we wanted to hear to make a sale.

"We were told bags to store our gear on the donkeys would be provided," Amanda says to the guide.

"No, but there are some sacks you can buy."

Great. Jen is especially unimpressed with this; she has brought most of her gear in plastic bags. Amanda is slightly better off, bringing her stuff in our travel laundry bag, and I fare best, bringing mine in a dry bag. Three sacks later and it's problem solved...for the time being.

With no further surprises we hit the trail at 9am. One of the tour company websites I found during our research phase describes the first day on the trail as *"following a wide, well-established track."* I would call it a road. So would nearly every other human on the planet, especially the people who drive past us every now and then.

For the next seven hours we follow this road, heading uphill towards snow-capped mountains. Danny (from Pucon) was right; we can go at our own pace. It's a scorching day and, despite my recent illness in Bolivia, my dehydration and blisters in Colca Canyon plus the fact that I'm twice as old as the majority of the group, my pace is a lot faster than most. Amanda only knows one speed, fast- and Jen's right up there too. This results in long rest stops waiting for the tail-enders, which is a little annoying. I like a good rest just as much as the next person...but three hours rest in seven hours strikes me as a bit much.

As fast as team Kiwi/Aussie is going, none of us can compete with French Guy. Tall and lanky, he's built for speed, and shoots off after every rest stop like he wants to get this trek done in a day. Harking back to the 1987 Rugby World Cup final, NZ (the All Blacks) vs. France, and more recently the 2011 final, with the same two teams (both of which ended in All Black victories), we decide to let French Guy win this day. His prize is first choice of rubbish tents at our camp site for the night. Not the sturdiest looking things to be sleeping in at 3900m, but erected in a much sturdier looking tent shelter which gives a little peace of mind.

As is my habit after a long run or a day's trekking, the first thing I do when I hit camp is find a place to lie down and elevate my legs for ten minutes.

"What are you doing that for?" one of our party asks.

"It helps with blood circulation and promotes recovery." I reply, trying to sound knowledgeable.

The next thing you know, almost the entire group is lying on the ground with their legs in the air. Amanda is one of the few still standing.

Amanda- I've ALWAYS thought it was a bunch of bullshit and I'm highly amused as I watch people follow Tony's lead.

Wherever you stand (or lie, as the case may be) on this theory, one thing is fact...after 44 years, my fifteen minutes has come: I'm a trendsetter at last!

Dinner is a new experience for us. We're used to arriving at camp, setting up, then cooking dinner, and it's a pleasant change to sit down and be served copious amounts of food. Not to mention an endless supply of popcorn and coca tea. This is a local tea, brewed from the leaves of the coca plant...the very same plant that produces cocaine. Possessing none of the mind-altering qualities of its highly processed counterpart, the tea is very good for relieving the symptoms of altitude sickness.

Over dinner, Isay, the head guide, tells us about the next day's activities.

"Tomorrow is the hardest day. We will be climbing over the 4650m Salcantay pass. It is a very steep climb and is very hard, on a bad trail. If you have any doubts about your ability to do this climb you should hire a donkey and ride over."

Ok, sounds tough. In his next speech he tells us about a ceremony which will be held at the top of the pass, featuring coca leaves and rocks.

"You must carry a rock up with you for the ceremony."

A bit tougher now!

Over the course of the evening, Isay brings up the donkeys several more times, reiterating how hard tomorrow's going to be. It seems to have the desired effect; a couple of people are more or less terrified into taking up the offer. Isay will no doubt be collecting a healthy commission. Eventually, everyone decides to turn in for the night. There's only so much popcorn you can eat.

Day 2

At 6am we're served a hot cup of coca tea in bed. I am especially grateful for this: it's usually my job to get up and make tea, and mornings are cold at 3900m. The hearty breakfast that follows is just what the doctor ordered for the day's 750m climb. After breakfast we select our rocks for the ceremony at the top. It's a pretty easy selection really: the ones we choose are more pebble than rock. Then, the race is on...

New contenders show their faces today for the King of the Mountain stage. The Italians, with their passion, and the Dutch, with their abnormally long legs, enter the fray. Along with the New Zealanders, the lone Aussie and the French, these new contenders bring the promise of great battle to this, a now truly international race. A final rest stop is called before the big climb, then it's all on...

"GO!!" screamed Isay.

Well, that's what we heard anyway. What he actually said was: "Take it slow, pace yourselves. See you at the top."

After the posturing and the mental games that have been playing out during the warm up, it's now down to business. And it's the Dutch that set the pace. The Italians quickly fall behind; they seem to have used up the entirety of their passion just making it to the final rest stop. The Kiwis and the Aussie are right up there...but French Guy is about to make his move, incorporating his "start at the back, pass everyone and win" strategy. Unlike on day one, where we let him lead the way, this time Amanda is having none of it. As he passes her she settles in to the drafting position close behind him; they go flying past the Dutch team, and into the lead. I up the pace too; hoping to stay in view of the leaders just so I can watch this trek duel. It's going to be an awesome battle.

The pace is relentless, too hot for Aussie Jen and Dutch Girl, but Dutch Guy hangs in there, the dark horse, doing all his climb-training in a country with no hills. When it comes to the crunch though, there are only two people in this race: Amanda and French Guy, slugging it out. They're soon out of sight and my focus switches to the battle for third place. It's a short battle. My initial speed burst to get into the leading bunch has taken its toll; Dutch Guy also disappears into the distance. With a large gap back to the next person, it looks like I'll be settling for a solid fourth.

As I reach the top I see two clues as to the result of this epic battle. Amanda is standing there smiling, gazing contently at the awesome vista that is the Salcantay mountain range. French Guy, on the other hand, is lying on the ground, clutching his stomach-and a roll of toilet paper. He is a broken man and Amanda is responsible for the breaking, the undisputed Queen of the Mountain.

Unsurprisingly, the climb hasn't been as hard as Isay made it out to be. As far as I'm concerned, the people who rode donkeys up the mountain looked to have a far more torrid time than us. I'm far happier to have trusted in my own two feet on these narrow trails rather than sitting in a precariously elevated position and leaving my fate to a mule. As usual we have a very long rest at the top but I'm more than happy to rest here. The snow-capped mountain scenery is simply stunning.

The ceremony for Pachamama is a simple affair. Isay places five coca leaves on a large flat rock and then asks us all to place our rocks in a pile on top of them. It is at this point that the majority of the group goes hunting for rocks. Amanda, Jen and I are among the few who sit back and relax, having done as we were asked, bringing our rocks up from the bottom. The ceremony asks for safe passage and, with our passage now pretty much guaranteed, all we need protecting from is the feeling of smugness. We place our rocks on the leaves first and look on in amusement as people, returning from their illegal stone gathering, try to balance much larger stones on our little pebbles. Once the ceremony's out of the way, and knowing by now how long these rest stops last, I find a quiet place away from the hordes and have a little sleep in the sun.

Luckily, Amanda remembers to wake me when it's time to leave.

After claiming the Queen of the Mountain stage, Team Kiwi/Aussie settles back into the group for the trek to camp. One long, hot and dusty 1750m descent into the valley later, we arrive, once again, to tents already erected. Jen buys Amanda a beer at the local store in recognition of her stage victory and we retire to the already waiting mountain of food. Walking by a couple of independent trekkers cooking noodles on their little cooker on our way to the dining room, we can certainly relate to their undisguised contempt for us soft, fully catered for, group trekkers. As much as I can relate, I don't care; I could easily get used to this. French Guy, barely making it to camp, has an early night.

Day 3

The morning's trek turns out to be my favourite part of the trail. We've hit the jungle and are trekking down a river valley. It reminds me very much of Kauaeranga Valley back home. As awesome as snow-capped mountains are, you just can't beat a good old-fashioned piece of bush! I'm enjoying it so much I leave Amanda chatting with someone and head to the front to test out the second guide. We're neck and neck for a good 45 minutes before he hears something in the bush and we stop for a look. There's nothing there; I have a strong suspicion he just needed a rest. Confidence is high in Team Kiwi.

The further down the valley we head, the less like New Zealand it is. Bananas, papaya, passionfruit (on trees, not vines!), sugarcane, coffee beans and the biggest avocado trees I've ever seen, all growing freely here at the lower, hotter altitude. We even spot some very rare Andean strawberries, the smallest in the world apparently. With our group nineteen strong, we only get to try one each...they don't taste great so we're not overly concerned that they're possibly now extinct.

After lunch something happens that has never happened to us before on the third day of a five day trek: we board a bus! Well, more precisely, a ten-seater minivan...into which we manage to fit our entire group for the hour long ride to camp. Not all of the group are actually *in* the vehicle. Some ride on the roof. Isay spots a mate on the way that needs a ride: yeah, hop in! Plenty of room!!

And that's how we arrive at Camp Techno: a heavily populated campsite complete with bar, bonfire and techno music blaring when we arrive. It's at this precise moment I begin to miss independent trekking. Seeking a little solitude I decide against going to the hot pools that are on offer (Amanda decides to go, solely for a wash!) and retire to the tent to nurse my continuing blisters, even managing to get the music turned down a bit. But the solitude doesn't last long. As group after group return from the hot pools, the partying starts, and continues well into the night. I **hated** techno before; now I've reached an all-new level of loathing.

Day 4

Today is another road walk. When the option of taking a bus to Hydro Electrica is tabled, we jump at the chance, and happily avoid a long, hot, dusty and quite pointless walk.

> Amanda- Pointless because it was along a road through an industrial landscape, with new dams being built.

In Hydro Electrica we have to wait...as part of the tour group returns from a morning zip-lining. Only a ten kilometre walk stands between us and our final destination, Aguas Calientes.

Sack of belongings over my shoulder Santa-style, in the absence of a good sized backpack, we hit the trail easily enough. It's completely flat, shaded, in a nice bush/river setting, following the train tracks from Hydro Electrica to Aguas Calientes. Occasionally spotting Machu Picchu in the distance is the only thing that sets this rail walk apart from the movie "Stand by me." It's 32°C; I'm hoping the dead body in the movie doesn't end up being me.

We're walking along happily when suddenly, the heavens open and our leisurely stroll takes a sinister turn. It's almost kill-or-be-killed, every man for himself. I'm not too fussed about my gear, it's in a dry bag; Amanda's, however, which I've managed to squeeze into my sack as well, has only the protection of the sack. This is all the motivation I need and I'm off, almost at a run. I'm sick to death of all the stopping anyway; they can't call me back if they can't catch me. It's my turn to win a stage for the team.

But this is terrain made for the Dutch- and their abnormally long legs. Not only do they catch me, they pass me with ease. I'll have to settle for third. Jen, also suffering from a waterproofing problem, is a close fourth. Together, as we wait for the others to arrive, we abuse the tour company for making us carry these ridiculous, non-waterproof sacks.

> Amanda- We were pissed off because they NEVER told us we would have to carry our stuff. If we'd known this we would've brought a decent backpack- or less stuff!

Surprisingly, after such an average day, the hostel we book into is excellent. We have a private room, complete with ensuite. While Amanda is battling with the water temperature in the shower, eventually having to settle for cold, I get the chance to look back on the trail that was named in the National Geographic Adventure magazine, one of the 25 best in the world. In reality, I'd struggle to put it in the top 25 treks in South America. Take away an excellent second day and a pretty great morning on the third and it would actually be quite shit. With Amanda's cold water screams echoing throughout the hostel, I'm no longer able to concentrate on quiet reflection, so I relax and wait for my shower. Fifteen minutes later I pop in and the water has warmed to perfection. Amanda is not happy.

Machu Picchu: day 5

Climbing four hundred metres up: one thousand steps- of the stair variety, not the foot. A 4:15am start.

Ever since Amanda tore her anterior crucial ligament skiing, her still-mending knee has rebelled against stairs. The more there are, the more it complains. Me, I've never liked mornings; the earlier I rise, the grumpier I am. We wonder what the hell we're doing this for.

It's an early start to beat the crowds, most of whom will be taking the bus up to the gates. It's only the hard core trekkers (and tight bastards like us) that decide to walk it. And it's a tough old climb first thing in the morning. We make good time though and arrive at the gate entrance, managing to stake a position very close to the front of the quickly forming queue. Unfortunately for me, I need to form a queue of my own, waiting for the toilets to open. As people start queuing behind me, the buses begin to arrive. I stand there watching my early morning advantage quickly disappear. By the time the toilets open and I've finished my business, it's a physical impossibility to get back to where Amanda is waiting in line. I've no alternative but to join the mob at the back of the line and hope to find her inside.

Luckily the queues move quickly and Amanda is waiting inside the gate with the rest of our group, which, in turn, is waiting for our guide. Poor old Isay has lost his identification and, without it, is unable to finish the job he started. With the gates open, we're all impatient to get in amongst it but our new guide is late. People stream past us to get their first glimpse of this world famous ruin. And still we wait...

Finally New Guide turns up (blissfully unaware that he is no longer getting tipped) and we're off. I've never been all that keen on guides, preferring to go at my own pace but this guy is actually quite interesting. Or maybe it's more accurate to say that the history of Machu Picchu is. Our first stop is to watch the sun rising up over the mountains and beaming its first rays on this ancient site. Not a bad start to the day. For a further two hours we wander around listening to story after story, and theory after theory. It's fascinating stuff.

Once the tour's over, our trekking group sits down for a picnic together. We're all catching different trains and buses back to Cusco so this is a farewell breakfast. And a slightly naughty one at that. Outside food and drink are not allowed into the grounds, but on the advice of Isay we've all brought food -and plenty of water-because of the extortionate prices charged in the only restaurant outside. While waiting for the toilets I noticed a vending machine selling cans of coke for a whopping US$5. Quite frankly it would be un-Peruvian to actually follow rules so, although we witnessed a few people with blatantly displayed food being asked to dispose of it before they were allowed to enter the ruins, a stealthily hidden sandwich and drink are easy to bring in...

After breakfast we finally get the opportunity to explore on our own. The main ruin is so big that even over the course of two hours, the guide missed stuff, so another loop of the one-way system is the first order of the day.

Then, with tickets to climb Machu Picchu Mountain, we decide to head in that direction. Unfortunately, after four days of being guided, I have a few navigation issues and we're halfway up to the sun dial (and the end of the famous Inca trail) before I realise we've missed the turn off. Committed, we continue on to the sundial...another 300m up.

Whilst taking in the view (and contemplating sneaking off down the unguarded exit of the Inca trail), I overhear someone saying that Machu Picchu Mountain closes to climbers at 11am. I look at my watch; its 10:55am. SHIT! Once again the race is on.

At 11:10am we get to the gate and are allowed to enter as long as we turn back by 12.30pm. No chance. With a 600m climb ahead of us, we promptly sit down and fuel up, eating all the food we have to lighten the load for this super steep ascent. And the stair climb begins. Amanda, the hill climb expert, quickly leaves me behind. Her knee complaining on every step, she decides it's better to get this done as quickly as possible. I'm more of the slow and steady climber, stopping for plenty of...photo opportunities.

In 50 minutes I reach the top and am rewarded with a fantastic view of the ruin and the surrounding valley on a perfectly clear day. Amanda's been there for fifteen minutes. With an expected ascent time of between an hour and a half and two hours, we've both nailed it and are able to spend a good half hour on the top, looking down on the much more popular climb of Huayna Picchu, which has been booked solid for months. Who on earth is that organised?

Eventually we are moved along by a friendly official. I manage to keep up with Amanda on the downhill leg, her knee liking the stairs down even less. Before you know it we're back at the ticket box signing out. Time in: 11:10am. Time out: 1pm.

"You went to the summit?" the ticket lady asks.

"Yes."

She looks suitably impressed.

With only one attraction left to visit Amanda decides to call it a day. Seven hours of climbing up and down stairs has taken its toll on her dodgy knee so I'm off to see the Inca Bridge on my own while she heads off in search of a $5 Coke. Our water has long since run out. Luckily, my solo expedition is a quick round trip on a completely flat trail and I'm back in less than 45 minutes. The Inca Bridge is, well, a bridge; it's where it leads to that's significant, for sheer astonishment value. It seems that the builders of this trail simply cut a bit out of a sheer cliff face. Considering the thousand metre drop to the bottom, I would've demanded a hand rail as well. And a parachute.

I arrive back at the overpriced restaurant to find Amanda has saved me half of the $5 Coke. I knock back this final "nutrition" and we set off down the one thousand steps back to Aguas Calientes, stopping for a quick look around a museum on the way, mainly because it has air conditioning. It's been a long, hot and tiring day. And it's not over yet.

With our train not leaving until 9.30pm, we spend the evening in a restaurant with the remaining members of our trekking group who are booked on the same train as us. Over dinner, from information we've collectively gathered over the last five days, we bestow awards on two of the groups who are no longer with us. The four person South African team gets the *"value"* award because they paid the least for the tour, US$180pp. They took a local bus back to Cusco (from Hydro Electrica) earlier in the day. The *"saw you coming"* award goes to the Belgian team, who booked through an operator in Europe and paid around US$1000 each, for four days. As for which tour company we actually went with? No one knows. It certainly wasn't the one *we* booked with. Award ceremony completed, we head for the train station.

One train and one minivan later we arrive in Cusco at 2am. Expecting to be delivered back to our hostel, as per our pre-trek discussion, we are nonetheless unsurprised to be dropped off in a deserted plaza outside the city centre. Knowing that Cusco after dark doesn't have the best of reputations outside of the well-lit and heavily policed tourist area, I decide to extend a menacing looking walking pole for the walk back to our hostel. You'd have to be mad to attack a man with a sack slung over his back, carrying a pointy weapon, grumpy because he needs his bed. Thankfully there are no other mad men roaming the streets, we get back safely and collapse into bed after a 22 hour day.

Over the next few days we relax in Cusco, hoping to recover enough to take on the Ausangate trek. It is reputedly one of the ten best treks in the world, and a lot less commercialised than the trails to Machu Picchu. Once again we're accosted by hordes of street vendors. If you sit or stand in one place for too long you're surrounded by vendors selling everything from sunglasses to paintings to photos with a cute llama.

"No thanks, you've already asked me...twelve times today."

In a step up from Arequipa, with its death defying intersection rule, there are traffic lights here. Strangely, there are also police officers directing traffic at the intersections...completely ignoring the lights! Or even more strangely, directing traffic exactly how the lights are directing it.

Unfortunately, Ausangate is not to be. After five days rest Amanda's knee is still not right and Jen hasn't recovered from an injury she picked up along the way. Injuries aside, a long spell of bad weather is about to hit the mountains and that's enough for us to reluctantly cancel our trek plans and move on. Jen is off to Bolivia; we are heading north, further into Peru. With this in mind we decide on a farewell dinner. It's finally time to try *cuy*.

Cuy is guinea pig, and has been a staple food in the Andes for hundreds of years. Putting aside memories of my childhood pet "Aqua Man," we walk into a restaurant, find a table, sit down and order two plates of *cuy*. Vegetarian Jen is relieved to sit this one out but happy enough to bear witness.

Never in the history of food has a meal been photographed (or discussed) more! Jen is in on the photo action too but does spend a good part of dinner putting napkins over the head of Amanda's *cuy*- to stop it staring at her. Amanda just seems to be pushing it around the plate anyway, napkin-hat and all. I happily chomp away on mine. It tastes good, but with more bone than meat on such a tiny creature, it takes a disproportionate amount of energy to eat for very little nutritional gain.

After posting the photos online we receive plenty of abuse from friends and family who have obviously had guinea pigs as pets in their youth. Sister Sandy though, sees it differently...

"It's what Aqua Man would've wanted."

The next day we bid Jen farewell, and book a bus north to Huaraz. Our final walk around Cusco reveals a knick-knack emporium-type shop. Its name is Kevin...

14- The best trek we've ever done

After 33 hours on a bus (with a quick stopover in Lima, where I spot another knick-knack shop named Adrian), we are determined not to make the same mistake we made with the taxi driver in Cusco. As the bus pulls into Huaraz station, Amanda puts on her negotiating face; we disembark and enter the fray.

Just outside the terminal we're accosted by at least ten taxi drivers. Amanda asks how much...

"Ten soles," is the unanimous reply.

But Amanda's already cottoned onto the fact that it's a buyer's market; it's only us and one other gringo couple looking for rides.

"Three."

Every single taxi driver looks at us as though we've just murdered their first born children. Eventually realising no one is going to take us for three soles, Amanda grudgingly accepts the counter offer of five and we have a ride. We also have another passenger as a tour operator joins us for the ride to our hostel. Little do we know, but this man is to become our stalker. For now, we're just pleased to be off the bus.

A major goal of our South American adventure was to walk the ten day Huayhuash circuit, also reputedly one of the top ten treks in the world. It was plunged into the limelight back in the eighties by two British climbers and their attempt to be the first to climb the west face of Siula Grande, one of the mountains in the Huayhuash range. Battling cataclysmic weather and catastrophic events, their tale of survival, immortalised in the book and movie "Touching the void," is without doubt one of the most inspiring tales of survival I've ever come across. I want to be where it all happened.

We wonder if we should do a warm up trek first but after more than four months at altitude, barring the occasional trip to sea level, we're already well acclimatised so decide against it, dreading the possibility of injury that'll prevent us from achieving our main goal.

How shall we travel? Should we sign up with another tour group? Should we hire an *arriero* (a man who transports gear on pack animals)? Or should we travel independently, carrying our own gear? We're only at the decision stage and things are already getting interesting...

After no less than half a dozen phone calls the next morning from yesterday's taxi-sharing tour operator, in which he badgers us to sign up for his tour, we find ourselves in Mr Persistent's office to see what he has to offer. He has a tour going in two days time, but it's an eight day trek which doesn't cross the San Antonio pass to the Cutatambo campsite in notorious "Touching the void" territory. The price is a good one, but he wants an answer within the hour.

"No chance," Amanda scoffs. "We're considering all our options."

The already excellent price drops and he wants an answer in six hours. OK, we can live with that.

Walking around town, checking out a couple more agencies, we come to realise that the companies offering tours are all basically offering the same option. It's late in the season and numbers are down. The companies that are going for ten days, and crossing the San Antonio pass, seem to be very expensive private tours, a little out of our price range. And we simply don't need a guide, two cooks, a cooking tent, and the extra donkeys required to carry the additional gear.

Another option is to hire an independent *arriero*. Making enquiries at the *Casa de Guías* (The House of Guides), apparently *the* place to hire independent operators, we find out we'll need to provide a tent, sleeping gear, cooking gear and all the food...and we'd have to cook for anyone we hire...unless we hire a cook! A bit of a hassle really- and it doesn't actually work out much cheaper than the tour we've been offered either. Communication could also be an issue; with nightmarish thoughts of asking the *arriero* to meet us at one campsite, and arriving to find he's gone to another, playing on our minds. We leave *Casa de Guías* with the email address of an independent *arriero*. Impatient to get on the trail, we'd hoped for a little more.

Enter Tristan and Phoebe. With his climbing options in the area almost entirely exhausted, Tristan approaches us as we're leaving our lunchtime restaurant. The hope shining in his eyes at finding new arrivals in town is evident at twenty metres.

"Are you guys climbers?"

We let him down gently.

Nearing resignation to the fact that his climbing aspirations are all but over, Tristan, together with partner Phoebe, finds a new spark of hope in our Huayhuash plan. We set a lunch date for the next day to share information, and then wander off to continue our search for the perfect tour, hoping that a group of four has a little more bargaining power.

Excitement mounting at the prospect of hitting the trail again, I simply can't wait for lunch the next day and fire off an email to Tristan that evening. I place special emphasis on the excellent value offered by one particular tour company that has agreed to simply supply an *arriero* and hire us the gear needed, for a very good price...split four ways. We're completely gutted when he replies that they've decided to carry all their own gear. Lunatics. Still undecided, we manage to put the tour company off until morning.

Neither of us really wants to do Mr Persistent's tour, it's too limiting. I lie awake most the night mulling over our options and come to the only conclusion I can in the face of severe sleep deprivation...for the freedom we want, we'll just have to carry our own gear. It's only nine 4300m-plus passes after all...how hard can it be?

When I put this idea to Amanda in the morning, she is unexpectedly open to it. We head off to the tour agency to offer our apologies because we've decided to go it alone...but we find ourselves strangely reluctant once we get there.

"Last chance," I say, as we hover at the bottom of the stairs.

Mr Persistent seems to sense our presence on the street outside and comes down the stairs to meet us. Amanda tells him of our decision to walk the trail independently and stands firm while Mr Stalker protests. Then he says:

"We can supply you with an *arriero* if you don't want to join the group."

Before you know it, we're back in his office, this time discussing terms. Neither of us wants to carry a big bag for ten days at altitude so, after a few reservations, we sign up, having procured complete freedom on the trail.

The next question is...what the hell do we cook for an *arriero*? Mr Persistent, having finally divested us of some money, completely loses interest and hands us over to another man, Mr Helpful, who takes us shopping. Judging by the food he fires into the shopping trolley, *arrieros* are inordinately fond of biscuits and jam. Never in my life have I taken a litre of jam (in a glass jar, no less) on a trek. Luckily we get some things we like as well. With food and cookware purchased, and tent for the *arriero* hired (we are assured he will bring his own sleeping gear), we head off to a restaurant to discuss our route plans with Tristan and Phoebe. We're all set to depart the next day. Walking home that evening I step in a hole in the pavement, twisting my ankle slightly...and am then bitten by a dog! But petty things like this aren't going to stop me; I've been looking forward to this for too long...

Huayhuash circuit; day 1

Well, it wouldn't be a trek without some sort of screw up at the start! After two days of frantic preparation we awake to our alarm at 4.10am, aiming to catch the only bus at five. Our taxi arrives ten minutes early and gives us the toot. Amanda wanders out to the hostel entry to let him know we won't be long...and finds that we're locked inside! Panic! We hear a car drive off; was that the taxi leaving?? Double panic!! After what seems like ages, the hostel owner is woken by the commotion and finally arrives to unlock the door, which we frantically rush out of...and discover a still waiting taxi. Phew! The best laid plans, almost foiled by a deadbolt...

Two buses, five hours, one strange transaction (a seemingly random man flagging down the bus to give us money to pay the *arriero*), and a bunch of singing and dancing rubbish collectors later, we arrive in the small settlement of Pocpa, elevation 3450m. Here, we meet Octavio, our *arriero*, his three donkeys, and the horse he is riding!?! Apart from his animals, he doesn't look like he's brought much with him.

"Do you have a sleeping bag?" Amanda asks.

"No."

Off to a great start then.

After farewelling Tristan and Phoebe, who are hoping to hitch a ride up the road to the first camp site, we leave Octavio loading up the donkeys and head off to check out "town." Luckily, one of the two buildings in town is a hostel and rents out gear. Not knowing us, and never having heard of Octavio, they are very reluctant to rent us anything without some kind of security. We have just the thing: Amanda hands over her expired passport, which they happily accept.

Finally, we're on the road. Unfortunately it is an actual road, constructed for the mining that goes on in the area.

"Donkeys take two hours to camp, you will take three." Octavio informs us. With that, he gallops off after his nimble asses and we are alone.

We spend the next three hours walking through a very picturesque...mining area, hoping to get a ride ourselves. But there's no traffic going our way. All we can see, as far as the eye can see, is the many signs posted liberally en route proclaiming the wonder of this environment- and the need to protect it. Amanda especially is struck by the obvious irony, that the signs are the work of the same mining company that is raping the land.

Apart from a 45 minute hail storm welcoming us to the mountains, the walk is uneventful and uninspiring and we arrive at camp (elevation 4180m) in a little over three hours. It's been tough going, but good acclimatisation for the higher stuff to come. Octavio greets us with a smile.

"Where is your cooking tent?" he asks.

"We don't have one."

"Where will you cook?"

"Outside, like we always do."

That answer horrifies him, so to show it's possible, I set to making a massive feast in the biggest pot I've ever brought into the wilderness, channelling Michael and Jo (Dientes) to help me.

After dinner, while Amanda's washing the dishes in the stream, and having scary barking contests with wild rabid dogs (and winning), I wander around camp aimlessly, checking out the toilets, reading random signs and generally amusing myself. During these wanderings I spot something that looks slightly out of place. Investigating further, I discover a note addressed to us, from Tristan and Phoebe! As planned, they've managed to catch a ride up the road, and have set out for the next campsite immediately.

We'll need to be on our game if we're to catch them so, without further ado, we head for bed...and spend the night listening to mining trucks driving up and down the gravel road. "Ahhh, the serenity..."

Day 2

As I cook breakfast in the morning, I watch two fully-catered tour groups wake up, breakfast, and then hit the trail with their guides and emergency evacuation horses, leaving the cooks and *arrieros* to break camp. Octavio, on the other hand, complained about dinner, complained about breakfast –before it was even made- and has slept in. We begin to wonder if he's a little bit of a mummy's boy. It's certainly a late exit from camp.

Fresh from her Queen of the Mountain success, and with no suitable humans to challenge her, Amanda decides to race some donkeys to the top of our first pass of the day, the 4700m Qaqanan pass. The two kilometre climb for a 520m elevation gain is a tough ask straight out of camp and, as we near the top, the donkeys are breathing down our necks looking for a passing opportunity. Amanda puts in a final burst and hits the top first...only to discover that it's not the top. It's only about halfway. Hate it when that happens. We let the donkeys pass and continue on at a more manageable pace...that is, more manageable for me.

When we finally do reach the top, the Cordillera Huayhuash opens out in front of us and we get our first indication of how special this place is. With cloud, rain and hail in the area, we only get teasing glimpses of its grandness but it's already a million times better than walking up a mining road. We have a quick chat with one of the guided groups, some American Peace Corps workers we've caught up with, and continue on our way.

We head down into the valley, and then up again, tackling the 4650m Carhuac pass, finally arriving at Lake Carhuacocha campsite in six and a half hours. We spot Tristan and Phoebe as we walk in and invite them over for dinner. Given their weight-conscious packing, of largely freeze-dried and rationed food, they're not really in the position to turn down burritos and hot chocolate.

"I need to talk to you," Octavio informs us once we've set up camp. We are about to learn that there may be more to our witless *arriero* than meets the eye.

It seems that Octavio has managed to get cell phone reception at the top of the pass and has been talking to his friend...who has told him that he isn't being paid enough and that he should abandon us. We have given him every cent that Dodgy Transaction Guy gave us after he waved down the bus. Apparently it's not enough.

"I'm not a bad guy, so I will take you to the next village where you can get a bus back to Huaraz." Octavio continues.

We can't quite believe what we are hearing. Amanda lets rip, with a few choice suggestions, and we offer to make up the shortfall, just to save our trek, but it all seems to fall on deaf ears.

Amanda thinks she may be losing something in translation so employs the services of Tristan who has just shown up for burritos. He isn't able to understand the situation any better than we are so Phoebe walks off to find a more fluent Spanish speaker and returns with Patrick the Peace Corps worker.

Surrounded by five people, two of them VERY angry, Octavio is now severely outnumbered...and shitting himself.

"He says he's been underpaid." Patrick confirms. "He wants 300 soles before he continues."

"We've agreed to pay him that," I exclaim, "but he's not getting a fucking cent out of me until the end of the trek!"

Amanda hasn't let up either, telling Octavio he should be ashamed of himself for even thinking about abandoning us. I was unaware my wife knew the Spanish word for arsehole but it's coming up thick and fast now.

Eventually a solution of sorts is reached.

"He's going to ride to the nearest village, phone the agency and sort it out with them," Patrick tells us. "He said he'll be back in the morning."

"Fine." Amanda answers hotly. "His donkeys stay."

With that, Octavio is gone, and I try and remember how to load a donkey...

Our burritos and hot chocolate are a lot less fun after that and we head to bed, an anxious and sleepless night ahead. If Octavio leaves us, our trek is over.

> Amanda- I spent all night awake thinking I could hear Octavio returning and sneaking off with his donkeys.

Day 3

With no sign of Octavio in the morning, it's Patrick that comes to our rescue again, asking his groups' *arrieros* if they can transport our gear. They agree, for a price of course, but we know we'll have to work to their itinerary if we go with it. It's certainly not ideal but at least we'd still be in the game. Patrick then walks off to the freezing cold lake and dives in, the Peace Corps glacial lake swim record in his sights...

We're saved from having to decide however, when Octavio eventually returns, all smiles. It must be said he's somewhat sheepish after the bollocking Amanda gave him last night. The good news is, we are continuing.

"So; we pay you the 300 soles at the end of the trek?" Amanda confirms.

"Yes."

No problem, the extra will be coming off his tip. We suspect this is less about the money (although we know now that the money wasn't the best) and more about the lack of creature comforts out here. He *is* a mummy's boy; the evidence is now overwhelming.

Once again we're last to hit the trail but our late start has its rewards as the clouds part momentarily and we catch a fleeting glimpse of Peru's second highest mountain, Yerupaja, standing tall at 6634m.

"It's not going to rain today." Protection Money Man proclaims, as we hand over our cash.

Protection Money Man isn't actually here to predict the weather though. He represents a scheme initiated by an assortment of locals in the area, aiming to ensure the safety of trekkers from the robberies and occasional murders that have happened in the past. Once a stronghold of the now defeated "Shining Path" guerrillas, this area has certainly seen its fair share of violence. We're heartened with his weather forecast, and his local knowledge, all the same.

For the next two hours we play hide and seek with the mountains and lakes. They hide, we seek! We do manage to spot the north face of the famous Siula Grande though. Has anyone ever taken that on? Maybe next time...

Just as we start the climb to 4800m Siula pass, it starts hailing... for the third day in a row. As we climb higher, hail is replaced with snow. Protection Money Man was spot on with his predictions, no rain whatsoever. It's a long, steep and cold climb to the top, our only respite a short break for lunch under a large rock, out of the weather, along with the Peace Corps party. Patrick has added one more lake to his tally, foregoing another two because he was a bit cold.

It certainly isn't weather for sitting around in, so we don't stay long. As we press on to the top I feel a sudden pain in my chest. Self-diagnosis says I've pulled a muscle, trying to gasp in the thin, cold air that my body needs to continue exerting itself at this altitude. Things just got a little bit tougher; the top can't come fast enough.

And who do we meet there? Coke Lady! I read about Coke Lady in several blogs I was trawling for information. A mysterious woman who climbs a 4800m pass armed with nothing more than a couple of dozen bottles of Coke. It would be rude not to buy one, even if there's a blizzard.

But Coke Lady isn't Coke Lady today. When we approach her, she tells us she only sells Coke during the summer. Instead she asks *us* for chocolate and lollies. We hand over some of our plentiful supply and continue on our way, wondering if she's part of the local protection plan, ensuring everyone gets over the pass safely. It certainly makes more sense than walking for three hours to the top of a 4800m pass, sitting in a blizzard, with nothing more than a worn looking tarpaulin for protection, and begging lollies from the gringos walking by.

The downhill journey is a lot easier on the legs but the pace is not a lot faster, the trail having all but disappeared under snow. A few wrong turns later we manage to find the trail...and Tristan and Phoebe. Each is looking distinctively mulish, with heavy packs weighing them down; it doesn't take us lightweights long to catch them up. We walk into camp together...in glorious sunshine.

After four hours of hail and snow the sun is very welcome in our new camp ground. As we're setting up camp and putting out our wet stuff to dry, a group of gun-toting locals wander over to collect the protection fee. The irony is not lost on me. There's a fair chance that in such a remote community the people who are doing the guarding of the Huayhuash campsite were once doing the robbing. Having said that, they're very friendly armed men and, after a bit of a chat, they retire to their military compound (a shack) and leave us lying in the sun, thawing, for the rest of the afternoon.

Day 4

Last night, we caught wind of an alternative route into the high mountains, being taken today by an Israeli group- a middle aged man and his two sons. Once we'd cottoned on to their plan, we spent the rest of the evening in their cooking tent, looking at the possibility we could do it too- after bribing their English speaking guide with copious amounts of chocolate. Tristan and I updated our maps eagerly before retiring. I wake up excited and stick my head out of the tent to welcome the new day.

I'm greeted by pea soup fog. Not the best conditions for attempting a high mountains route. A quick consultation with the others confirms our change of plans for the day. New destination: hot pools!

It's bloody cold so, after serving Octavio breakfast in bed, we get moving. Not wanting to sit around for long in the icy fog, only early starters Tristan and Phoebe leave camp before us. The local dog, for whatever reason, decides to come with us. It's good to have some canine company on the trail again. Amanda wants to call him Hamish, because apparently, he looks like a Hamish (sorry Hamishes!), but I manage to persuade her to go with my name, Limpy Poo Fur. He walks with a limp, and has a big wad of donkey poo tangled up in his fur. I'm a big fan of keeping it simple.

As we climb towards the 4750m Portachuelo pass it starts snowing again and I can honestly say this is the coldest I have ever been on a trek. We carry on at a good pace, purely to keep warm. With pea soup fog and driving snow, it's not the most scenic day, but we do manage to spot a lake. Even the conversation with Tristan and Phoebe, as we catch up to and pass them, is a short one. The conversation we have with a local, who asks us if we have seen a stray donkey is slightly longer, even though we haven't seen his donkey.

"Where are you from?" he asks.
"New Zealand."

For the next ten minutes Amanda tries to explain to him where New Zealand is. Eventually she gives up; we dig ourselves out of the mounting snow, and continue on our way.

Finally, after three and a half hours: salvation. The steam coming off the hot pools at the Atuscancha camp ground beckons. We have a slight problem though. In our efforts to keep warm, we've completely blitzed the competition, arriving at the pools ahead of even the *arrieros*. With no swimming gear, we've no option but to sit by the pool and stare longingly at its inviting waters. I give my hands an emergency dunk in an effort to restore circulation and we find a sheltered spot to sit down and wait.

> Amanda- The local Peruvian men did invite me to go in nude. Even though my waterproofs are soaked and I'm chilled to the bone I decline their kind offer...

Everyone else dribbles into camp and eventually Octavio turns up as well. He is surprised to find that we've been here for two hours and will no doubt be getting a ribbing from his fellow *arrieros* for being beaten to camp by his group. With an icy cold rain still falling, we get the tent up quickly and change into our swimming gear. Amanda emerges from the tent first. Jo (Dientes) graced us with her sleeping bag attire on the Puerto Williams-Punta Arenas ferry in Chile. I considered myself even more fashionable, in my shorts, socks, jandals and puffer jacket. But as far as fashion statements go, Amanda soundly defeats us all, in a glamorous and imaginative bikini, beanie, waterproofs and jandals combination. We head for the pool.

And that's where we stay for the rest of the afternoon. We're all fully aware of the energy it'll be sapping from us for tomorrow's climb...but none of us care. It feels too good to be warm again.

Once we get to prune stage, we decide it's time to get out. I cook up a speed feed in the rain, serving dinner to Octavio and Amanda snug in their respective tents, wishing we had a cooking tent for the first time. I give our new best friend Limpy Poo Fur a sausage or two, and quickly retire to the tent myself.

Day 5

We emerge from the tent 12 hours later to a beautiful day. After a miserable cold one yesterday, the restorative powers of the sun's rays are welcome relief. Basking in the sun, we are last to leave camp by a long way. Even the *arrieros* who pack everything up beat us onto the trail. Good old faithful Limpy Poo Fur has waited for us though and the three of us walk out of camp together.

It doesn't take Limpy Poo Fur long to realise we're not the front runners today, and he runs off ahead, completely forgetting who fed him sausages yesterday. I don't really remember much about the four kilometre climb to the top of 5000m Cuyoc pass, except that it's a stunning day. And that, even after popping several painkillers before I start out, sucking in the thin mountain air is excruciatingly painful with a chest injury. That said, my memory of the climb was pretty well obliterated anyway by our arrival at the top.

"Wow, this is the best mountain scenery I have EVER seen!" exclaims Amanda.

No arguments from me. And coming from New Zealand, with its fair share of amazing mountain vistas, that is no small accolade. The difference here is that we're actually standing 1000m higher than New Zealand's highest, Aoraki/Mount Cook, and there are still peaks soaring above us into the sky. Snow-capped mountains seem so close we can almost touch them; it is truly spectacular. Tristan and Phoebe think so too, they've been unable to leave since they arrived here an hour ago. We sit down next to them and take it all in.

After 90 minutes, hunger sets in and a cold breeze makes its presence felt. We leave Tristan, reigniting his climbing aspirations, and Phoebe still sitting on top of the world, and begin making our way down into the next valley. In the distance we can see the Peace

Corps group, and Patrick heading for another lake. He rejoins his group just as we catch up.

"Eighteen." He smiles in quiet satisfaction.

He's closing in on the record. Whether he made it or not, we'll never know, for this is where we part ways. One of the groups' guides, Patrick and his co-worker mate have plans to climb to the top of San Antonio pass today before returning to the valley and camping at a site further down it. Another guide, the Old Guy in the group and Emergency Horse are not attempting the climb and will just carry on down the valley. We bid both parties farewell and carry on ourselves.

We're making such good pace we manage to completely miss the turn off to our camp site. As we stop and regain our bearings, getting ready to take a bit of a short cut cross country, Old Guy catches up to us. It's clear that he's struggling.

"You should ride the horse for a bit," I suggest, only half joking.

"That would be cheating," he replies.

A man after my own heart. We veer off trail and eventually walk into camp Guanacpatay from completely the wrong direction. At 4480m in perfectly clear weather, it could get a bit nippy here.

Later on in the evening as Amanda's dishing out more chocolate to the Israeli party, their English speaking guide imparts some more inside information when she hears that we plan to cross the San Antonio pass into the next valley.

"The climb to the top of the pass is good," she says, "but the descent down the other side is very steep and very dangerous. There's an alternative route just to the east of that one. It's a steep climb up, but a much easier descent to the bottom."

I'm sold; our chocolate bribery is paying off big time. Tomorrow, we Touch the Void.

Day 6

"That was, without question, the coldest night I have **ever** spent in a tent." I tell Amanda, who, snuggled up in her 30-below sleeping bag, can't understand what the fuss is about. Until she gets out of her sleeping bag, that is.

> Amanda- We woke up to find that, despite our body heat, the tent is covered in a thick layer of ice.

The rising sun- and a 600 metre climb- should get the blood flowing.

We zigzag up into the heavens on another gloriously sunny day, then head up a gully towards the unnamed pass. Enclosed by rock walls on both sides, we are completely unaware of what we're walking towards. We crest the pass and our jaws drop.

"WOW!"

Further words escape me. Yesterday's stunning views have just been rendered insignificant. It's hard to believe these are the same mountains we were walking beside on days two and three, and we now start to wonder what we might've missed in those first four days of bad weather. 5095m is the highest our legs have ever taken us. Once again we join Tristan and Phoebe, sitting down, marvelling at nature's awesomeness.

We then descend into legend...

Quickly setting up our tents at the Cutatambo camp site, the four of us set off. Destination: What the locals now commonly refer to as Joe Simpson Base Camp (Simpson being one of the climbers, and the writer of Touching the Void), a further five kilometres into the mountains.

Amanda has promised her family she won't attempt to climb the west face of Siula Grande, but I have made no such promises. I am under quite a time constraint though. After breaking his leg, falling off a cliff, then into a crevasse and taking about a week to crawl back to base camp, crawling through the camp latrine on the way, Joe Simpson had it pretty easy. I need to be back to cook dinner. That gives me about two hours. I approach the first challenge in my summit attempt, the glacier. It is at that moment that I realise I've left an important piece of kit back in Huaraz: my trusty all-purpose jandals, perfect for glacier travel. Summit attempt foiled, I break my own leg and crawl back to camp for dinner, not forgetting to crawl through the latrine on the way...only to find that Amanda's burned all my clothes. (Read the book folks!)

Ok, now here's what *really* happened:

Tristan and Phoebe humour us all the way up the valley to Lake Sarapococha as we continuously stop to take re-enactment photos and video footage of Joe Simpson's ordeal. At one stage they wait, rather patiently, it must be said, while I make a splint for my broken leg out of my walking pole, and tie it on with Amanda's spare shoe laces.

Satisfied with the footage we have, we head in the direction of the lake, but climb a path winding up a giant moraine rather than heading directly to the lake itself. It offers a far better view of the area.

Totally spent from my re-enactments (you try crawling over rocks with a broken leg at 4400m), my chest injury *and* a major climb already today, I plonk myself down on a large rock to rest. I can go no further. Phoebe sits down beside me, happy to have the big pack off her shoulders and equally happy for the rest. Amanda and Tristan press on.

Phoebe and I sit in relative silence simply taking it all in, Siula Grande and several other massive mountains crowding our view. I look down to the lake and try to remember the details of Joe Simpson's crawl back to base camp, my imagination filling in the blanks. It was nearly thirty years ago; I wonder how much the place has changed.

Our attention then turns to Amanda and Tristan, striding off into the distance. It looks like a trek duel is materialising before our very eyes.

"How far do you think they'll go?" I ask Phoebe, a little concerned about the changing weather and fading light.

"Too far, if I know Tristan," she replies.

Suddenly we see Amanda turn back, leaving Tristan to go it alone.

"And if I know Amanda, she's just worked that out" I say.

"That guy's a *machine!*" Amanda exclaims as she returns to our temporary base camp. "I got all demoralised because I couldn't keep up with him."

It's official: Amanda, Queen of the Mountains, has met her match. Tristan eventually returns from his solo expedition with eagerly awaited photos of the west face of Siula Grande. We head back down the valley together as darkness approaches.

Day 7

After the last two days, the river valley we walk down away from the mountains seems quite uninspiring. Amanda actually walks backwards for the first hour, preferring the view. For the first time in trekking memory I manage to keep up.

The further down the valley we go, the better the scenery seems to get. Dropping below 4000m for the first time in six days, it's a lot greener on this part of the trail- and there are some great waterfalls.

Suddenly a local draws up beside us and we offer a friendly "*hola*". We don't recognise him from camp so Amanda asks where he's come from. He tells us the name of his village and I consult the map, but I can't find it anywhere so ask him to point it out. He points at a trail snaking off the map...

"Down that trail"

It appears that he's crossed the 5000m pass to get into this valley. "Wow, that's a long way; when did you start?"

"This morning."

Our pace is clearly not up to man-machine's standard and after our quick chat, he speeds back up and quickly disappears into the distance.

As we approach Huayllapa, the most populated village we've seen in six days, our thoughts turn to soft drinks. It's a scorcher of a day and I'm tired of having to filter drinking water. We reach a crossroads; one trail will take us back into the mountains, to our next camp site. The other will take us down to Huayllapa, elevation: 3500 metres. Already facing an 800m climb, we decide we can't face a descent, followed, as this one would be, by a larger *ascent*. Banishing all fantasies of Coke, I find an irrigation ditch and fill up my bottle for the climb to come.

This part of the trail is Colca Canyon steep- and Colca Canyon hot. Another near-death-from-dehydration episode is neatly avoided by a well-placed river. What begins as a drink stop turns into a swim, which quickly becomes more of a wash when I discover how cold the water is. Patrick must be completely bonkers!

The climb to camp, at 4400 metres, is by far the hardest section of the trail to date...for me anyway. Amanda is once again happy to be kicking someone's arse after the trouncing she got yesterday.

It's great to be back in the mountains at another very picturesque camp site but the two new, and very large, groups joining us somewhat spoil the serene and intimate camping experience we've had so far. We set our tents up as far from the new arrivals as we can; Tristan and Phoebe, who walked into camp just before us, go even further away! Then, with the soft drink fantasy still fresh in our minds, Amanda decides to brew up some lemonade. It goes especially well with the popcorn.

The rest of the evening is spent listening to a bunch of morons trying to buy a sheep off a shepherd who just happened to bring her flock through camp. It doesn't work out for them when their offer's turned down and, not happy with the outcome, they're getting ruder by the minute. No barbeque for them tonight; good job too, rude, arrogant arseholes.

Day 8

The newly named Rude Arrogant Arseholes group beats us out of camp the next morning but it doesn't take us long to catch them. Out of a group of ten or so, three are already riding their emergency horses, and the rest are struggling alongside, obviously waiting for their turn. Old Guy from the Peace Corps group has just made a bunch of young people look pretty pathetic. It dawns on us that we could've been in this group if we'd signed up for the tour. We thank our lucky stars we didn't.

We've been told it's a long day on the trail today, with two 4800m passes to climb, so we decide to get some pace on to reach our next camp quickly. Tapush pass, a gradual climb and only a kilometre or two from last night's camp, is quickly conquered. Having seen only cows, sheep and donkeys (but surprisingly only one llama) on the circuit so far, we finally spot non-domesticated beasts on the ascent. After close analysis, I decide these creatures are some kind of hybrid-squirrel-wallaby (-the animal, not the Australian rugby player). These squillabies are fast little critters so photographic evidence is unobtainable.

The next climb, Yaucha pass, is a killer. As I'm shuffling up a rather steep part, Amanda looks back and offers me some less than encouraging words.

"It looks like you're walking on the moon."

I feel like I'm as high as the moon. The terrain is certainly barren enough to *be* the moon. And I'm certainly suffering from a distinct lack of oxygen as I look towards the top...and spot salvation.

"There's another Coke Lady!" I fair scream in triumph.

"Where?" Amanda's immediate reply indicates that her anticipation matches mine.

"Up the top there, just to the left of the trail."

That's all the motivation we need to soldier on. But my oxygen impaired vision has let me down horribly. Three quarters of the way up the mountain I manage to lift my head and take another look at Coke Lady, patiently sitting there, waiting for our business. I am surprised- and devastated- to find that she's been replaced by a cairn with a piece of plastic wrapped around it. I reluctantly break the news to Amanda; there will be no coke for us today.

After four hours on the trail, we reach the top and have a quick bite to eat with the Israeli group, who's also just arrived. It's a quick stop at the top of this pass though; the scenery is nowhere near as spectacular as what we've just seen and we head down into the valley, hitting the lead for the first time today.

An hour and a half later we're sitting in the sun at Lake Jahuacocha campsite, having an ice cold beer, courtesy of the camp shop. Peru's second highest mountain, Yarupaja, soars majestically above its glacial lake and we are reminded, yet again, of why we came here. Easily the third best scenery we've encountered on the circuit!

It's over an hour before the next group shows up...and it's Tristan and Phoebe! Carrying all their gear over two passes, they've beaten people half my age riding horses, and having their lunch carried for them. No one deserves a beer more than they do so I track their trajectory, and meet them at where they're headed with a cold one in each hand. I leave them with an invitation to dinner and decide we'd probably better set up camp, rather than sit around drinking all day. The Rude Arrogant Arsehole group stumbles into camp many hours later. They look totally spent, which is great news for us; the expected party never eventuates.

Dinner is burritos, which Tristan insists on cooking after deciding that he and Phoebe have eaten pretty well on this trek considering the limited food they actually brought with them. We, on the other hand, haven't even touched the litre of jam our donkeys have carried for eight days. We sit around into the night, partaking in a few more beers before the cold mountain air drives us tent-ward. Before bed, we successfully wash the dishes *and* our teeth in the river without falling in; it's no mean feat after a few beers.

Day 9

We're not at all interested in rising sufficiently early to get the only bus out of town at 11am, so we decide to sleep in, and then take a leisurely walk out to Llamac at the end of our circuit.

Octavio, who, we've since discovered, has done this trail only once before, lets us in on a little inside information...for the first time in nine days. There's an alternative route, not marked on the map, which misses the final climb up and over 4300 metre Llamac pass. It's not a huge climb in the grand scheme of things but why walk up a hill if you can walk around it?

And that's how we find ourselves on a narrow trail at the top of a cliff, following the river, 300 metres below. Judging by the debris we encounter on this trail, it's very prone to rock falls so we don't dawdle. It's an uninspiring trail, but we were always going to be relatively uninspired after seeing the best mountain scenery we've ever seen. We're similarly underwhelmed with Octavio's "inside tip" and entirely unsure we've saved any time at all taking this route...arriving in Llamac in just under four hours.

Octavio and his donkeys are waiting for us at the hostel we picked. He is keen to get on his way in order to catch up with his uncle for the two day journey back to their village. But he can't turn down a final free lunch. Realising he'll be doing this trip without all the gear we'd hired for him, Amanda asks the obvious question.

"Where will you sleep?"

"Under the stars on my donkey blankets," he replies. "I have a tarp in case it rains."

He complained about the tent, he complained about the sleeping bag...in fact for the first five days of average weather he complained about everything...and *now* he's going to rough it under the stars?? *Really??*

His demeanour changed noticeably when the sun came out however; God forbid, he almost looked happy. A true fair weather camper! We pay him the 300 soles we agreed on and tip him slightly less than planned. The untouched litre of jam goes to a good home, along with most of the other leftover food, and the big pot. Loaded with freebies, Octavio is on his way, galloping off into the sunset, going home to mum.

We deposit what gear we have left in our room. The bathroom is our next stop, looking forward to our first showers in nine days and, for some strange reason, staff decide to clean it for the first time in at least a decade *after* we've used it.

> Amanda- It was the most disgusting bathroom I've seen in my entire life, I'm sure I came out dirtier than when I went in...

Next up, a bit of a lie-down in a real bed; then it's off to explore Llamac- and its dinner possibilities. It eventuates that we gave away most of our food a tad prematurely as we find there's a total of zero places to eat. We return to our room for two minute noodles on the gas cooker; a huge come-down from the gourmet menu of the past nine days. Not long after tea, I start feeling a bit off colour and head for bed.

Day 10

I wake up feeling quite awful but dig into breakfast eggs hoping food might help. It doesn't. Amanda feels fine and I begin to go over what I may've eaten or drunk that she didn't. It doesn't take me long to work it out; in Bolivia and Peru, the set menu for lunch usually includes a *refreshco* which is basically a tap water and cordial mix. I've been drinking these for over six months without a problem. Amanda stopped drinking them when she developed food poisoning in Bolivia, so I've been drinking hers too...as I did yesterday. Finally my blasé approach to hygiene has caught up with me. Unfortunately, we have a bus to catch.

We meet Tristan and Phoebe (who decided to stay in the last camp site another night) at the bus station and all board the bus together. But that's where 'togetherness' ends for me. Over the course of the next five hours I'm in my own world, MP3 blaring, buttocks clenched, trying desperately not to shit myself, knowing full well that if I start I won't be able to stop. Astonishingly, I make it back to Huaraz incident free.

Only a quick stop- to return the hired gear- now separates me from the hostel toilet, and salvation. Unfortunately it's anything but quick when Amanda brings up the near abandonment incident of day two.

"Yes, we talked to Octavio on the evening in question and didn't realise he was taking an extra donkey so we agreed to pay him more money so he wouldn't abandon you." Mr Helpful explains.

Really, I couldn't give a fuck.

"Where's your toilet?" I ask, and am out the door and down the street looking for the public toilet to which he directs me...or at least begins to. I'm gone before he actually finishes the directions. Suffice it to say, it is an unsuccessful search.

When I return Amanda and Mr Helpful are deep in discussion, Amanda holding her own in this Spanish conversation. Finally an agreement of sorts is reached. Mr Helpful will get Octavio's side of the story and we can talk about it again tomorrow.

"Great!" I yell. "Let's go!"

I've told Amanda I'm not feeling so well but she finally realises the magnitude of my problem when, after suggesting we now take the hired sleeping bag back, I reply with a very firm NO and flag down the next taxi. Finally we arrive back at the hostel, and I spend the evening- and most of the next day- in the toilet.

Amanda's next day is more productive. Armed with advice from the tourist information office, she turns up to the tour office with two Tourist Policemen in tow. A stunned Mr Helpful quickly explains Octavio's side of the story. He didn't like his tent, he wasn't fed properly and the 300 soles we gave him was a tip.

"Bullshit!" Amanda is especially pissed off with the food comments. "It was *your* tent, *you* helped us buy the food, we fed him what we ate ourselves, and we paid him *a hell of a lot more than* 300 soles as a tip. I want my money back."

After some more discussion Mr Helpful offers 200 soles. It's now become clear to Amanda that this isn't really his mess; he's just the guy sharing an office with another guy...Mr Persistent, who is conspicuous in his continued absence. The 200 soles he offers looks to be coming from his own pocket, so his company isn't taken to the cleaners online...as Amanda is threatening.

Amanda accepts the 200 soles and walks out with her police escort. It was never about the money anyway. All in all, it's a rather anti-climatic conclusion to the best trek we've ever done.

15- Sun, surf...and boobies

Although eventually I shake off the worst of my food poisoning bout, and resume the eating and drinking necessary for trek recovery, it'll be weeks before it's completely gone. During my recovery, I also manage to get bitten by the same dog that bit me before we went trekking. Amanda wants to bite him back on my behalf; I don't have the stomach to take such a risk.

> Amanda- Its worth pointing out here that in Bolivia when I had hideous food poisoning for two months, Tony wasn't overly sympathetic. In fact he regularly trotted out the line to people that unlike me and my weak constitution he had a stomach of steel and could eat anything with no ill effect. It felt like karma when he finally succumbed.

We hang out with Tristan and Phoebe for the next few days, discussing our plans and swapping information and books over hot chocolates or beer. They introduce us to their favourite street vendor, and treat us to the most delicious pork sandwiches. This is a big step for Amanda who hasn't eaten street food since her "Boli Belly" in Bolivia, nearly three months ago.

During this period of downtime, I even get to watch some rugby! I haven't seen a game in six months so this is no small thing for me. I've kept up to date with the All Blacks schedule and I know they're playing Argentina, in Argentina soon. It's the right time zone so we should be able to catch it at a reasonable hour. Our number one goal over the next two days becomes finding a bar that'll show it. No mean feat in football mad Peru.

But find one we do! Walking down the main street on the way to the bar, I can hardly contain my excitement. We pass a home appliance store. On a big screen TV in the front window the game is about to kick off. I quicken my pace.

We get to the bar- and have to remind them why we're here. We wait impatiently as they flick through more than 20 sports channels. No game. Noooooooooooooo! They apologise profusely:

"The home appliance store probably has a different service provider."

And that is how I end up watching my first game of rugby in six months: standing on the main street of Huaraz watching a big screen TV through a shop window, with no sound. By the time I curse, swear and cheer my way through the first half, quite a crowd has gathered, more to watch me than this daft sport with an oval ball, I think. And we're winning; I'm as happy as Larry. Nothing will stop me from watching another great All Blacks victory. Well, almost nothing...

There is a city wide power cut just as the second half kicks off. I stand there for ten minutes hoping the power will come back on, looking like a complete idiot as I stare longingly at the "all black" screen in front of me...until Amanda snaps me out of my coma.

"It's not coming back on Tone."

I am completely devastated. It takes twenty minutes to walk back to the hostel- ironically on the first street outside the city centre blackout. By the time I fire up the internet and attempt to locate a live stream for the final ten minutes, it's all but game over- I end up watching the final five minutes on a live score update website. At least we won...

Eventually, rather than letting me dwell on fate's miserable hand, Amanda cleverly tempts me out of my sorrow with our To-Do list.

"The Santa Cruz trek is supposed to be good." Music to my ears, nourishment for my broken soul.

Tristan and Phoebe have already done it so we pump them for information the next day. "Is it as good as Huayhuash?"

The simple answer is no. As Iguazu has ruined us for waterfalls, so it seems Huayhuash has ruined us for mountains. Our trekking friends have another option. They're planning an Amazon River trip and invite us to join them. A boat journey up the Amazon River is right up there on my To-Do list and we think long and hard about it. But, in the end, since we're well behind schedule already, we grudgingly turn down this awesome sounding adventure. There's just too much uncertainty around the timing and every day away eats into the time we've allocated for

Colombia, which is also a frontrunner on our list. Besides, after five months at altitude we reckon we deserve some beach time...

So, we bid farewell to Tristan and Phoebe, and Huaraz, and board an overnight bus to the highly rated beach town of Huanchaco, hoping for a bit of sun, sand and surf. Unable to sleep on a bus thus far, it's no surprise that I'm unable to sleep on this one as it winds its way down narrow mountain roads to the coast 3000m below. Possibly whilst attempting to break the land speed record. Arriving in Trujillo at 3am, we taxi to Huanchaco, where we feel slightly guilty ringing the hostel doorbell at such an early hour. But with consistently stupid bus arrival times, these guys seem quite used to it. They show us to our room and we're straight to bed.

After a nap it's time to check out this beach town. Our first impressions are not good. Sun? Non-existent: a low fog hangs over the town giving it anything but a beachy feel. Surf? Looks good, the best waves I've seen for quite a while. But would I swim here? No chance. The beach is littered with rubbish of all descriptions. Conclusion? One of the most over rated "attractions" we've seen so far. We sit down for lunch; a plate of Peru's famous *ceviche* (like Island-style raw fish, marinated in lemon or lime juice) so the afternoon is not a total waste.

"Do you want to buy some weed?" One of the local tourist tack vendors asks as we walk past his stall on the way back to the hostel, showing no interest in his trinkets.

"No thanks," we reply in unison, both quite used to being approached by now.

As we walk down the road and out of ear shot of the local drug dealer, Amanda asks:

"Why did that guy selling souvenirs offer us a sandwich?"

Amanda's ears seem to be playing tricks on her.

Amanda says- It's not my ears, it's their accents- and my innocence!

We arrive back to the hostel, without drugs, and sandwiches, to an email from Aussie Jen. We consulted her a few days ago for information on travelling north. The subject heading of the email is:

"Don't bother going to Huanchaco."

Bugger. The body of the message begins with "it's a shit beach." Luckily however, it contains some information that we don't already know. We decide to head into Trujillo the next day to go to the Jen-rated ancient ruin, Temple of the Moon (*Huaca de la Luna*) on the outskirts of town.

How many people can you fit in a mini...van?

The next day we forego a taxi in favour of the stalwart of the Peruvian public transport system, a ten-seater mini or microbus affectionately named after the German version, the combi. We head into Trujillo, passing another highly rated ruin on the way. It's Jen-rated "shit" though so it's not on our itinerary. It looks pretty rubbish too; nothing more than piles of sand. We're happy to have dodged a bullet there.

We wander around town for a while looking at (and occasionally inside) the old colonial buildings. Then, to honour Danny and Karen, who we met in Chile, we take advantage of the facilities at the local fast food restaurant for the first time in our travels. As I'm having a McShit, Amanda sits in the McAir-con and checks out the McWifi hoping to gather some information on the ruin we're off to see. With nothing useful online, we head down the road to the IPeru visitor's office and get directions to the local combi stop that we need.

After a short walk we board a near empty combi and are on our way. It doesn't take long for the seats to fill. Whilst we were walking around Trujillo, I was amused by the signs in every single room of every building we entered, stating how many people are allowed in a particular room at any one time, by law. If only this was the case in vehicles as well.

The ten seats may be occupied but the driver decides that the vehicle is by no means full, stopping to pick up more and more people along the way. Amanda, whose view is *not* obscured by the large arse in her face, counts 27 passengers in the ten-seater vehicle when the driver's assistant finally stops trying to squeeze them in. The driver's assistant isn't counted as being "in"- given that he's hanging out the open door.

"How the hell are we going to get out of here when it's our stop?" I mumble at the arse in front of me. Thankfully it doesn't answer.

Luckily nearly every single person hops out in the small town before the ruin site and we are able to exit easily when our stop comes...after I have woken up my foot. I do this by putting some weight on it, then falling out of the van door when it's unresponsive.

Blood flow –and ability to walk- restored, we proceed to spend an interesting few hours being guided around this partially excavated ruin. The site is comprised of five religious buildings, all built on top of each other between 100AD and 800AD. With only the fifth layer visible, we catch but a glimpse of the vast history of the site, but what we can see, along with the tales of human sacrifices, keep it interesting.

Interesting would also be an apt way to describe the trip home. The first stage is no problem. It's the same combi we caught out here, and with only 20 people catching a ride this time, it's the height of luxury. After being dropped off on the outskirts of Trujillo we immediately start looking for an "A" combi- the IPeru lady has assured us this is the one we need to get back to Huanchaco. We spot one and jump in.

"This doesn't look familiar," says Amanda, looking out the window 15 minutes later.

I'd been thinking just that but, not wanting to be dropped in an unfamiliar part of town, we decide to stay on the combi thinking it'll return us to where we came from. The combi driver has other ideas.

"This is the end of the line, get off." With that he parks up and walks off.

OK.

Where the hell are we? It looks like we've been dropped off by the beach in what looks to be a very dodgy part of town. With more ruins here than the ancient ruin we just visited, and with people staring at us as if they've never seen a foreigner, we get a little nervous. As I stealthily consult Google Maps on my tablet, Amanda sneaks a peek at our travel guide on her phone.

"We should have taken a "B" combi," she says as she eventually finds the information she's looking for.

"OK... An "A" combi takes us to Buenos Aires."

That's my contribution, when I finally work out where we are.

As well as being the capital city of Argentina, however, Buenos Aires is also the name of a beachfront suburb of Trujillo. We aren't as far off course as we thought! With nothing better to do we start walking, purposefully, and keeping our eyes peeled for a combi back to town. A taxi turns up first...

The search continues

The next day, in search of a beach we can relax on with water we can swim in without fear of rogue nappies, we hit the road again, destination Chiclayo. We know there's no beach there but the only direct bus from Trujillo to reputedly Peru's best beach, Mancora, arrives at three in the morning which is something we prefer to avoid.

Chiclayo is a destination in itself though: as we bus into town I realise they take their rubbish quite seriously here... I spot a guy watering it! At dinner that night we find that it's also home to the world's smallest and most expensive pizza- a dubious honour. The reason we're foregoing the beach in favour of this place is another Aussie Jen recommendation, The Royal Tombs of Sipan museum (*Museo Tumbas Realas de Sipan*). AWESOME, she wrote in our personalised travel guide, underlined twice.

Well over combi travel for the time being, we sign up for a tour. At 50 soles per person it seems good value, considering an English speaking guide at the museum costs 30. Although it doesn't cover museum and site entry, it does include an English speaking guide; transport to two archaeological sites, Sipan and Tucume and their adjoining museums, as well as the Jen-recommended main attraction.

Sipan and Tucume archaeological sites are ordinary. With most of the ruins still being excavated, you need far too much imagination to make it come alive. The small onsite museums are interesting without being extraordinary. But the **Royal Tombs of Sipan museum is AWESOME!** And, as per the norm here, it's free on a public holiday. The detail in some of the gold artefacts found during tomb excavations is so stunning it makes you wonder how on earth it was manufactured 1700 years ago. Easily one of the best museums I've been to in South America. Worthy of an AWESOME underline!

The next day, still seeking a bit of sun, sand and surf, we board a bus to Mancora, full of hope. Arriving in town, we take a short *mototaxi* ride to our beach front bungalow...this is more like it. The only thing still eluding us is the sun.

"Don't go on the beach at night." The hostel owner starts off in his welcome briefing. "We're close to the Ecuadorian border here and smugglers operate in the area. They don't tend to stray far off the beach anymore."

OK, no romantic evening beach strolls then.

"Also, don't walk through the neighbourhood the *mototaxi* just brought you through. There have been recent robberies in the area."

Not exactly the best start for our relaxing beach holiday; still, our accommodation is nice, the view from the balcony is a sea view and the beach looks...OK. Around about now, we decide our beach standards are way too high: in New Zealand great beaches are a dime a dozen. If we're to enjoy beach holidays around this part of the world, we might have to lower our standards.

The 15 minute walk up the beach to Mancora town does little to improve our impressions of this place. The sea is threatening to claim coastal Mancora and the owners of beach front properties here are doing everything in their power to stop their homes being washed away by rising sea levels. What this amounts to is dumping massive piles of concrete rubble- and, by the looks of it, anything else they can get their hands on- in front of their houses, in an effort to hold back the waves. It's not working; all it does is make the place look like a huge rubbish tip.

Mancora town is slightly more picturesque but in just as much danger of being washed away. Sitting in a beach front bar, we're endlessly amused by people who look like they've never seen the sea before. Our 'misfortune of others' highlight comes when a wave rolls into the bar next door, knocking over tables and washing drinks, cameras and wallets away. We sit smugly in our bar, safe and dry on a raised concrete platform.

Safe and dry though we are, we've still not found a peaceful little beach town where we can relax. Mancora might fit the bill in the beach sense but it's also a party town, not our scene. After a couple of days waiting for the sun to shine, we decide to move on, and continue our search in Ecuador.

Of course, on the day we're due to leave, the sun finally shows itself. It's a hot walk up the beach with full packs; even hotter wandering up and down the main road looking for the bus station. With conflicting information, this takes a lot longer than expected- luckily the bus is late. We sit down in the ticket office and wait.

Four hours later, still no bus. Being constantly told it'll be here any minute, we haven't dared to go and find something to eat but now we can wait no longer. There's a Thai restaurant next door and we dash across and order Pad Thai. Oh Pad Thai, how we have missed you.

Just as our meals arrive, I spot a bus. Having spotted several already I'm not really holding out much hope; but of course, according to Murphy's Law, this one is ours.

"SHIIIIIIIT!!!!" I yell.

"GO!!!" Amanda commands.

And I'm off, running down the road with two backpacks, leaving Amanda to pay for our uneaten meals. My mission is to hold up the bus until she arrives. I load the bags then join the queue. Just as I'm about to put my stall tactics into motion, Amanda saunters up...with two takeaway boxes of Pad Thai. I could kiss her, in fact I do.

...In to Ecuador

Our destination is Guayaquil, and to get there we have to cross reputedly one of the most corrupt borders in South America. Reaching the border we file off the bus into immigration, alert for con men and dodgy border officials. The process is a lengthy one, but incident free...unless you count the idiot who tries to push to the front of the line, gets into a fist fight with the person he pushes in front of, is ordered to the back of the queue by officials...then tries again...with the same results. At least we're entertained during the process. We all file back onto the same bus and continue on to Guayaquil, arriving at midnight.

Sleep is impossible in the hot, sticky hostel room in Guayaquil and we press on first thing in the morning. Destination, the tiny coastal town of Puerto Lopez. We're still in search of a decent beach...but now we've added boobies into the equation with a planned visit to Isla de La Plata (dubbed the poor man's Galapagos), just off the coast.

It is 8am and we're on the bus. As we're sitting there, patiently waiting for the bus to leave, it's suddenly boarded by police. All the men on board are marched off the bus and searched. I'm still sitting in my seat wondering what the hell is going on when a female officer tells Amanda that I have to get off too. I'm marched off the bus and told to "spread 'em." Amanda and I find this hilarious, and I'm trying not to laugh as the officer assigned to me gets a little too intimate. Amanda's leaning out the window taking photos, having temporarily put down the policewoman's hat that she'd been asked to hold. The officer gets so intimate I think he should now buy me dinner.

We are the only ones *not* taking this seriously though: the locals don't see the funny side. Apparently, this kind of procedure is regular, as robberies on buses around Guayaquil are common...especially on the tourist routes, with would be thieves posing as passengers and robbing everyone as soon as the opportunity arises. Police molestation over, we finally get on our way.

The bus doesn't stop for more passengers until we're well clear of the city, and it's a relatively quiet day on the road. Amanda only sees one road rage incident involving a machete as we drive through...

While our bus is waiting at a set of lights, a 4x4 pushes into a gap and we hear the usual horn blast from the car that's been cut off. We think no big deal: in Bolivia and Peru people lean on their horns liberally and no one gives a shit. Not so in Ecuador. Amanda watches as Mr 4x4 steps out of his car and threatens Horn Guy with a machete. Horn Guy suddenly wishes horns had never been invented and apologises profusely, thankfully defusing the situation.

Arriving in Puerto Lopez without being robbed, we check into our hostel without incident. It's a bit on the expensive side so we book a night, then wander off for a look around town, and to find cheaper digs. Only a seasoned traveller would understand that we eventually commit to three nights at a less flash, more expensive room just down the road. Sixteen hours on various buses, and about five hours of attempted sleep in a stinking hot room in Guayaquil, is blamed for the temporary lack of sanity.

The next day, after settling in to our less flash, more expensive accommodation, we search out a boat tour to the Isla de La Plata. US$35 each later, we're at the wharf awaiting our ride. It's not exactly a slick tourist operation; in fact, it seems we just join the queue and get on the next boat that's available. Whether it is our tour boat we have no idea, but at least we're heading in the right direction...out to sea.

After about 45 minutes at sea we spot three humpback whales, two adults and a baby. No one's told them that the whale watching season has ended. The baby is breaching, having a great old time. It is easily the size of the boat we are on. The adults are acting their age a bit more and we catch only glimpses of their enormity. It's always a special moment seeing these guys at sea but after about half an hour we leave them to their fun. After all, we have boobies to see...

But first, the turtles, which seem almost as big as the whales! As we motor into the bay I spot one and keep my eyes peeled for others. I needn't have bothered; within five minutes there are four of them around the boat. They know where their next feed is coming from, that's for sure. It feels a little unethical feeding wildlife for the sake of tourism but still, it's amazing to see these massive turtles feeding close up.

Finally it's booby time! Luckily we're in a group of relatively fit, young people, and all agree to walk the biggest loop the island has to offer. It's a booby fest from the start. Star attraction of this windswept island is the famous blue-footed booby. Watching them strut around reminds me of Monty Python's ministry of silly walks skit. They're a little bit shorter than John Cleese, with more feathers, but they certainly give the great man a run for his money.

Boobies don't seem to integrate. A little further up the trail we enter Nazca booby territory. Not as abundant as the blue-footed variety, these ones are easy to tell apart. Instead of blue feet they have...Nazcas?? Maybe they're from Peru's famous Nazca lines region. Same silly walk though, it's awesome.

The final booby in this soft porn session is the red-footed booby. We see one from a distance; it's a very rare sighting for this island apparently. This booby *has* integrated...into a flock of frigate birds. Male frigate birds are known for puffing out their big red chests to attract mates. There's not a lot of posing going on today though; we only see that one puffy red chest. Is that guy trying to attract the sole red-footed booby? Naughty boy.

Our day is rounded off with a quick snorkel on a reef just offshore. It's a refreshing swim after getting a little hot under the collar during the booby fest. I'm not sure it's possible to get more value out of $35 in a day. Having never been to the Galapagos Islands, I can truly say that, from what I've seen of both islands, Isla de La Plata is far superior in every way. With an el cheapo tour of the Galapagos Islands costing around $1200pp, the price is certainly right.

Los Frailes Beach just down the road is our final hope for a decent surf beach before we head back into the Ecuadorian mountains for a bit more trekking. A short *mototaxi* ride brings us to the entrance of, reputedly, Ecuador's best beach...which is already occupied by a shit load of people. This beach is well and truly on the tour company radar. It's just as well the bulk of the people who've arrived on tourist buses don't like to walk; we take a short stroll over a small bluff and enjoy the complete solitude of the next bay for a couple of hours before heading off to meet our *mototaxi* driver for the ride back to Puerto Lopez.

And it's Puerto Lopez that finally takes the prize for most idyllic beach town (ok, fishing village) of our search. We enjoy a few days dining at the shacks that line the beach, watching the locals going about their business; a well-earned rest before we head back into the mountains.

Not quite paradise, but it's close enough...for now.

16- Rainy season sucks!

Trekking in the mountains of Ecuador cancelled...

17- Protest in Bogota

Continuing on up through Ecuador, we soon arrive in Quito, where we check out a few sights and immerse ourselves in the local culinary delights, including the Ecuadorian delicacy of hot chocolate and cheese. It's as nice as it sounds (which is disgusting!) We walk the streets of the La Ronda district, the bohemian centre of Quito, and accidently end up in a dodgy karaoke bar, eating dreadful overpriced food and listening to horrific singing. This is quite enough to scare us fair out of town and we find ourselves up the road, in the market town of Otavalo. As luck would have it, we're just in time for the market.

> Amanda- No luck involved, good planning!

The Otavalo Market is apparently the most famous street market in South America. It all kicks off early Saturday morning with live animal markets that take place well before most of the day tours from Quito arrive for the western take over. And what a sight! It's a melee of pigs, cows, horses, chickens, guinea pigs, dogs, cats, goats and sheep, all being bought or sold. Buyers prod their potential purchases, looking for the best value for money; sellers stand firm on their prices. We watch people waiting to board buses with their newly acquired livestock. There is NOTHING funnier than seeing a pig walk onto a bus behind its owner.

From the hilarity of the animal markets, it's off to the artisan market where we've pencilled in some Christmas shopping. Expecting a more authentic market, I'm quite surprised by what I see. Having worked in the exhibition industry for 15 years, I know a filler stall when I see one and there is a good amount of crap on sale here. Luckily for our families there's also some decent stuff. For the first time in my life I last the distance on a shopping trip...without complaining too much. After a little over five hours we head home for a siesta before hitting the final market of the day, the textile market. I'm all marketed out though. Amanda goes by herself, and is back in less than an hour. Turns out that "textile" actually means factory-produced souvenir tee shirts.

Tours to the local lake, Laguna Cuicocha, apparently cost US$100pp. Roberto, the most helpful hostel owner ever (Hostel Chasqui), tells us how to get there for US$4.25. A friendly local lady we meet on the 25 cent bus to Cotacachi asks if we'd like to share a taxi to the lake. "Share" in this town turns out to be...we pay. Our "friendly local lady" simply walks off when we reach our destination and the two other locals put their wallets away when Number Five Taxi Man informs them that we will be paying. He then charges us $5. It's only $1 more than we expected to pay but it pisses us off all the same.

"Trek will take you four hours," Number Five Taxi Man says. "I will be back in four hours."

We knock it off in two and a half (it's not that inspiring after all we've seen) and find another taxi down the mountain. Hopefully Number Five Taxi Man is still waiting.

The Ecuador/Colombia border crossing

Although looking forward to visiting Colombia, we're quite apprehensive about what's allegedly the most dangerous border crossing in South America, the area around it holding perils of its own. Off the Pan American highway, it's home to drug runners, bandits and FARC guerrillas.

The advice we are given by Roberto is: don't travel at night, and clear the border area quickly. Departing Otavalo, we jump on a local bus to the border town of Tulcan. From there it's a short taxi ride to the border. On Roberto's advice, our first Colombian stop is Pasto.

"Where are you going?" the Ecuadorian immigration official asks me.

Is this a trick question? Do I have options? Is there a second country that shares its border with Ecuador here?

"Umm, Colombia," I reply, deciding truth is the best option...and not seeing any others.

"Colombia is that way." He smiles, pointing over my shoulder.

Maybe he just wanted to practice his English.

Colombian immigration is also a breeze, and we're across the border looking for a taxi to Ipiales bus station within ten minutes, noting the signs stipulating a set price for all taxis going to town, 7000 pesos. Handing our selected taxi driver a 10 000 peso note upon arrival at the bus station, and receiving 2000 pesos change is as close as we come to an incident at this border crossing. Suddenly I speak *very* good Spanish...and suddenly he *does* have change. It only equates to 65 cents but once again it's the principle.

After braving a night in a less than desirable area somewhere in Pasto, we jump on another bus to Popayan. You wouldn't know this was a dangerous area by night; from the only clue, the occasional military bunker overlooking the odd bridge of obvious strategical importance. One settlement we pass has four watch towers on the surrounding hills and a large bunker on the edge of town. I wonder who they've upset.

The Ipiales taxi driver has probably phoned through to his mate in Popayan. Our new taxi driver, Mr Dodgy, dumps our packs upright in the boot so it won't close. As we jump in, we see other taxi drivers scratching their cheeks in some weird gesture and calling out something Amanda can't decipher. As we hit traffic, we're both concerned about the vulnerability of our packs in the open boot; we keep a close watch when the taxi slows or stops. Then Amanda starts noticing some locals trying to get our attention...and she finally works out what the other taxi drivers were saying. Thief! Taking advantage of a traffic jam we throw some money at Mr Dodgy, jump out, retrieve our packs and walk the rest of the way. And that's how we arrive in Popayan...the third "white city" we've visited in South America. It's white.

I've certainly felt an edge the first few days we've been in Colombia. It's hard not to be edgy when you see the military presence in the area we've travelled through- and when the local visitors' centre in Popayan is manned by armed police. Maybe rural Colombia will put us more at ease.

Archaeology overload

San Agustin is a six hour bus ride from Popayan, unless you have a formula one racing car driver at the wheel. After four and a half hours of the worst road we've been on since Bolivia, we're dropped off at a crossroads, 5km from town. From there we're transported to town in a "free" service the local tour companies provide.

"Do you have somewhere to stay?" Tour Guy asks. "I know a place..."

"I bet he does," I mutter to Amanda after she's filled me in on what's going on.

Our accommodation standards have risen since we tried dorm rooms at the start of our trip ten months ago. Tour Guy asks us what sort of accommodation we're looking for...

"We'd like a private room, preferably with an ensuite; it needs to be quiet, and have hot water and Wi-Fi, and it needs to be cheap, 40 000 pesos maximum." Amanda stipulates.

"I have just the place," Tour Guy replies.

"I bet you do," I smile, speaking English.

Tour Guy drops off his local passengers then drives us to a place just out of town. We have a look at a room, and it looks good.

"How much?" Amanda asks the owner.

"60 000 pesos."

Tour Guy has a quick word with the owner.

"40 000 pesos."

Welcome to Colombia, the discount capital of South America.

Accommodation sorted, Tour Guy jumps in his car and drives off. Within 30 minutes he's back, intent on selling us a tour we've shown some interest in. Deciding to mix things up a bit, we've enquired about a horse ride in the countryside and are offered one our travel guide says is a good price. But Tour Guy has a 4x4 jeep tour going tomorrow for 40 000 pesos per person. I've cottoned on quickly though; he needs us to make up the numbers.

"Discount?" I enquire.

"OK, 30 000 pesos per person. But only tomorrow."

Sold! We haven't had to lift a finger yet. I like it here already- and I haven't even made it into town.

San Agustin used to be smack bang in the middle of FARC guerrilla territory which probably put a bit of a damper on tourism. Now though, it's apparently completely surrounded by carefully hidden army outposts that serve to keep the guerrillas away. The police in this town are also carefully hidden, or more precisely, non-existent. This allows every motorbike owner in the area (and there's a lot of them) to be a complete nutter, racing around town and accelerating through intersections with complete disregard for their own (or anyone else's) safety. Throw in the noise pollution and the exhaust fumes the motorbikes create, and San Agustin won't be winning any tranquillity awards.

Its saving grace is circumstantial; we've arrived just in time for Halloween. We sit ourselves down in the plaza, away from most of the motorbike noise, and observe the festivities around us. Kids and adults alike, all dressed up in costumes, getting ready for a parade (that never happens!) While they wait for this parade (that never happens), they have a bit of time for some trick or treating. Kids run into shops, with no regard for what *kinds* of shops they are, and are given sweets by the owners. One little girl, completely unafraid of the only two gringos in the vicinity, gives us some of her sweets... candy from a baby anyone? Food always wins me over; I like this town again.

The next day we're joined on our tour by an Austrian couple, who annoyingly got *their* room at *our* hostel for 40 000 pesos *including* breakfast. We jump into the 4X4 and head off into rural Colombia.

Our first stop in this colourful countryside is a place where Colombia's largest river squeezes through a two metre gap. It sounds a lot more impressive than it actually is. Still, this is my chance to jump a river. I was junior long jump champion in high school some 35 years ago; two metres shouldn't pose a problem. I was also a school swimming champion as a five year old, so falling in shouldn't be cause for concern either.

"***Do not** jump the river!*" The guide says, seemingly reading my mind. "If you fall in the river you will die."

That warning, and the memorial cross we pass on the trail down, convinces me not to jump the river.

Eventually, as we're being driven around the countryside looking at archaeological sites (statues, dating back over 3000 years), the inevitable question comes up.

"Does FARC still operate around here?" Someone asks.

It seems to be the opening the guide's been waiting for.

"A few years ago, I was driving a French group on a similar route to the one we're taking today," he begins. "The vehicle broke down and left us stranded...until another car came along. We all squeezed in and the sole occupant drove us to the nearest town where I was able to call my office and arrange a rescue. While we were waiting, the French group found a local bar and started buying drinks for our rescuer. Everyone was having a great time. Eventually our ride turned up and we left a happily drunk rescuer drinking his last beer. The French group were quite drunk too, and couldn't stop talking about their new friend, and what a nice guy he was. When we were all safely in the new car I told them...you've just been drinking with a guerrilla. They were stunned."

Part of me wills our 4X4 to break down; what a story that would make! Our driver winds up his story telling with a woman in town that has four sons: two are in the army, two are guerrillas. I wonder if they get together for Christmas. Awkward.

Our drive takes in a couple of waterfalls: one, the second highest in South America; and one, we...don't...actually...see from the "viewing platform." One hit, one miss. But then, without question, the day's highlight...

"STOP!!" I yell.

I've just spotted the back end of a cattle truck in a shed by the side of the road. It's being hand crafted out of timber. I walk as close as I dare, close enough to see that the joinery is impeccable. I feel honoured to be witnessing the work of a true craftsman...who is away, perhaps having a well-earned smoko. Not being tradies themselves, the four other people in the vehicle waiting for me don't understand my fascination with this work of art.

"Hurry up!" This from Amanda, probably on behalf of them all. I sense it's time to go.

Day two's excursion features more history at the San Agustin Archaeological Park, the area's main attraction. We visited a lot of archaeological sites on the tour yesterday so I can't say I'm overly enthused about visiting another one. It must show:

"Try and be a little more enthusiastic." Amanda, again.

On the 2km walk to the park I try my best to get into the spirit of things...

"Look, a tree...WOW!" I enthuse.

"Look, there's a rock...WOW!"

My 'enthusiasm' completely wanes when we hire a guide just inside the gate. The planned quick run-around-then-wait-for-Amanda-at-the-gate tactic (my usual modus operandi when it comes to museums, art galleries and the like) just went out the window.

It takes us about 20 minutes just to get to the first sign and we quickly realise that this guide likes the sound of her own voice. I'm vaguely interested in the various statues but I really don't need a 20 minute description of each.

The day improves considerably for me when we start comparing the statues with TV characters. Amanda spots Muttley from Wacky Races.

There's also a very good rendition of The Face of Boe from Doctor Who. I spot a cartoon penguin as well but when I point this out, the guide tells me it's actually an eagle- and to be quiet so she can talk more. Then she tells Amanda off for questioning what she's saying- and continues to spout some more.

"That one looks NOTHING like a Maori carving." Amanda whispers to me. "She's making shit up."

Finally my favourite part of the tour: after four hours, we leave.

The next evening we board an overnight bus, destination Bogota. I feel a protest coming on...

Amanda vs. Russia

How many travellers have taken time out of their busy itineraries to stage a protest at the Russian embassy in Bogota, Colombia? Well, there's a first time for everything.

Whilst campaigning against drilling for oil in the arctic, a Greenpeace vessel, The Arctic Sunrise, was stormed by Russian Special Forces and the crew, arrested and charged with piracy. Taking a boat by force in international waters...isn't that what pirates do? The crew, dubbed "The Arctic 30," were thrown in jail, and that is where they remained, despite worldwide condemnation. Paul McCartney and Madonna were among those to speak out against this outrage and protests were happening all over the world. Amanda, it seems, is feeling a bit left out. The driving force behind her decision to single-handedly protest these actions is a little closer to home though; one of her friends, a Kiwi, is part of the detained crew.

In between checking out some of what Bogota has to offer, in weather that can only be described as atrocious, she obtains the materials to make a banner. After she's made said banner, she writes a letter to the Russian authorities, with Spanish spell checks courtesy of our Chilean friend, Gonzalo, via email. It's all on for the next day.

And what a day for a protest! We wake up and it's absolutely pissing with rain, again. But protests aren't cancelled. After a short taxi ride we find ourselves at the fortress-like Russian embassy. Three metre high brick walls, razor wire, security cameras and solid steel gates and doors, guarded by soldiers with machine guns. And that's just the stuff we can see.

"Are we going inside?" I ask.

"Don't be bloody stupid!" Amanda replies. "It's Russian soil, they might arrest us!"

> Amanda- You NEVER said we! It was always very clear this was MY protest!

Conflict averse, I've designated myself cameraman and taken up a good position...across the street.

The first photo I take is of Amanda, chatting with the armed guard at the gate...then going inside the Russian Embassy!

Luckily, after a few very nervous minutes, she comes back out again...and takes up position with her "Save the Arctic, free the Arctic 30" banner at the front entrance. The armed guard is indifferent to her presence. After about 15 minutes a police officer walks out of the embassy and approaches her, and I start snapping photos. Amanda and Mr Colombian Police Man talk for a while. Then he walks around the corner and gets on the walkie talkie, probably to fill in his bosses.

Unfortunately I take one too many photos. He spots me across the street and starts walking my way. Should I scarper, paparazzi-style, with my potential prize-winning photos? No, I decide to play the dumb tourist and walk towards him smiling.

"*Hola! No hablo Espanol.*" I manage to get out. "I don't speak Spanish!" -just to confirm the fact.

It's pretty clear what he wants though, and Amanda, who has joined us, confirms that he does indeed want me to delete the photos I've taken of him. All of them. He stands over me while I delete them one by one, all the while desperately trying to save one. Finally I get to the last photo...

"This is a really good one of you," I say. "Can I keep it? I'll email you a copy."

"No," he smiles.

He then disappears back into the embassy and Amanda continues her vigil in the pouring rain. Over the next hour or so she gets good support from the Colombian public, who are tooting, giving her the thumbs up and stopping for a chat. Russian officials walk into the embassy past her, trying not to look. It seems they don't mind her standing there. So stand there she does, smiling, waving at cars and engaging in conversation with the people that stop to ask her what she's doing.

It's around two hours into the day's action that I learn the first lesson in successfully staging a protest: eat first! I realise I'm starving so I decide to go and look for somewhere to buy some food; it seems we are here for the long haul. As I walk off down the road, I'm passed by two trucks carrying ten or so soldiers apiece. I turn around to look where they're going, and see that they've stopped at the embassy door. Running back, camera in hand, I clear the parked cars blocking my view to see an "oh shit" look on Amanda's face. I ready the camera, thinking what awesome photos these'll make- until Mr Colombian Police Man reappears, as if by magic, and waggles his finger at me as if I was a naughty child. I do as I'm told and put the camera away. The two truckloads of soldiers depart and thankfully, Amanda isn't with them. She has survived this full frontal assault, and continues to stand there bravely. It turns out the soldiers were just dropping a raincoat off to the lone guard.

For some bizarre reason, the guard then ups and leaves his post and walks off down the street into the pouring rain- perhaps taking his newly acquired raincoat for a spin? Seizing the opportunity, Amanda starts taping her sign to a glass fronted notice board by the main entrance. Sensing the end is near, I risk crossing the street to help her.

The last thing we see as we make our escape is the guard returning to his post, practically on top of the banner, apparently completely unconcerned by its presence.

At the debriefing back at the hostel, we decide the day's action has been a great success and Amanda decides she's going to protest at every Russian Embassy we pass on our travels. Next stop Panama City. But as it turns out, her first Latin American protest is her last; a few days later, after two months in a Russian jail, the Arctic 30 are freed.

18- A mud hell

We've been sitting in Bogota for three days now, waiting for the weather to clear in El Cocuy National Park, and we're at a loss what to do next. We wake up on the fourth morning and check the long range weather forecast, just to make sure. It's clear we won't be trekking there any time soon. Amanda consults the travel guide.

"Let's go to Salento."

"OK." Just quietly, I'm a little past caring. I've had my heart set on what has been described as one of the most diverse treks in the world, and am still coming to terms with the fact that we won't be doing it. Salento isn't even on my To-do list. Still, anywhere's better than Bogota in the pouring rain.

We board a bus for Armenia, where we'll need to catch another bus to our destination. We're totally unprepared, though, for the length of this bus journey. As the day marches on, darkness approaches, and the traffic on the narrow winding road gets heavier. We start to worry we'll miss our connection. On cue, traffic grinds to a halt, and for half an hour we don't go anywhere.

Eventually moving again, we manage to get past the holdup, a small convoy of military vehicles that've pulled over to the side of the road, completely blocking one of the two lanes. Men with guns roam the area, unconcerned that they're holding up traffic, for what appears to be a toilet stop. After 11 ½ hours (rather than the six hours scheduled) we finally roll into Armenia at 9:28pm. We have two minutes to find our connecting bus, the last one of the night. Unfortunately, it takes us seven.

Standing at the bus stop wondering what to do next, we're approached by another bus driver who's spotted our dilemma.

"My bus is going to Circasia, about halfway to Salento. Hop on and I'll arrange for one of our company taxis to take you the rest of the way."

We jump on, deciding that this guy's wearing a uniform, and driving a bus which is a good indication he's above board, and we're not about to be taken hostage. An hour later, with no idea where we are, we're ushered off the bus and into a waiting taxi. It whisks us, not into the jungles of the Colombian interior, but to the tiny village of Salento, finally arriving at about 11pm. Thankfully the hostel we pre booked has a night manager, and unlike the rest of town, she is awake. We check in, then head straight to bed. It's been a long day.

The next morning, in the light of day, we realise we've found a home-away-from-home. We're surrounded by hills covered in vegetation; the greenery reminds us very much of New Zealand. And though Salento is obviously a tourist town, it's well kept and almost traffic free. And it's sunny. We've been awake an hour and this place already feels like it'll be hard to leave. Especially after I see a dog...walking a horse. *That's* how awesome this place is.

Speaking of horses, we finally have the opportunity to go riding. What better way to explore the country side? Well, actually, I can think of several better ways; I've been on a horse four times in my life- not even the same horse. This way is certainly a novelty.

On one of the four horse rides I've ever been on, I realised my horse was heading for a jump...so I jumped off. On another, the damn horse bit me- so on direction from the guide I punched it. I was 13 years old, and the guide was surprised- I think he thought I wouldn't do it. I decide to pay close attention during the safety briefing.

"I'll go at the pace you guys go," the guide tells us.

Safety briefing over, Amanda trots off. Against my will, so do I.

For the next few hours we trot down jungle paths, ford rivers and, dare I say, gallop, when the terrain allows. It doesn't take me long to realise that the faster you go, the less painful it is, so I happily gallop at any given opportunity...sometimes even when the horse *isn't* running after Amanda's with no prompting from me. It's a battle of wits- man versus horse- and man is getting the upper hand. Although it must be said, he's never fully in control. He is, mind you, humming the theme tune to Bonanza.

Eventually, we dismount and a short, very bow-legged walk brings us to our destination for the day, a swimming hole at the base of a very powerful looking waterfall.

"Where do we swim?" Amanda asks the guide.

"At the base of the waterfall," the guide replies.

"Bugger that." Amanda says emphatically.

It's left to me to take one for the team. As I wade into the water I encounter my first problem. It's freezing. I've been in colder water though, so a quick dive should sort that out. Herein lies my second dilemma: there's more waterfall than there is swimming hole, and a dive will take me straight underneath the water crashing into the pool. With the current that's being produced, I'm even struggling to get deep enough to get my knees wet.

But I persevere, finally get there, and take the plunge. I'm up and out pretty quick, helped on my way by the current.

"I missed the photo, do it again," Amanda laughs.

After being visited by hundreds of colourful butterflies that keep the camera clicking, and our minds off our already painful arses, it's back on the horses for the ride home. We're confident now and Amanda sets a cracking pace; we're back in no time. The 20m waddle to the hostel, from across the road where we've parked the horses is, without a doubt, the toughest part of the day. We cancel our mountain bike plans, and retire to the comfort of the hostel hammocks.

Give me coffee!

Neither Amanda nor I drink the stuff usually, but I've taken it up for the Colombian leg of our journey. Being one of Colombia's major (legal) exports, it'd be rude not to, and besides, I'm enjoying the copious amounts of free coffee the hostel provides. Salento is one of the more famous coffee growing regions and we decide to pay a visit to a local coffee plantation.

Shunning the mountain bikes again, we decide to take a stroll through the countryside to the small *finca (farm)* we've seen advertised at the hostel. The sun is shining; it's a great day for a walk. Until Amanda steps on a snake. Luckily it's dead. One military check point later, we arrive at the *finca*.

This *finca*, of the coffee variety, is a real family affair; we're greeted by the grandson of the owner, who works here. He shows us around the fields where the coffee beans are grown, and tells us that they grow two different kinds of beans, to ensure at least one of them will thrive...and that banana trees make excellent companion plants, offering the coffee plants some shade. We're shown around the drying facility, which basically amounts to a poly-tunnel in full sunlight on a concrete pad, where the beans are laid, once picked. We even get to roast (on an open fire), then grind, enough beans for two cups of coffee.

The grandson brews up our coffee and places it in front of us. It's only then that Amanda decides to 'fess up.

"Um...I don't like coffee."

The grandson looks like he's just been shot: not liking coffee is obviously unheard of here, and very un-Colombian.

"Just try a little bit," I suggest, hoping to avoid a diplomatic incident.

She does, and then pulls seven different faces in as many seconds.

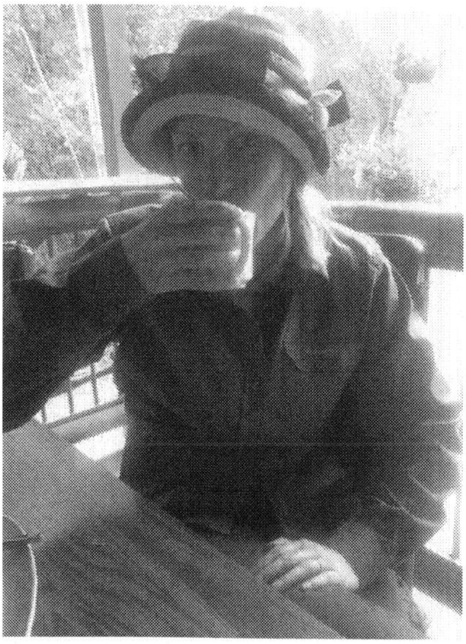

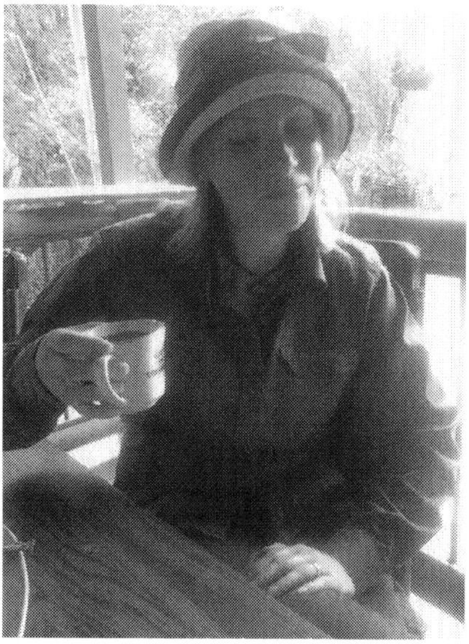

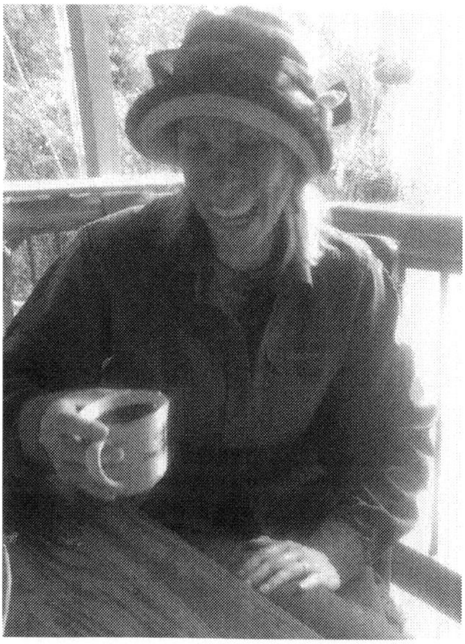

"Nope, still don't like it," she grimaces, adding "you'd better buy something!"

I drink both cups, and then we depart the *finca* after purchasing 300 grams of Colombia's finest...coffee. Everybody's happy.

On the way home we stop at a house-shop for a fresh juice and I make a startling discovery. Perusing a map on the wall, I discover we're right beside Los Nevados National Park, and a trek I researched, and then discarded, hoping to do El Cocuy instead. Making enquiries with the owner of the house-shop, we learn that she knows a guide who might be willing to take us out into the park. Amanda grabs the guide's phone number and we dare to dream...all the way back to the hostel and, for me, another cup of coffee...or two.

Red Bull gives you wings...

During the week, Salento is a sleepy little town. Men wandering around in ponchos and cowboy hats are common, and getting a seat at our favourite local restaurant for the 3000 peso set lunch is a breeze. Not so in the weekends, when the rest of Colombia comes to town: tourists snap up souvenirs and men walk around in what are described as "ironic" ponchos in our travel guide, obviously feeling pretty good about themselves, but looking very much out of place. And especially not so in holiday weekends, as this particular weekend is. And there's a special event on to boot: an international Red Bull Motocross enduro event, right outside town.

We're not big fans of motocross but, come event day, we think what the hell, and grab a bus out to the track. Johnny Walker from the UK is the star attraction. Even with my limited motorsport knowledge I've heard of him...or maybe I've heard of the whisky? We don't know enough to do anything else so we decide to try and find a Kiwi to support. Our first mission is to find a starters list. Our search is thwarted initially by a stall selling rice pudding...then completely, when we are told no such list exists.

For the next two hours we wander around the track, watching bikes doing a few warm up laps. That gets a bit dull so we decide to go for lunch before the real race starts. On the way out Amanda asks an official when things kick off; we've come this far, we don't want to miss the most exciting part.

"It started four hours ago," the official replies. "It's a time trial."

We still have no idea who's racing. We come to the conclusion that this event is not for us, have lunch, then catch the bus back to

Salento. As we climb on board, it starts pouring with rain. Our good timing proves to be the highlight of an otherwise dull day.

That evening, after Amanda makes a phone call, we meet the guide offering to take us into the mountains. I've been furiously researching the possibility of trekking independently but information, and more importantly, good maps, are non-existent, so we decide to play it safe. A few cups of coffee later, when all our questions are answered to our satisfaction, the guide confirms we're on for tomorrow. Giuseppe from Switzerland, who sat in on the meeting, decides to join us.

Los Nevados; day 1

Bright and early the next morning, Mr Guide introduces us to Mr Apprentice Guide, who will be coming along to learn the trail. He also introduces us to our snacks! It's an all-inclusive trek so food is provided. The snack bag alone is more food than we would take into the wilderness for three days; it must weigh at least five kilos. We won't be going hungry.

After a quick breakfast we catch a jeep to the trail head and start walking up a well-trodden path into the Cocora valley. This part of the trail is a very popular day walk, and it's not hard to see why. Is there anything better than walking through the jungle beside a raging river, taking in abundant and glorious bird life? Not for me there isn't. It's still rainy season and we set off in a light drizzle. It's pretty muddy under foot, but nothing we haven't coped with before.

Our lunch stop is the lodge where most people turn back. The two guides disappear into a house beside the flash new lodge and leave us sitting on the steps in the sun, which has finally shown itself.

"Are these snacks our lunch?" Amanda wonders out loud.

That's all the prompting I need to start eating. Fifteen minutes later, the guides emerge with our freshly cooked lunch. Knowing what's to come I hungrily scoff that as well. There's nothing like a climb from 2300m up to 4000 to get the system going.

We knew about the climb. In all fairness we knew about the mud too. But as we break free of the jungle we're not really prepared for what we're about to face. Energy draining, shoe stealing, high altitude mud...for as far as the eye can see. Oh how I have missed this! Amanda, on the other hand, has not. It is her kryptonite.

> Amanda- I'd like to point out that being only 5ft 3, having to wade through knee deep mud is a lot harder for me than it is for you gangly legged men. Not to mention having to carry my body weight in snacks!

As we continue climbing above the tree line, plants that look like cacti, but without the spikes, appear, and we get our first view of the mountains. But something else catches my eye.

"My God, that poo is HUGE!"

Amanda bursts out laughing; I probably just said what she was thinking.

"That must have hurt coming out," she adds.

We detour around the poo and continue walking along the trail, still laughing, Amanda's battle with the mud temporarily forgotten.

> Amanda- Because we're now having an in-depth discussion as to what kind of animal did that!

Just as the laughter dies down...
"WOOOOOWWWW!"
That's Giuseppe, walking behind us. It starts us laughing all over again, and we turn around to see him take several photos.
"These photos are going to be captioned 'Holy Shit'," he tells us happily as he catches up.
As the rain resumes, it doesn't take long for laughter to be replaced by frustration as Amanda continues her battle with the vast quantities of mud we're traipsing through. A lot of her problem stems from our inability to keep up with the guides...who are making light work of this climb and are quite a long way ahead. Amanda is a front runner by nature, and not coping well being left behind. I, on the other hand, am in my element; I love this shit. I even surprise myself when I go striding past Amanda, determined to catch up with the guides. As Amanda, then Giuseppe (who's having a few problems with his hired gumboots) finally catch up to where the guides and I have stopped for a rest, I can see the terrible mistake I have made...written all over Amanda's unsmiling face.
"You're going well darling," I offer.
"Don't be so bloody condescending," she snaps.
As we set off again I return to my rightful position, and follow her into the dense fog that greets us just as we reach our cruising altitude, just over 4000m. Finally, after eight tough hours, we reach our destination. Happy to be at the *finca*, Amanda's humour returns as she makes reference to my superhuman effort.
"What have you done with my husband?" Am I an imposter? Only time will tell.

Day 2
After another near death-by-crushing under the sheer weight of blankets we need to survive our freezing room, we wake up and head straight to the warmest place in the house, the kitchen, where the *finca* host is cooking breakfast on an open fire. Then, a quick visit to the bucket flush toilet and we're on our way. Today's destination is the hot pools, a mere 12km away.

"There is less mud on the *paramo*," Mr Guide tells us as we head out. It would be a physical impossibility for there to be more...

The *paramo* is the high plains in this part of the world. Not since Huaraz in Peru, nearly two months ago, have we been above 4000m, let alone walking for 24km at that height. On top of yesterday's 1700m climb, we're breaking all the altitude gain rules. But surprisingly, I'm feeling absolutely fantastic, still riding high on yesterday's endorphins.

Unfortunately, Amanda is looking down the barrel of another bad day. It seems as though she hasn't adjusted to the altitude gain as well as I have. She's struggling for breath, her arms and legs are feeling very heavy, and she's feeling faint. Mr Guide orders her to lie on the ground then proceeds to hold her legs in the air. Fifteen minutes later she no longer feels faint but her other symptoms linger. What she hates most about this situation though is showing signs of weakness; being thought of as the weak little girl the men have to wait for. More than anything, it's a battle against herself, her own demons. I remind her of all the times when I've been that weak little boy, lagging behind her. It doesn't help.

Neither does the horse we happen across that's sitting in the grass, with a freshly broken leg. It's a distressing sight, but there's not a thing we can do so eventually we carry on, reluctantly leaving it to its fate.

Eventually we turn off the main trail onto a very indistinct track and start following a river up a valley. It's been three hours since we set off...surely we must be nearly there... With Amanda still struggling, the rest of the group are quite a way ahead and we are alone. With the ball on the other foot now, and me in charge of the motivational speech for a change, I give it my best shot:

"See that waterfall up ahead?" I say. "That's sulphur on the rocks where the water's running over the cliff. I reckon that's the hot pools. Dig it in darling, we're nearly there; half an hour at the most."

Just as I finish the sentence, Mr Guide turns away from the river and starts climbing towards the ridgeline. Amanda looks up and notices this as well.

"The canyon must be impassable; he's probably climbing to get a better trail," I say, trying to sound confident, but not entirely convinced I'm telling the truth anymore.

When we get to the climb, I realise that Mr Guide, Mr Apprentice Guide and Giuseppe have all continued walking away from the river- and the waterfall beneath which my imaginary hot pools were situated. I try another tact.

"It's just over this hill darling, I'm certain of it."

"It better be."

And luckily for her -and me- it is! It's taken us just over four and a half hours. The guides disappear into the shack to make lunch and Amanda and Giuseppe lay down on the grass in the sun, happy for the rest.

"Who's coming for a swim?" I ask, bounding all over the place like the energiser bunny.

"What have you done with my husband?" Amanda wonders out loud again.

I haven't trekked for nearly five hours for nothing so, in a flash, I'm down to my undies and lowering myself into the hot water. It doesn't take Amanda long to join me, quickly seeing it as a chance to wash. It's not exactly what we were expecting though. For a start it's not a natural pool, rocks cemented into place line the banks. And the water is very murky, the rocks underfoot are covered in a thick slime. When we emerge a short time later, all too aware that we still need enough energy to walk home, we're both covered in an orange algae. It's the furthest I've ever walked for a bath, by a long way, and we've both come out dirtier than when we went in.

It seems as though the orange algae has restorative qualities though. We set off back to the *finca* after lunch and Amanda keeps up with the group, who are travelling a lot faster now, hoping to get back before dark. After the trials of the outward journey, it's only now that we get to fully take in the surrounding landscape. And a desolate landscape it is. We're walking beside the snow-capped mountain of Nevado del Tolima and for as far as the eye can see in every direction, cactus-like plants dot the *paramo*.

"Those plants are called *frailejones*." Mr Guide tells us after Amanda asks; "they suck the moisture out of low clouds."

I wonder why; there's certainly no shortage of moisture around here. I notice their soft, broad leaves. Any Kiwi who's spent some time in the bush back home will be familiar with a native plant affectionately known as "bushman's friend." Its soft, broad leaves make it great natural toilet paper. With my observation of the similarities, I decide to take it for a test drive.

"I'm just going to the toilet, I'll catch up." I say to Amanda. She rolls her eyes...

"Ah yes, *here's* my husband." She walks off to catch up to the others who don't seem that interested in my toilet paper theory either.

But if they were to wipe their arses with these leaves I think they'd become interested very quickly! If bushman's friend is the kind of el cheapo paper found in public toilets that spreads rather than wipes, this stuff is veritable quilted four-ply. I pull up my pants and run to catch up with the others, delighted with my discovery.

With Amanda back to her normal self, we knock off the return journey in less than four hours, stopping briefly to admire the courage of the horse with the broken leg. Hunger has outweighed pain and he's hopping around chomping on grass. He's not going down without a fight.

As darkness engulfs the *finca* and the temperature drops rapidly, we once again retire to the kitchen and sit around watching our dinner being cooked- and the owners' four year old grandson running around playing with a machete he just happened to find lying around. The evening's conversation turns to the 24km day's walk, which has taken us nearly nine hours to complete.

"There's no way that that walk was 24km's," I announce. "It's definitely closer to 30, at least."

Amanda and Giuseppe nod their heads in agreement, but the guides are not convinced. What would they know? I know that even a severely depleted Amanda can walk faster than three kilometres an hour.

Day 3

And just to prove that point, we knock off the final day's trek (22km) out of the mountains in a little over five hours. Amanda's finally come right and even manages a laugh when she attacks the mud with a vengeance- and disappears up to her knees on more than one occasion.

Off the *paramo* and back into the jungle by a different trail, we're treated to the most amazing bird life. Jungle, river, bird life...I'm like a pig in shit, again. I am invigorated. To what do I owe my new found strength? I hope it's not coffee.

Arriving back at the hostel, the rest of the day is spent cleaning mud off shoes. Until now, I didn't know how muddy a shoe could get. Three scrubs and two rinses later and I can just about see the brand name again. Unfortunately it still reads "Bolivian Clog".

Over the next week, Salento does indeed prove difficult to leave. So difficult, in fact, that hostel staff start giving us a discount rate- and even cook us breakfast one morning. We spend the days lying around in hammocks in the sun, wandering around town, and eating at our favourite local restaurant. We also discover the best curry in South America. Very, very hard to leave...

But Amanda, lacking a purpose and growing tired of "being a passenger on the planet" doesn't like to lie around too long and finds herself getting useful; writing a campaign strategy for a UK immigration group that she recently became involved with. After our 14 year relationship, and ten years of marriage, I still can't emigrate with my wife to the United Kingdom. Naively we thought it would be easy, what with Amanda being British and all. Unfortunately it's been anything but easy, meaning Amanda has effectively been exiled from her own country. She's not taking that lying down- although she did write the campaign strategy in a hammock!

Eventually though, we have to hit the road again. The Caribbean Coast is beckoning. If Salento had a beach we may never have left...

19- Hot enough for ya?

Yearning for some beach time, we decide to make a move, destination the Colombian Caribbean, a mere four buses and thirty hours away. Giuseppe joins us on the first two bus rides but we wave goodbye in Medellin, where he's staying, and board a local bus to the other side of this massive city. From here, it's an overnight bus to Santa Marta. We pull into town the next afternoon...well nourished by the remaining snacks from our Los Nevados trek.

The first thing that strikes us is the heat: It is oppressive, temperatures hovering in the mid-thirties, which is somewhere in the mid-nineties Fahrenheit. It's so humid you could almost drink the air. Unsurprisingly then, the second thing we notice is the pool at the hostel. Well, of course we notice the hostel first; it's a house that used to belong to a drug cartel. But at this stage we only have eyes for the pool.

The Drop Bear Hostel is so named to attract Australians to its doors; apparently only Aussies would get the drop bear reference. We certainly don't and we decide not to ask...on our first visit anyway. Tayrona National Park is calling so, after a few nights' rest, and after being told that Santa Marta's beaches are a bit shit anyway, we vacate our stifling hot room and head for Colombia's most visited natural attraction.

Too hot to move...

Except to do this...

The only things working around here...leaf cutter ants.

That three picture montage was my only blog update on our Tayrona leg of the journey, posted solely to make friends and family jealous. Our *actual* experience was a little different though. Yes, it was too hot to move-; unfortunately, to get to the beaches, we would have to.

Already near heat exhaustion just from the bus ride to the park, our first stop is a strategically placed juice bar. We drink as much as we can in a futile attempt to cool down. A beat up old minivan is parked up at the entrance. Assuming it's there for the ride in, we pay the entry fee and ask what the schedule of departure is.

"We go when van is full," the driver announces.

Looking behind us at the distinct lack of people following us through the gate, we decide that that's not going to be for a very long time and set out on the four kilometre walk to the beach.

Despite the heat, it's a pleasant walk through the jungle and we soon happen upon our first beach. Already hot, we instantly feel refreshed on seeing the sea. Unfortunately, it's only a psychological refresher: "**No Swimming!**" signs, and an obvious rip tide keep us out of the water and it's an easy decision to press on and find a more suitable place to experience our Caribbean beach fantasy.

Walking back to the main trail we decide to head to the Cabo San Juan campsite, a further two hours up the coast. I'm desperate for a swim; surely we'll pass a swimmable beach soon.

Over the next hour, we pass a lot of beautiful beaches but all of them have the same **"No Swimming!"** signs as well as, occasionally, a sign depicting the number of drownings. It's a sobering statistic; the ocean around here is certainly not to be taken lightly. We pass a lot of people walking in both directions; there's bound to be one or two amongst them who don't heed the warnings.

After a leisurely lunch stop at a restaurant just off Arrecifes beach, and a bit more walking, we arrive at our destination. We're at what is supposed to be the best beach in the park, and we can barely see it through the hundreds of people. We promptly turn around and start walking back to where we just came from. In my opinion, a good beach is a deserted one.

At around 5pm, with dusk approaching, we finally get in our first swim of the day. Long overdue, it is simply bliss. Sadly, there's no campground at La Piscina beach so we walk back down to Arrecifes, a long, white-sand, surf beach, surrounded by jungle, with mountain views. At times, the day's been frustrating; rolling in here just as the sun's setting is a pretty good way to wrap it up. We arrive at Bukarug campground just on dark, secure our hammock space for the night, then sit down and polish off a huge plate of *ceviche* for dinner. It's our kind of crowd here, a small one.

After dinner, we're walking back to our hammocks when we hear what sounds like a low flying aircraft coming in to land. Suddenly: *CRASH*! Something hits the light on the path right beside us, smashing the bulb into a thousand pieces and engulfing us in darkness. Always prepared, I flick my trusty head torch on to see not a horrific plane crash, but the biggest beetle I have ever seen. It's easily the size of my palm (that's a two litre water bottle in the photo below) and I get in a bit of a photo session as it regains consciousness. Later research suggests it was the aptly named elephant beetle...obviously with poor night vision.

Sleeping in a hammock is a bit uncomfortable for Amanda, who sleeps on her front, and for me, a dedicated side-sleeper. Add the stifling heat of the night, from which there is no escape, and inadequate mosquito netting, and 'a bit uncomfortable' quickly becomes a bit shit! But the next day we finally get to do what we came here to do...

At the far end of Arrecifes beach is a picture-perfect bay- the one you can see in the second photo at the start of the chapter. Here we finally get to laze on the beach and swim when we like in complete solitude. As the morning wears on and the park becomes busier, people arrive to share our little piece of paradise. Eventually, the growing crowds and the strengthening heat of the sun conspire to move us on our way, savouring the relative cool of the jungle as we walk back to the park entrance. This time we wait for the minivan to take us back to the road, and board a bus back to Santa Marta. It was just too damn hot to stay longer.

Back at the Drop Bear Hostel we are completely devastated to find out the only rooms left are the deluxe rooms with air conditioning. Not! We happily fork out the extra cash. When they say deluxe, they mean deluxe: our room is easily as big as an entire hostel. Well, the hostels we normally stay at. When notorious Colombian drug lord Pablo Escobar was on the run from the (US) DEA, there's evidence to show that he stayed at this house. We settle into air-conditioned comfort wondering if we're sharing space with infamy. It's a strange feeling. Amanda threatens to call in the mercenaries on the bedside intercom if I even think about snoring tonight.

> Amanda- The room would have been deluxe in the 80s, maybe that's why Tony felt so at home! With its turquoise bathroom suite and kitsch decor it looks like it's straight off the set of Dynasty or something.

Outside the air-conditioned comfort of our room, the unrelenting heat continues to kick our arses. It's time to head back into the mountains to escape it.

"Off again? Where to this time?" The Aussie hostel owner Gabriel enquires as we check out.

"Minca."

"Oh, ok...do you have a place to stay?"

"No."

"In that case, you should stay at Oscar's Place; you guys will love it."

Standing outside some less than enticing accommodation in Minca a couple of hours later, Amanda decides to give Oscar a call. Before you know it, we're walking along a steep, muddy jungle trail in the pissing rain carrying full packs...wearing jandals. Oscar has gone into Santa Marta for the day so we make ourselves at home on the balcony overlooking his back yard: 60 acres of jungle with a view all the way to Santa Marta and the coast.

He eventually arrives home and offers us a beer.

"Mind if I smoke some weed?" he asks. "It's very stressful going to the city."

"No problem." says Amanda.

"It's your place Oscar," I agree, slightly taken aback by normally anti-drug-Amanda's casual reply.

He then spends the next two hours looking for his stash. We pass an enjoyable evening with plenty of interesting conversation, broken only by a quick meal a local restaurant has delivered up the muddy jungle trail in torrential rain. We talk about all sorts of things but what I remember most is Oscar's story of the night a battle raged in the hills all around.

"About five years ago, when I'd just come back to Colombia after living in the States for a long time, I was lying in bed one night and a gun battle erupted in the hills around us. All I could do was lie in bed hoping that the good guys were getting the upper hand and we'd all still be here in the morning. It was the most terrifying night of my life...I slept with my boots on, ready to run at a moment's notice."

"Have you seen my shower?" he asks, in an abrupt change of subject.

His shower is practically an outdoor shower with a view all the way to Santa Marta.

"Yeah, I was REALLY stoned when I designed that," he tells us. "Hello Santa Marta...look at me, I'M TAKING A SHOWER!"

Guess he's found his stash.

We've come to Minca to escape the oppressive heat of the coast. Amanda has visions of floating down a river on an inner tube. Possibly with cocktail in hand. I'll just be happy not being so hot- and maybe getting in some hammock time. We're both a little surprised the next day, therefore, to find ourselves a couple of hours in to a six hour hike.

Our surprise abates after another hour or so, as we reach our destination: a lookout point, 1000m higher than where we started. We've put in a sterling effort...to see a bunch of clouds in no more than 20m visibility.

At least it's all downhill from here, and a nice walk through a jungle full of interesting bird life. We even spot a cocaine processing factory...cleverly disguised as a school. We hired a dog from the local dog hire kiosk, the breakfast café in town, partly for protection in exactly this kind of situation. He seems completely unconcerned as locals swinging machetes saunter casually past us, all offering a friendly *"buenos dias."* Then he barks rabidly at a 106 year old man carrying two heavy loads of firewood home. This dog with no name seems a little confused as to who would pose the most danger to his clients...

In a little over five and a half hours, we finish the loop and treat ourselves to a very nice hamburger from a cafe in town. No-name-dog gets treated to a few chips and a piece of grilled cheese...at which he turns up his nose. We're reminded of both Fussy and Poo Breath, our first two dogs in Chile at the very start of our trip. Like Fussy, this canine protector goes home very shortly after not eating the food we've given him.

Heading back to Oscar's, we see how truly dangerous this place can be. A man on a motorcycle has his duffel bag searched at the local police/army checkpoint. He unzips the bag and out pops...a couple of chickens. It's nerve-racking stuff.

After a couple more days of just hanging around Oscar's Place, enjoying his easy way as much as the cool breeze of the jungle, the time comes to head back to the oven that is Santa Marta. From here, it's on to our final destination in Colombia, Cartagena.

Our final stay at the Drop Bear Hostel is the most memorable, not only for the fact that we have a choice of rooms this time, (and select the most expensive one with air conditioning) but also for the house tour.

Aussie owner Gabriel meets a group of us at the bar, a bar that still sports the original decor from the cartel days. For the next hour we walk around the hostel and Gabriel shows us underground passages (for escape purposes), and hidey-holes where the owners stashed their cash. Complete with a running commentary of the history surrounding the house, it's a dead interesting evening. The inevitable question comes up...

"Have you ever found anything valuable?"

"No," replies Gabriel. "But we have found a couple of hidey-holes that we're pretty sure no one's opened yet."

"Where are they?"

"I'm not telling you guys that!" He laughs. "Put it this way: we're renting this house at the moment; if you hear that we've purchased it, then you'll know we found something. Watch the news for the rest!"

Later on, back in our room, I start tapping walls and looking for false bottoms in cupboards. The treasure hunt is on. With several hidey-hole possibilities in mind, I saunter out to reception...to see just how far this hostel is willing to go to keep its guests happy. Gabriel is on duty.

"Maaaate! Can I borrow a sledge hammer? And...maybe a crowbar?"

"No."

I wonder how many times he's heard that one. Nothing ventured and all the rest... Doubting I'll crack him any time soon, I take the opportunity instead to ask him about the name of the hostel.

"What's a drop bear?"

"A drop bear is a large, vicious, **carnivorous** marsupial from Australia that inhabits treetops and attacks its prey by dropping onto their heads from above. At least that's what we tell tourists...it's not actually real."

Aussies...weird race.

Cartagena, briefly

Oh how I've missed the street vendors of Cusco! Luckily I can get my fill of saying no to the same one a dozen times right here in Cartagena. I especially enjoy being approached by people selling hats and sunglasses. I'm already *wearing* a hat and sunglasses; do I *look like I need more?*

Cartagena is getting a makeover...slowly. The walled historic centre is very picturesque but you don't have to stray far to come to the more run down areas. It's still nice to walk around the old town, and along the defensive walls that were used to keep the likes of Sir Francis Drake from flogging all Spain's gold. Hang on a minute; didn't they flog it themselves in the first place? Easy come, easy go...

Our stay in Cartagena is cut short by the schedule of yachts leaving for Panama. There are two yachts scheduled to leave in two days' time. One is a 60ft catamaran with 15 people signed up to make the trip- plus crew. The other is a recent arrival that's turning round and going back to Panama to pick up another group of people. With no passengers, save for two: us. It's a no brainer.

It seems the heat is affecting our brains though. By the time we get around to signing up, the Austrian boat owners have found and confirmed two other people and brought forward the departure time one day, to the next morning. Bollocks! We really wanted a day or two more in Cartagena; we're most reluctant to leave Colombia, it's such an awesome country.

Put on the spot, we're umming and ahhhing over whether to accept the new terms. In the end it comes down to simple math: six people on this boat; at least 20 on the other.

"We hadn't planned to leave so early," Amanda tells their negotiator. "Can you move on the price?" It wouldn't feel right leaving Colombia without asking for a discount...

George the Austrian skipper agrees and we sign on the dotted line. The name of the vessel is Cool Running 2. I go to bed that night wondering what happened to the first one.

Cool Running 2; day 1

Amanda boards the boat armed with enthusiasm and a bottle of rum. I, on the other hand, am carrying sea sick tablets and a book called "Deep survival," which, among other things, tells the story of a man lost at sea for 53 days. Joining us on the boat are Mara from Austria, and Louisa from Germany.

We motor out of the harbour eating a leisurely lunch.

"Right then; let's do some sailing!" George orders, surveying his motley crew. "Everyone who's *not* helping, get behind the wheel please! The rest of you, let's go!"

Always up for a bit of sailing, Amanda's in her element. Mara and I follow George's instructions and settle in out of the way to spectate. Up go the sails, off goes the motor...stop goes the boat. You can't sail without wind. The motor restarts ten minutes later.

As we motor into the setting sun we're visited by dolphins and, once completely dark, we're also treated to a spectacular lightning display as three storms hit the Colombian coast simultaneously. Thankfully, we have clear skies above us. After dinner I retire to our cabin, or, as we quickly come to call it, our sauna. I'm hoping for some sleep, as much as for some time to give my numb arse a rest from the hard deck. Amanda joins me soon after, but doesn't last long, heading back out to sleep on deck after a restless few hours roasting. I wish I could say the drone of the motors was soothing...

Day 2

As the motoring continues, the lovely Caribbean cruise we were expecting has already started turning from pleasure cruise into endurance event. Rather than risking 'roids from sitting on the hard deck, and in an effort to hide from the blazing sun, I opt to stay in bed, rising only to eat.

I finally venture out onto deck right on dusk, happy to've missed the heat of the day. George has put a fishing rod out and he and wife Sandra are cooking dinner; Amanda is monitoring the autopilot and Mara and Louisa are otherwise occupied. It's only me that sees the rod bend as a fish takes the bait. I've only just got up really so it's a rude awakening but I get busy attempting to land dinner anyway.

After 15 minutes playing the fish...whilst trying not to fall off the boat in the heavy swell, and somehow managing all the while to avoid tangling the line in the trailing dingy, I am completely knackered. I'm not devastated about the fish getting away. Obviously, it was huge.

At 10pm, after 36 hours of drone, the motors are finally switched off when we reach our destination, dropping anchor at an outlying island of the San Blas group. Silence is golden.

"Pool's open!" George declares.

I'm into the water in a flash.

Day 3

Daylight gives us our first view of the area and we're not disappointed. We spend the morning lazing around on our very own deserted Caribbean island, and the afternoon snorkelling its surrounding reefs, only returning to the boat to be fed. The food so far has been plentiful- and very tasty- and The Cool Running crew go above and beyond the call of duty, turning Amanda's bottle of rum into a fresh fruit cocktail. We drink our way late into the night. The perfect day in paradise...

Day 4

We wake up to a picture perfect day- for Amanda: the wind has picked up, the sails go up...and the sails stay up. Off we go to the next island.

"And...we're racing!" That's me, yelling from the comfort of the spectator's seat. There's a catamaran on our tail, closing fast.

"Ignore it," George instructs his crew.

With Amanda on board? I'm thinking.

But George knows his stuff; we're easily out gunned by the cat. Just when I start thinking George is a bit boring, he's lined up a yacht closer in class to ours, tacks onto its tail and goes to work. And the race *is* on: the front boat crew obviously sees our moves and suddenly there's action there as well. But they're no match for George (already on his third glass of wine), and we overtake them easily before tacking away and returning to our original course.

"Good work crew," says George.

I am quietly chuffed at the role I have played in this victory: from spectator to instigator, and motivator.

Our new destination is a bit more populated than last night's mooring, in terms of both people and yachts. We forego the opportunity to pay a tenner each to land on one island, and head instead for a free one that seems to have pretty similar sand, palm trees and surrounding ocean. Free, that is, until some random guy turns up claiming to be the son of the two elderly island residents, whose permission we've already sought.

"How do we know you're their son?" Louisa asks.

"Ummm, ask them?"

So we do. The old folks look slightly confused by all this, but eventually agree that the extortionist is, in fact, their son. We're not convinced and get ready to leave, expecting a hefty price tag. While we're readying, the discussion continues and the fee is set at...$2 per person.

"Let's pay the man," I suggest. That's cheap, for paradise *and* principles.

More lying around on the beach, and more snorkelling, ensue. Eventually we head back to the boat for dinner and tell George about our day.

"Some islands charge $20 per person; $50 if you want to bring a video camera," he says. "We don't take people to those ones."

Four plates of yummy curry later, I hit the sack. It's tiring work lazing around.

Day 5

What **not** to do when you have seven hours of open water sailing to look forward to? Eat four plates of curry the night before: it certainly won't go down in history as my greatest day on the ocean but at least I manage to keep my dinner down.

We sail into Puerto Lindo around 2pm.
Hello Panama!
Hello Central America!
Hello Customs!
Oh, wait, what, *no* Customs?! No wonder this is a smuggling route...

20- Bikes we have pushed

After we spend the night in Puerto Lindo, George and Sandra give us a ride to neighbouring Portobelo, where they have to bribe an immigration official to get him to open up and stamp our passports. Seems it's a public holiday.

Passports returned, it's time to farewell our skipper and first mate and head deeper into Central America, destination Colon. (It's not just a clever name, it really is a shit hole!) This leg of the journey sees us experience the notorious Central American chicken bus. What an experience! A chicken bus is basically a retired school bus that's skipped the border from North America. The ride's like a party! Mara and Louisa entertain the kids while I enter a haggling match with the man in front of me.

"I like your shirt, we swap?" He suggests.

"No thanks." I reply; his shirt's not that flash, and a bit sweaty!

"We swap hats then." he states.

"Ah, that's another no, mate." For the same reason as the shirt.

The guy's going after all my good stuff; but while he's been trying, I've been sussing, and I note that his sunglasses are rather excellent. Two can play at this game: "We swap sunglasses?" I offer.

"No."

Amanda interjects before I lose my pants.

As we're attempting to secure our baggage at the Colon bus terminal, Louisa has her backpack snatched, and gives chase. It's a short chase: the thief loads it onto the waiting bus to Panama City, then demands payment. At least we now know where the bus going to Panama City is.

An honest taxi driver...

Bidding farewell to the girls at the Panama City bus terminal, we pencil in three days to check out the sights.

After pirate Henry Morgan destroyed the original Panama City in 1671, Panamanians moved their city 8km up the road to a more readily defendable position, and Casco Viejo was born. As far as old towns go, it's better than Bogota: not quite as good as Cartagena; and absolutely nothing on Quito. Or maybe we're just over old towns...

Next on the agenda is Panama's famous canal. We're here; we figure it'd be rude not to check it out. Engineering marvel the Panama Canal may be, spectator sport it is not. We spend the 45 minutes we're there working out ways to make it more interesting. We come up with one: Lake Miraflores is 45 metres above the Pacific Ocean; if they did away with the lock gates and let the ships run the rapid, they'd get at least double the $5 entry fee!

A short bike ride along a peninsula; a stroll in a local national park (where I spot my first ever live armadillo) and that's Panama City done. It would be fair to say it was a bit underwhelming. It's time to move on.

So far Amanda's been able to negotiate pretty good taxi fares around town- usually around $5-$6. With one thief trying to charge $30 (he drove off when we both burst out laughing), it's a full-time job negotiating anywhere close to the going rate. We vacate our hotel and hail a cab to the bus station.

"How much?" Amanda asks, steeling herself for the inevitable battle.

"$2.50," the taxi driver answers.

We are stunned: have we found an honest taxi driver? We quickly jump in before we wake up and realise it was all a dream, or he realises his mistake. Amazingly, at the bus station 15 minutes later, the price is the same. I hand over a five dollar note then practice my limited Spanish on him.

"No nessicito cambio amigo." Keep the change mate. Amanda takes over with her more advanced Spanish to thank him profusely for being our first honest taxi driver in Latin America. The smile on his face is priceless.

Bussing on to the town of David, then on to the North American retirement village of Boquete in the Panamanian hills, we struggle to find anything to catch our interest. Whether it's because South America was so awesome, or after eleven months travelling we're suddenly on a deadline (-to meet Amanda's family in Costa Rica for Christmas), it's hard to say. Maybe it's just travel fatigue. Thinking along the lines of the latter, we decide we need some more beach time to work it out. We make a beeline for Bocas Del Toro on the Panamanian Caribbean.

Bocas Del Toro; day 1

We are welcomed back to the Caribbean with torrential rain, rain that starts the minute we board the boat heading for Bocas Town on Isla Colon. With no map, no accommodation booked, and no let-up in the rain that looks to have set in for the day, it's not exactly the smooth transition to a golden sand beach we were looking for. We step out into the downpour and walk aimlessly, hoping to find some signs of life. Finally we find some, in the form of the local accommodation tout.

"What sort of accommodation are you looking for?" Mr Tout asks.

"Cheap." I reply.

He shows us to a cheap hotel in the main street.

"Not really what we're looking for. Let's try cheap AND waterfront." Amanda suggests.

We head back out into the pouring rain and follow him to another hotel. It looks a bit scummy. Mr Tout seems to read our minds.

"If you want nicer water front you will pay more. I will show you another place close to the water that's tidier."

At the next place, we're greeted by the North American owner, who shows us around a very tidy room with cable TV (*and* English channels!), a valuables safe, air con, *and* a fridge. We decide this is the place for us. After over an hour of walking around in the rain, Mr Tout has certainly earned his commission today. We sign up for his full day snorkel tour tomorrow to express our thanks- after the hostel owner vouches for him. Hopefully the rain eases in time.

Day 2

The sun is shining as we board the boat. The first stop on our snorkel tour is a 'secluded' bay where dolphins are known to frolic. Alas, no, we're not allowed to swim with them: with all the boats out here it wouldn't be safe to jump in. Ok, so...not such a secluded bay then.

We, along with the other eight boats in the vicinity, spend the next 30 minutes following four dolphins around the bay. It's more like a hunt than a watch, and finally the boats have them surrounded. Luckily dolphins aren't as stupid as humans- they escape easily. We continue on our way, already itching to get into the water and cool down.

Next stop is a waterfront restaurant to order lunch for later on in the day. It's US$23 a meal so we're quite happy we brought food with us. After everyone's done getting ripped off, we're taken to a deserted island that we have the run of... until all the other tours turn up. Luckily it's big enough for us to find our own private spot. During our private island time, Amanda tells me she never actually learned to dive.

"Can you teach me?"

By the end of our first lesson, she's diving like a pro and has even mastered the 'run from the beach and dive into the water' method. I can almost feel "Baywatch" auditions coming on. Delighted to be back in the waves myself, I instinctively body surf in on an awesome wave I spot forming. Alas, forgetting how close they break to shore, I'm unceremoniously dumped on the beach, permanently engraining part of the Caribbean in my chest. After about four hours of this bliss (and 30 minutes of snorkelling), our group heads back to the waterfront restaurant for the overpriced lunch or, in our case, some snack bars. After lunch we head for home, willing the boat to stop on another reef for a bit more snorkel action, but it's not to be. It was a nice day out but it probably shouldn't be called a snorkelling tour.

Day 3

Waking up to another glorious day, we decide to head for the local surf beach. Red Frog beach, a short water taxi ride away on Isla Bastiementos, is named for the poisonous red frogs that call this island home. What do you do on a picture perfect beach when the sun is shining? Swim, sunbathe, swim, sunbathe...rinse, dry, repeat...lunch.

And after lunch, more of the same. To mix it up, I enter into a somersault-over-a-wave competition with a young local lad. Eventually, taking full advantage of the language barrier, I call it a draw and stumble back up the beach to collapse on my towel. I'll sleep well tonight. We don't see any red frogs but we do see a couple of sloths in the trees on the walk back to the jetty. After two days of this, we're ready for a change of scene: time for a bit of land-based exercise. We turn in early, in preparation for tomorrow's adventure.

Day 4

The first bikes we hired were in Puerto Rio Tranquilo, Chile. That day it was my body that broke down, and I only managed a very short ride. The second time we hired bikes was in Pucon, also in Chile. Half of *that* ride involved me standing on a pedal, using my bike as a scooter after my chain broke. Still in Chile, pushing heavy bikes up sand dunes, and through sand in the driest place on earth, we almost lost our cycling spirit forever in the Atacama Desert.

But nowhere on our travels has a bike ride been *such* an epic fail as it is here in Bocas Del Toro. Brace yourself to feel our pain...

Our first destination today is Boca Del Drago, reported to be one of the best beaches on the island. It's a 16km ride through the centre of the island on a paved road, which the travel guide describes as "taxing." From the beach, we plan to head east along the coast on a little known trail to Playa Bluff, another beach that warrants a mention. Hooking up with the road again at Playa Bluff, it's a 9km ride back to Bocas Town. Sounds easy...

The most taxing thing about the first leg of our journey is, as per usual, the rented bikes. Amanda swears her bike is heavier than she is, and with gears slipping all over the place, the ride is much more difficult than it should be. We decide to take a break and stop off at the local bat cave. To see real bats, not superheroes.

As we take those first tentative steps into the cave, we quickly realise that bats aren't the only things that live here. Our entry comes to a screeching halt as we come face to face with hundreds of cave spiders. Just as I'm talking Amanda through her fear of spiders, in an effort to coax her along, a rather large eight-legged specimen jumps towards us, yes, jumps! Amanda breaks all speed records leaving; I fire up the torch and continue alone.

As I explore further, with bats swooping alarmingly close, I come face to face with the mother of all cave spiders, without doubt the biggest spider I've ever seen. Not even Bear Grylls would eat this fucker! I back away slowly; if this one jumps on me I'll be crushed. I carry on exploring 'til I'm tired of bats swooping and spiders jumping. Returning to daylight, and Amanda, who's watching over the bikes, we continue on our way.

After a quick lunch, a look around, and a swim at Boca Del Drago, we head east...towards adventure. For an hour we cycle down the only road we can find, not entirely sure if we're on the right track. There's a nagging doubt in our minds but with no other obvious options, we press on until we come to a crossroads.

Left or right; the age-old crossroads conundrum.

I choose left, towards the coast. It turns out to be a track to nothing as we hit the coast within five minutes and have nowhere to go beyond.

"Ha! I knew we should've gone right."

We cycle back to the crossroads and fork right. Within five minutes we've stopped at a gate with a large, and very new-looking, "Private Property" sign beside it.

"What now smart arse?" Amanda, to me.

Back home, a private property sign in the wilderness wouldn't really worry me; I've run down trails leading out of parks and onto people's farms. I've just kept running as if I'm supposed to be there- and pled ignorance if approached. "Sorry mate, I'm a bit lost," works wonders. But this is Panama: people carry machetes!

"I think we need to turn around," Amanda says. I'm relieved she's saved me from making this decision, going, as it does, against everything I stand for.

Our 40km loop has now become a rather more epic 55kms out and back.

As we cycle back to where we came from, all the while looking for a route we may've missed on the way in, we come across a German woman walking down the road with a Panamanian survey team. We finally get the direction information we're looking for.

"Yes, this is the right road," German Lady confirms. "But there's no trail. We have rescued many people in here; there's no way you'd get through the jungle on bikes. And besides, its private property and the owner doesn't like people walking through."

Hence the big new sign. We resign ourselves to the 25km cycle back to Bocas Town.

But German Lady hasn't finished: "You look hot. Turn right in about 100 metres and go for a swim at our beach."

No arguments from us. As we cycle into this little piece of paradise, I can't help but think of our own home in New Zealand, a house on stilts surrounded by native bush, so similar in its' natural beauty to this place. But this is nature on a much grander scale. Trees tower over us and sloths look down on us from the branches. Oh, and it's beach front; my dream property location.

After our swim at this private Caribbean paradise, we pop into the house to say thanks and German Lady's husband invites us in for some much-needed refreshment. We sit on the deck chatting with this hospitable couple for a good 45 minutes before we reluctantly leave. We have to get back before dark.

Invigorated, we set off again on our piece-a-shit bikes. Just 8kms of rough track and 16kms of paved road stand between us and a well earned beer. 2kms later I'm descending a hill on one of the rougher pieces of the track when all of a sudden...
SNAP!!!!
My pedals stop turning and my back wheel locks up. It's not the ideal occurrence at speed. I manage to bail before I'm thrown, luckily, and I yell for Amanda to stop before she disappears into the distance.
"What happened?" Amanda asks.
"My bloody derailleur snapped." I'm thoroughly pissed off at another rental bike failure.

For the next 30 minutes I attempt to render the bike if not *ride*able, then at least *scoot*able- as per the Pucon rental bike failure, but to no avail. The pedals aren't turning and the back wheel just keeps locking up; I'm going to have to drag this bastard out of here. Luckily I'm wearing my all terrain...jandals. Swearing, and covered in grease from the attempted bare-hand-repair, I start walking. Amanda joins me in my misery.

It's a frustrating and hot 6km walk back to the main road, whereupon it's decision time. Turn left and walk 16kms back to Bocas Town, hoping to catch a lift, or turn right and walk 1km to Boca Del Drago. Either way we're relying on a taxi to get us home. The restaurant at Boca Del Drago seems the best option...at least they might have a phone. There's certainly not much else there.

As we turn right towards the restaurant, we get our second lucky break of an otherwise pretty rubbish day (German Lady was the first). We spot a ute-taxi (yes, a **ute-taxi**!!!) heading our way. We don't so much flag it down as we do stand on the road and block its way. Our hearts break just a little when we see it's already occupied. It stops anyway and an American guy winds down the passenger seat window.

"What seems to be the problem?"

"My bike's broken down mate. Could your taxi man call a taxi for us? Please?"

"Meh, hop in," he replies after a quick conversation with the driver...who proceeds to throw our bikes on the back. It's a good thing mine's already broken.

Back in Bocas town over a meal and a few beers, we can't help feeling just a little bit of animosity towards a certain travel guide. It's true that this trail was never touted as being bike-able, and we like a good adventure as much as the next (adventurous) person, but for them to describe the trail with no mention whatsoever of the fact that it goes over private land? Plain bad form.

The day wasn't a complete write-off. We saw some more lovely beaches, got some exercise (more than we were expecting), had fun in the jungle, and finally managed to spot the elusive poison dart frog we were hoping to find at Red Frog Beach (although this one was yellow!). On top of that, we met some great people who helped us out in our time of need. Chalk it all down to experience.

That said, my lasting memory of this trip is our last day in Panama, spent trying to get the grease out of my bright yellow- brand new- Colombian football shirt.

21- The in-laws

My first holiday with the in-laws came at the start of this trip, almost a year ago in Scotland. Thankfully our Christmas rendezvous in Costa Rica promises to be a hell of a lot warmer than Scotland in January. Amazing Race Costa Rica is about to begin. Albeit slowly.

The warm-up

Sneaking over the Panamanian border to Puerto Viejo, we arrive in Costa Rica four days before the planned rendezvous. With a bit of time to kill in the Caribbean, our immediate thought is, of course, the beach.

With the rental bike disaster of Bocas Del Toro still fresh, it may come as a surprise to you that the first thing we do is hire bikes. It surprised us a little too, but with 15km of beach stretching down the coast to Manzanillo, it's the best way to get around.

After a few hours of torrential rain early in the day, the sun comes out. What follows is probably the best day we've spent on bikes during our entire travels. We explore beach after beach, still managing to get in a little bit of off-road time on our street cruisers. We stop at deserted bays and spend hours in the water, cooling down and continuing Amanda's dive training. Bocas Del Toro's mishaps fade into memory.

Our final Amazing Race warm-up event is a coastal walk in Cahuita National Park, just up the road. It's another glorious day as we step off the bus and walk through the small town of Cahuita to the park entrance. After making a donation to (apparently) the only national park in Costa Rica that you *don't* have to pay to get into, we head off down the jungle path. This is awesome: thick jungle on one side, a golden sand beach and ocean on the other. And the further we walk, the less we have to share!

About 30 minutes into our expedition an eerie silence sweeps over the jungle.

"Do you hear that? I ask Amanda. Although *not* hear it would be a more accurate description.

"Yeah. I wonder what's going on."

We get our answer seconds later as the heavens open and it starts absolutely bucketing down. Enclosed in thick jungle, we didn't even see it cloud over. One mad dash later we're sheltering under the small roof of an information sign. It's not long until three North Americans, who arrive from the opposite direction, join us.

Half an hour later we're all still standing there- and the rain is still pouring down. The Americans realise through the course of our conversation that they're quite close to the main entrance of the park, and decide to make a dash for it. They bid us farewell and run off into the downpour. We have a lot further to go...

"How long are we going to stand here?" Amanda asks.

"Shall we go too eh?" I ask, by way of a reply. "This rain isn't stopping; we could be waiting all night!"

With any chance of wildlife spotting all but gone, our attention turns to the marine park we're walking beside. Rather than join an expensive tour, we brought our own snorkels to do a bit of exploring. We're completely drenched anyway; we may as well be in the water. Unfortunately that plan is also thwarted, not by the elements, but by a strategically placed park warden...with binoculars, who is standing at the tip of the peninsula where the reef begins. Sadly, there are a few irresponsible people damaging the reef and ruining it for everyone else. We wave a greeting to the warden, trying not to look guilty, and walk back off into the pouring rain, looking for a more secluded entry point.

But as the rain continues to pour down, our enthusiasm wanes. Time to get the hell out of here before we're washed away! We set off at a cracking pace and eventually come across a small settlement. It looks like a ranger station and there are two people sheltering beneath an information kiosk. We wave, but continue on our way. Not long afterwards we hear a vehicle coming up behind us and, before you know it, we're out of the rain and on our way to the park exit with a ranger- and the two people from the shelter. They're completely dry so they must've been there for hours. Just as we're leaving, three hours of torrential rain simmers down a notch to merely heavy, and the chatter of the monkeys returns to full voice. It's almost as if they're laughing at us.

The Amazing Race

The planning stages of the inaugural Briggs Family Amazing Race have put us at a distinct advantage; we're already in the right country for a start, a mere seven hours by bus from the first checkpoint. We're at the bus station, complete with pre-purchased tickets...

"You have to pay more," the man working at the ticket office informs us when we arrive at the station.

"Why?"

"There have been landslides across the road and the bus has to take a longer route to San Jose."

Paying more for a bus that's now going to take longer? Now I've heard everything. We pay up and are handed our tickets just as the bus arrives. As it pulls in, Amanda joins the rapidly forming queue to try and get us seats together, while I stow the luggage. Only the first leg of the race and we're showing team work at its finest.

A couple of hours up the road, the driver suddenly pulls over and makes an announcement. A huge discussion ensues.

"What the hell's going on?" I say to Amanda.

"I didn't really catch it but it sounds like we can go the original route if we want to."

"That's right; the driver just asked us which way we'd like to go. He's going to take a vote soon." A helpful, English-speaking local overhears us and chimes in with clarification.

I can't believe what I'm hearing. Sure enough, ten minutes later the driver walks to the back of the bus and starts moving forward, counting votes on his way. Eventually he gets to me.

"I don't care! *Vamos*!! Let's go!! A stationary bus isn't going *any* way!" Finally we're back on our way. I have no idea *which* way we end up taking but we arrive 45 minutes ahead of schedule. Do we get a refund for the shorter travel time? Er, what do you think?

From the private bus terminal we arrived at, it's just a matter of navigating our way to the Coca Cola bus terminal, San Jose's main transport hub. A wrong turn reaps huge rewards when we spot a Movistar, a mobile phone shop; Amanda pops in to purchase our secret weapon- a Costa Rican sim card for her phone. With Google Maps now fully operational we find the terminal easily.

We've just missed a bus to Atenas so we've got a bit of time to kill. Not wanting to stray too far from the station, we decide to head into the neighbouring market for some lunch. Since Amanda's Bolivian food poisoning, she's eaten street food just a handful of times, and has steered well clear of food halls in the local markets. She sits tentatively at the most hygienic looking food stall we can find and we order up and dig in. I idly note two police officers watching us as we shovel food in our faces. I hope there aren't any table manners by-laws we don't know about here.

Just as we finish our meals, Amanda is horrified to see a cockroach run across her cleared plate and vows anew to never eat at a market again. As we leave, I greet the police with a friendly *hola* and they return the greeting before disappearing further into the market. It seems the only two gringos in the market warrant police protection: have our Amazing Race opponents put the word out to the criminal underworld in an effort to slow us down? If so, we thwart their efforts, safely boarding the bus for Atenas.

We arrive in Atenas and decide to walk to the B&B after consulting the phone and finding it's not that far out of town. Ten minutes later we arrive at the B&B, only to find it *not actually there*. The Google Maps app's let us down, giving us the wrong location. Not to worry, we swing Plan B into action and ask a passer-by for directions. Three kilometres later, (a lot further than anyone should walk wearing a full pack in the Costa Rican sun) we arrive at a very flash looking B&B. Team Kiwi arrives a full nine hours before the competition, who are disqualified anyway for failing to arrive with all their luggage.

The competition

I guess I should introduce you to the team that we thoroughly trounced in the first stage: my father-in-law, Robbie, who we all think of as Grandad because of the kids; mother-in-law Mavis, or Granny; my sister-in-law Caroline and her husband Stephen; and the kids, seven-year-old Luca and Paolo, who is one. They all look completely shattered.

Amanda has spent the nine hours before they arrived pacing the B&B, barely able to contain her excitement. She hasn't seen her family for a year and she's ready to party. It's 1am; I managed three hours sleep but, now that I'm up, I could probably go a beer or two. I could just as easily go back to sleep though. Team Scotland has just come off a long haul flight, so it's pretty clear they and I are on the same page. The party will have to wait.

Never known for her patience, Amanda plants herself in the chair outside her mum and dad's room at 5am and settles in to wait. She's been looking forward to this moment since these plans were finalised. After almost a year on the road, this reunion has been her fuel. Me, I'm just looking forward to the accommodation upgrade.

> Amanda- I am as well. After a year living in the most basic accommodation without creature comforts and plenty of un-comforts, we now have a *very* tidy room with a real bed, an ensuite, and in that ensuite, a shower that pumps out *real* hot water.

The Amazing Race- special stage

After a few days lounging about the pool it's time to move on to our next flash accommodation, so it's off to get the hire cars. Amanda, Grandad, Stephen and I are assigned to this task. Because of Team Kiwis decisive victory in the first stage, we've agreed to mix things up a bit. Team Grandad/Tony vs. Team Amanda/Stephen is the new line-up. Shit is about to get real…

Initially though, we have to cooperate. We all take a taxi 40km up the road to Grandad's hire place. The plan is to pick up the first hire car and drive it direct to the next place. Our plans unravel and our quick pick-ups turn into a good old fashioned (Costa Rican) car insurance scam. Despite the fact that Grandad paid for full insurance back in the UK, where he organised this, it soon becomes clear that he's going to have to cough up something extra before they'll release the car. Like us and our fight with our tent manufacturers, Grandad's fight for justice would go on for a long time afterwards. Finally, well behind schedule, we're on our way to the next hire company.

Stephen has managed to find a much cheaper deal, but Grandad was more thorough. Stephen may have saved a dollar or two, but his hire car is only a two wheel drive. Apparently we need 4X4s for where we're going. Too late to change, Stephen resigns himself to his fate…and the race home begins.

Stephen takes the lead with Google Maps and Amanda navigating. I'm navigating for Grandad and it's easy:

"Follow Stephen!"

We're biding our time…

Rather than taking the easy navigational challenge of simply going back to the B&B, our first destination is a large shopping complex, to pick up some forgotten bits and pieces- along with some clothes for Granny, whose lost luggage still hasn't arrived.

We're on track to the mall when Stephen makes an abrupt turn. Is he trying to shake us off his tail?? I consult the map and direct Grandad to follow. We pull into...a shipping container yard just behind the frontrunners: way to go, Google Maps! We get back on track and, eventually, arrive at the shopping centre. It's 5pm on a Friday, five days before Christmas. The queue to the already full car park is long so Stephen drives past and continues driving down a small side road, where a couple of parks await us on a grass verge.

"I think I should stay with the cars," I say. I don't like the look of the area we're parked in- but I like the thought of shopping in a crowded mall even less. The shopping party departs and I begin guard duty, a duty that will fall to me for the rest of the holiday.

What feels like many hours pass; day turns to night before the shoppers return. It's time to head for home.

"Follow Stephen?" Grandad asks. He's cottoned onto my tactics by now.

"Yep."

I continue to check every turn Stephen makes and guide Grandad along, both of us waiting for the opportune time to make our move. Finally it happens, Stephen turns a corner.

"DON'T FOLLOW!" I yell.

Grandad hesitates:

"Are you sure?"

"Yes!" I quickly recheck the map. "I've got no idea why they turned there."

For the first time today we've taken the lead and, with a mere 5km between us and our destination, it's looking very good for Team Grandad/Tony. Sure enough, after checking and rechecking the map, we arrive at our destination and claim victory. Team Amanda/Stephen arrives 30 minutes later.

The Christmas house

The next morning we put our rivalry aside and head for our destination, the tiny settlement of Tambor on the Nicoya Peninsula. I join Grandad and Granny in one vehicle, while Amanda is emotionally blackmailed by nephew Luca to join Stephen, Caroline and baby Paulo in the other. In convoy we make a leisurely beeline for the ferry town of Puntarenas.

As we're driving through town, aware that we may've just missed a ferry sailing, a man jumps out onto the road in front of us with a "Ferry" sign in his hand. After a quick discussion with

Amanda and co in the front car, he walks back to our car, opens the back door and jumps in. I'm slightly taken aback, as are Grandad and Granny.

"You've missed the ferry so I've booked you on the next one. Now we go to a restaurant. Turn the car around." Mr Ferry Man orders.

With no movement coming out of the other car, we can only assume that they're in on this, even though to us it feels like a kidnapping. Grandad does as he's told and follows our new tour guide's directions. Stephen, much to our relief, follows. It's not until we arrive at the restaurant that we get a chance to communicate with the others and holes start to form in Mr Ferry Man's story. Actually, they're less like holes, more like enormous, gaping chasms. Luckily, we're used to this kind of thing by now:

"I have booked you on the ferry, and have brought you to a nice restaurant. Now you must pay me."

"How much?" asks Amanda.

"Thirty dollars."

"Ah ha ha haaaa. No." Amanda's response. "I'll give you two."

Mr Ferry Man doesn't like what he's hearing.

"I have done good work for you; I need to feed my family," he argues, keeping the conversation going in English to take full advantage of the recent arrivals. Holidaymakers have such nice, pliable heart strings. Unfortunately long-time travellers have long since hardened theirs. Amanda knows exactly how to handle this:

"You haven't done *anything* for us, apart from tell us lies. You have not booked the ferry for us! You're nothing but a con man, and you're scaring my family so now you're not even getting two dollars."

Mr Ferry Man opens his mouth to respond.

"If I were you, I'd leave now," I suggest casually. "You don't want to see my wife angry."

"OK, I go."

Even with Amanda at the helm, it helps to have three more people behind you!

The rest of our journey is quite dull in comparison, and eventually we arrive at our destination, a house we've rented just out the back of Tambor village, in a lovely jungle setting. As the letting agent shows us around, it strikes me that there don't seem to be enough rooms for everyone.

"We don't do dorms," I joke.

"You and Amanda are over in the guest house," Granny says, recognising the vague concern beneath my attempted humour. It's no secret that I'm not at my most tolerant when it comes to children. I like my (adult) space.

We follow the agent out the door and down a short, jungle-covered path. Arriving at the guest house, we're pleasantly surprised with what we find. The house itself is nothing more than a bedroom and a bathroom- but it's right beside a pool- and an outdoor kitchen and bar. There's even an ice machine. I think I'm going to like it here.

The next day, we wake to howler monkeys in the trees all around us and realise we're in photo paradise. We spend hours, fascinated, watching the monkeys watching us from the tree tops. Outgunned by actual cameras, my seven inch tablet struggles to compete. I may need to come up with a new strategy if I'm to hold out any hope of victory in the Briggs holiday photo competition.

> Amanda- Its all sounds very idyllic having monkeys in your garden but the monkeys weren't always happy to see us. One day while I was trying to get a close up shot of one, it proceeded to poo in its hand then throw the poo at me...and it had good aim!

After breakfast, with the wildlife long gone, everyone decides to head to the local markets. Everyone except me; I have a date with my brand new trail running shoes, which have thankfully been transported from the UK in Granny's bag that ISN'T lost! Newly shod, I run out the gate looking forward to exploring the surrounding country side. It feels good to get out of those Bolivian clogs. After half an hour I'm completely knackered; it's my first run in almost a year and, even at 10am, it's somewhere in the vicinity of 30°C (86°F). I turn around and head for home- and the pool. I stay there for the rest of the day and when the shoppers get home, they join me.

Over the next few days Luca and I spend most of our time in the pool inventing dives, including such gems as "The Monkey," "The Plank" and "The Snake." Channelling Monty Python, Grandad contributes "The Silly Walk," and even Amanda makes a contribution. While she's getting in some dive training, and making great progress, she unwittingly patents "The Eye Flop." A variation on the tried and true belly flop, it's such an impressive manoeuvre, I try it myself later in the week, with the same excruciating results.

We manage to get out of the pool and embark on a few excursions though, mainly to the air-conditioned comfort of the supermarket as the Scots continue to struggle with the heat. A bit of zip lining through the jungle canopy is really most memorable for Luca jumping off a five metre rock face into a pool at the bottom of a waterfall, to rapturous applause from the whole zip lining group. A fearless effort from a seven-year-old. On our way home from zip lining, we stop off at the supermarket, as has become routine, in a town called Cobano.

"I'll guard the vehicle," I offer, somewhat superfluously, as everyone else is already walking off.

Fifteen minutes later, as I'm amusing myself watching the local drunks, a man approaches the vehicle and produces a hand gun. FUCK! When I designated myself guard I wasn't expecting this! I make a quick decision to give him...*ANYTHING he wants.* He's holding the gun by the barrel; I'm thinking he's about to use it to smash the window. Not its primary purpose, but I'm really not complaining. Then he seems to notice me for the first time, sitting in the back seat. He's apparently so surprised to see me; he puts his gun away and walks off. I am clearly a menacing specimen indeed.

"Umm, you might not want to tell your family about that for a while," I suggest to Amanda when I relate my adventure later that day. Westernised Costa Rica is proving to be more dangerous than other, less "civilised" places on our travel.

It's not until Christmas Eve, after countless more supermarket excursions, that we finally get in some solid beach time. We have a lovely day out at Playa Hermosa, lying on the beach under palm trees, and swimming in the ocean at will. To top off the perfect day, we not only walk past a supermarket without going inside, but not long after we arrive home, Granny's lost luggage also arrives, only five days late. It's just in time for Christmas.

Our nightly search for wildlife is about to pay off as well- big time for me: I'm the one with the camera. When we call it a night, we're heading back to the guest house for bed when there's a rustling in the undergrowth...and out pops an armadillo!

"Quick! Go and get the others," I whisper.

Amanda races off and I keep my distance, hoping not to scare it away. Amanda returns with only Grandad in tow...and he's camera-less! It's up to my trusty tablet-camera to capture this. I move in as close as I dare, snapping as many frames as I can in the process. Eventually I move too close and Mr Armadillo runs off into the trees. I think I've just dramatically increased my chances in the photo comp.

The Amazing Race- water stage

Christmas Day is spent by the pool. A long-standing tradition of the Briggs Family Christmas is the "silly objects in the room" game. This involves Granny hiding items around the house that normally have no reason to be there. Over the years, a head of broccoli snugly hidden in the foliage of a pot plant has been one of my favourites. This year we have to adapt to our surroundings. After my suggestion of "silly objects in the rain forest" is discarded (-possible snake activity), Amanda comes up with the slightly safer "silly objects in the pool" variation of the game.

With Amanda as judge, and me as cameraman, the rest of the 'crew' line up poolside, awaiting starter's orders.

"GO!" Amanda yells.

All hell breaks loose as three adults and one child dive into the pool to start. Granny walks down the steps...slowly. Words can't accurately describe the next fifteen minutes as pots, cans of beer, coins, and other strange items are retrieved from the bottom of the pool. Amanda has devised game rules that reward teamwork, by requiring that items leave the pool in a specific order. The order is shown on a list strategically placed at the bottom of the pool in a waterproof map case. As Team Grandad/Caroline/Luca seems to struggle with the concept of working together, preferring instead a somewhat more random individual-collection method, Team Stephen/Granny comes up with an infallible strategy. Stephen dives to the bottom of the pool, reads the list then proceeds to recover things in the correct order, taking full advantage of his Dutch need for order and precision. Granny sits at the edge of the pool and waits for him to surface with the goods, then takes them straight to the judging table. It's a decisive victory.

A long, fun day by the pool comes to an end and Christmas dinner at the main house beckons. As we walk back through the jungle, the howler monkeys make a timely appearance, venturing closer than they ever have before. Have they been watching our poolside antics from a distance, and decided to get a better look at this strange bunch of humans? Whatever, it's the perfect end to a Costa Rican Christmas.

Our Christmas hangovers demand a couple more excursions. The one to the supposed best beach in Costa Rica, on Isla Tortuga, is really only memorable for some good snorkelling, some good food and a tame pig. The beach isn't much to write home about.

The second excursion is a whole lot better. Curu National Park starts off a bit lame as we walk down trails scanning the jungle for elusive wildlife. There are a few distant sightings but it's not until we arrive back at park headquarters that the monkeys really come out to play. Probably not that surprising really; wardens at park headquarters are feeding them. We spend hours getting close-up photos of three or four different species of monkey, and a couple of very large- and very fast- iguanas. The photo competition is heating up. But it's time to move on.

The New Year's house

We forego the opportunity for a race and instead form a convoy heading for our new destination, Ojochal, a 300km drive down the southwest coast. Granny, organised as ever, has booked a night's accommodation in Jaco to break up the journey. Just before Jaco though, is the one of Costa Rica's main tourist attractions, Crocodile Bridge. I walk out onto the bridge and look over the side to confirm the veracity of its name; yep, definitely crocodiles.

Jaco is memorable for one thing and one thing alone: Luca becomes the youngest barman I have ever been served by. With the help of his mother, he's bought some alcohol with the cunning plan to sell it back to the adults, at extortionate prices. It's more than likely the only bar in town run by a seven-year-old and, situated in the hotel, it's also well within walking distance. Deciding to settle in for the night, I try a few of the drinks on offer and go with the beer and coconut juice concoction; it offers by far the best value. Unfortunately, the night ends like several other nights I've spent in a bar- thrown out by 8pm. Only the reason differs this time: the barman's dad decides it's past his bed time.

When we reach Ojochal the next day we're impressed by what we see. After following the letting agent 10km up a dirt road into the hills, we arrive at a house that, quite frankly, makes the Christmas house look a bit ordinary. Our room alone is easily the size of the guest house in Tambor, and the large pool is metres away from all of us this time. Add to that ten acres of rainforest for a back yard, jungle as far as the eye can see, and a view all the way to the coast, and we have, without doubt, arrived in paradise.

Instead of monkeys, it's toucans that greet us to our new abode. One, then two...and finally eight park themselves in a tree close to the house. The photo competition is well and truly on again.

As awesome as all this is, the best is yet to come. For nearly a year now, because of the inferior sewer systems in Latin America, we've been placing our used toilet paper in waste baskets that are usually provided. Nine times out of ten, because of poor bin placement, this normally requires a degree of flexibility and some acrobatics. It is with great pleasure that my first act in this house is of a toiletry nature- and because the plumbing system has been built to western standards, I'm able to flush everything. Amanda is equally taken with this detail:

"I just *flushed toilet paper* down the toilet," she whispers to me a little later on.

It's the little things...

One of the nicknames I've acquired over the years is Couch Man, for my uncanny ability to find a couch wherever I go and completely take it over. This trip- and its lack of couches- has been very hard on me. My luck appears to have changed here, when I find a couch in a small outdoor area down the side of the house, a little bit away from the main pool area where everyone else is sitting. It is here that I stake out my territory, to enjoy a bit of "me" time.

"Where's Tony?" the rest of the family ask Amanda continuously for the first few days as we settle into our jungle retreat.

"If he's not in the pool, or hunting down photo opportunities, he'll be on his couch."

There aren't many things worth getting off the couch for. Excepting of course the nightly bar service provided by Luca; he's working for tips now rather than risking getting the authorities involved in an overcharging scandal.

The wildlife strikes back!

It's not all sitting around the pool drinking Pina Coladas though. The one thing missing in our-near perfect house is the proximity of an ocean, so we decide to take a few day trips out to the beaches along the coast.

Playa Ventanas is first port of call, a pretty, black sand beach with some nice caves- and the best body surfing conditions I've ever seen! Constant double breakers give the waves twice the power, and I body surf about 50 metres at a time...all the way into shore. It is AWESOME!

The local beach at Ojochal is less picturesque, with no surf, but it's still ruggedly beautiful in its own way. Here, we get to see how the locals live, barbequing and fishing at a beach that doesn't see many tourists. And the bird life is amazing: flocks of scarlet macaws line the trees, and the pro photographers who are entered into the photo comp run off to try their luck. Lying on the beach rather than pursuing the bright new bird life, I'm content to watch an old friend, *el carpintero,* happily pecking away at a tree.

The main attraction in the area is the Marina Ballena National Park, a marine reserve with beautiful beaches and very good snorkelling.

After picking a shaded spot on the edge of the jungle, Granny and Grandad set off for a walk down the beach; Stephen and Caroline grab the snorkel gear and head for the water; and Amanda and I are left with Luca and Paolo. How do you occupy children at the beach? Dig a hole of course! And we don't just dig it; we also manage to coax Luca into it, and quickly bury him up to his neck. That's one child out of the way! I hand child number two the spade, then take photos of him burying his brother, thinking I'll use the photos as cooperation leverage until his parents get back. All is going according to plan...until Paolo decides it's much more fun to hit Luca over the head with the spade.

Eventually Stephen and Caroline return to take over the child minding duties and Amanda and I set off down the beach, looking forward to once again being at one with the fishes. As we approach the snorkel point we see Granny and Grandad walking arm in arm. How romantic! Unfortunately it's not a romantic gesture at all; Granny has been nailed by a stingray. Doctor Tone steps up to the plate.

"You need ammonia to curb the pain. Would you like me to urinate on your ankle?"

I weed on Amanda's leg to cure a jellyfish sting less than seven days ago so I'm kind of on a roll. We look into this theory later and find that it's an old wives' tale anyway, which perhaps explains why Granny has an ammonia stick specifically for stings. I run off up the beach to grab it, while Grandad and Stephen carry Granny to our shaded beach spot. Amanda flags down a beach cop, who radios the paramedics.

"They'll meet you at the entrance," Beach Cop says.

We just need to get her there. With Grandad and Stephen still recovering from their rescue effort, it's my turn to do the carrying. That is how I come to be piggy-backing my mother-in-law along a Costa Rican beach...completely sober! We make it about 400 metres before I need a rest and just over the river, a police vehicle is waiting to take her the rest of the way. I'm still sweating three hours later.

There's no stopping a true artist though. Despite the excruciating pain, Granny still has the photo competition in mind.

"We should be catching this drama on camera," she says as the police crowd around, probably thankful of something to do. Luca takes the initiative and grabs some potentially competition winning shots.

"You can pop all this in your blog too if you like," Granny generously offers.

An hour later we're still waiting at the park entrance for the ambulance. When it finally arrives, the paramedic takes one look and declares there is nothing he can do. The stingray has been kind enough not to leave a barb in her foot and the only treatment is immersing the wound in hot water and taking some pain killers.

Not happy with this diagnosis, Amanda tracks down a local doctor. It's a quick visit: a couple of jabs in her bum, and confirmation of the advice the medic gave her, and Granny is on her way to recovery. Unfortunately it's going to be a long, slow one...with a fair bit of pain. And that's just the thought of sitting with a foot in a bucket of hot water in 35 degree (95°F) temperatures! We're grateful it was only a small stingray.

Back at home only a few hours later, Luca is attacked by...wait for it...a hairy caterpillar! It hurts like hell too by the sounds of his screaming and for the next few hours he is propped up beside Granny in the quickly constructed M.A.S.H unit. Luckily his recovery is a quick one. No one decides to walk the snake trail tonight.

The snake trail is the name we gave to the short jungle trail which winds down to the river, and a rather rubbish swimming hole. Our main expeditions down this trail were at night, on various photography missions, with mixed success. With the stingray and hairy caterpillar incidents fresh in our minds, we're all on edge as we wander towards the trail head the next evening.

As Grandad, Amanda and I are leaving the lighted area of the pool, heading for the trail three abreast, happily talking amongst ourselves, I suddenly spot danger. Actually, judging by our reactions, perhaps everyone spotted it at the same time...

"SHIT!" I swear, jumping backwards involuntarily. Grandad and Amanda may have said something similar.

We're face-to-face with...Carlos...a blow up crocodile, expertly hidden by Stephen, who is watching from the balcony, laughing hysterically. I can't speak for the others' actions but my first one is to go back and change my undies...

All good things must come to an end

Our last non-travel day with the in-laws is spent at Playa Dominical, a renowned surf beach just up the coast. Once again the others hire boogie boards and I continue my search for Costa Rica's best body surfing wave. Our final act on a beach in Costa Rica, just as the rain sets in, is to watch a whale breach just off shore. A fairy tale ending.

That night photo competition judging begins. As expected, Grandad, Granny and Caroline, with their flash cameras, dominate proceedings but I also have my fair share of success. In fact, the "crap camera" category has been introduced especially for me, and my rare shot of an armadillo takes first prize. It pays to be married to one of the judges! Surprisingly I also manage second place in the "Briggs family holiday" category with my photo captioned "Paolo hits Luca over head with spade."

On this family holiday I've endured rubbish music; I've sat in the car outside more supermarkets than I've been to in my life; I've washed a million dishes and I've eaten everybody's leftovers, every night, and once for breakfast too (curry for breakfast, mmm)! And I'd do it all again in a heartbeat. Christmas with the in-laws should be more of a trial but, floating on a tube in the pool, with a non-alcoholic drink mixed in a coconut on his lap, Luca sums it up nicely:

"Look at me! I'm even more relaxed than Uncle Tony!!

22- Knackeragua

Waving goodbye to the in-laws at 4am as they head back to reality, our own reality sets in. Before long we will be leaving the flash hotel in Alajuela, and back to slumming it. After three weeks of luxury, it's not a reality we're looking forward to. Add to that a fresh wave of homesickness on Amanda's part and it's certainly one of the low points of our trip: not the best circumstances for making good plans.

After reluctantly deciding to skip a three day trek in Corcovado National Park, which is eight hours by bus in the wrong direction, our focus moves to the Monteverde cloud forest reserve. It's closer and just as highly rated. But we realise we've just spent the last three weeks surrounded by wildlife in a rain forest, do we really need more of the same?

We're already well behind in our travel schedule, with six more countries to see and only three months allocated to do so. I'd pencilled in three months for Mexico alone but it's clear that something's got to give. That 'something' starts with the rest of Costa Rica; it's bloody expensive, and lacks the local flavour we've enjoyed so much in other countries. Schedule thus amended, and with no research whatsoever to back our decision, we head to the bus station, Nicaragua bound.

We get a late start, not wanting to check out of our swanky hotel until the last possible minute. Armed with directions to the bus station we don our heavy packs once more and walk away from luxury. I've completely misjudged my new girth and accidentally walk into a lamp post just outside the hotel; the price you pay for eating all the left overs.

"This doesn't look right," says Amanda as we arrive where the bus station's meant to be.

Not a good start. After scouting several streets in the vicinity, we eventually find the station, which is really more of a booking office. There aren't actually any buses here. We wait a full twenty minutes for the office lady to stop checking her text messages before we finally get to ask her a question.

"We want to go to Nicaragua," Amanda says. "Can you give us some information please?"

She makes a phone call...

"Quickly, follow me!" She hangs up the phone and leaps to her feet. "There is a bus going past any minute."

She races out the door with us in lukewarm pursuit, our heavy packs already feeling burdensome after less than an hour on our backs. We cross a busy road just in time to see a bus approaching. Office Lady waves it down, we jump on and, just like that, we're off to Nicaragua!

Safely on the bus, we decide now's a good time to research our destination. Amanda consults the travel guide.

"How far to the border?" I ask.

"Seven hours."

"OK, that puts us at the border around 6pm. Is it a 24-hour border?"

"No. But it'll still be open then."

That's a load off our minds. Our next thought turns to buses on the other side of the border to take us on to our final destination, Granada. There is a distinct lack of information on this but eventually, as we both comb the pages of our guide, I find the answer. It's not the news we were looking for.

"Shit, the last bus leaves at 5.30pm. We'll have to play it by ear."

These are Amanda's least favourite words, particularly when they're coming out of my mouth. Unfortunately, this time there's no alternative.

The most shambolic border crossing ever!

We jump off the bus on the Costa Rican side of the border and are immediately accosted by money changers. Luckily this is one thing we've been able to prepare for on the bus journey, thanks to the currency change app on the new phone Amanda has recently purchased. So begins shambles number one.

Here we are, standing at the border with a wad of cash. Far too much to be carrying around: we got a bit carried away with the excellent pay out rates of Costa Rica's bank machines.

> Amanda- WE? *You* were the one who got carried away!

Three money changers gather around us, and a bus load of locals looks on, as Amanda negotiates them down. Finally an agreement is reached, I produce the wad of cash, and the money changers spend the next 20 minutes trying to short change us. Eventually we all reach agreement on that too, not before I try a short changing trick of my own (unsuccessfully) and we conclude negotiations and head off in the vague direction of our next shambles, feeling like a couple of rookies. We've been incredibly stupid.

With no signage whatsoever to follow, we walk towards the largest of a small group of buildings and are relieved to find that it is, in fact, immigration. We are soon stamped out of Costa Rica, destination Nicaragua. Three police checkpoints later we cross the border.

"Where the hell do we go now?" I think out loud, knowing we need our passports stamped to complete our official entry into the country.

There are men standing by the side of the road with high powered hoses, spraying every vehicle that passes; "Danger-Poison" signs alert us to the fact that it isn't water coming out of the hoses. One Hose Man spots us and gestures for us to walk down the road so we can get sprayed as well. Whether he is joking or not, we decide to give this environmental disaster a very wide berth.

As we veer away from the road, we meet our first Nicaraguan "friend".

"You want taxi?" Nica Friend asks us as he approaches.

"No, we would like to know where the immigration building is." Amanda replies. He leads the way, indicating for us to follow.

"You want bus?" He asks again. "I will find you bus while you are at immigration."

"OK."

Little do we know, we are heading direct for shambles number two...

Just as we finish up at immigration, our new friend returns and leads us to the transport he's acquired for us.

"How much is the bus?" Amanda asks as an afterthought.

"US$20. Each."

Tired and sick of arguing, we agree to this extortionate price, board the bus, pay the driver and tip Nica Friend accordingly, acknowledging that he has, in fact, been quite helpful. The bus then leaves, with us its only two passengers. $20 each for a private bus to Granada doesn't seem so bad! We realise that this guy is probably off duty and returning to base; we're probably quite lucky to have found a bus at all. We're just hoping now that word isn't out about our huge wad of cash- otherwise we're probably being driven to a remote place to be robbed and killed.

Unfortunately for us, "base" isn't Granada. At a crossroads about 10km from town, the bus pulls over and the driver gestures to some waiting mototaxis that there's a fare available. The race is on and we watch with amusement as three drivers battle it out for the privilege of our custom. We board the winner's mototaxi for the final leg of our shambolic journey, the highly skilled driver driving with one hand and holding onto Amanda's backpack with the other. It's been a long and tiring day but finally we start to relax as we motor towards Granada.

Suddenly the driver pulls over on a dark, jungle-clad section of the road. We are instantly alert; this is it, the ambush. The locals are about to take the stupid travellers' wad of cash, the smartphone, and whatever else they want.

"There's no one on the road," Amanda whispers, checking in both directions.

"They must be coming from the jungle then," I decide. "You look left, I'll look right."

Just what we intend to do if we actually see anything is anybody's guess. If the driver senses our heightened awareness, he doesn't let on. He gets off his seat and reaches for...a coke bottle.

"*Gasolina*," he says with a huge smile on his face.

He fills up the tank and we continue on our merry way, finally reaching Granada around 9pm.

We're less than delighted to be back in budget accommodation- a stinking hot room with a fan that sounds like a low flying aircraft. However, we manage to grab a little sleep. We wake the next morning to an email from Michael and Jo (from the Dientes trek): they were here recently and their email tells *us* not to bother. Damn, too late! Wandering around town, we wish we'd got their email earlier. Granada is a run down version of what we've already experienced in South America. The only beach that gets a mention in the travel guide isn't worth crossing the street for, and one of the city's few redeeming features, the Spanish fort, is closed for renovation. It's pretty cool to see the locals going about their daily lives though, sitting on the pavement outside their brightly painted houses in rocking chairs, relaxing in the cool evening breeze. But it's not enough to keep us interested for long; it's backtrack time.

Isla De Ometepe

It is becoming clear that we're tiring of travelling when the rated destinations just don't cut it, and Isla De Ometepe is no exception. The chicken bus to get to the ferry town of Rivas, while a fraction of the price of our "private" transport from the border, seems to be more uncomfortable than normal. Our journey to board the Che Guevara ferry is made even more annoying by meeting several more Nica "friends" who, in the process of "helping" us, cause us to miss the next ferry crossing. By the time we reach the island we actually start to wonder what we're doing here.

We could climb a volcano? But, we've done it; these ones don't look worth the effort. We could swim in the "lovely clean waters" of Lake Nicaragua, on one of the "excellent beaches" of this island we've read so much about. Checking out the beach, we find dead fish and rubbish lining the shores for as far as the eye can see. Lovely indeed. I brave a quick swim but we don't go back.

Eventually we decide to check out "one of Ometepe's classic hikes" to the local waterfall, Casacada San Ramon. Most people hire motorbikes to make the 11km trip to the trail head. Having never ridden them before, we opt for our usual form of transport, mountain bikes.

Well, let's just say *bikes*. They don't feature suspension, and the limited gears continuously slip. They make the 11km journey over an undulating, rock-covered road a complete nightmare. Note to Nicaraguan mountain bike rental outfits: putting Shimano stickers all over a bike does *not* make it a quality bike! In fact, I'm pretty sure the stickers are the only thing holding these bikes together...

An hour and a half, and one very large argument later, we dismount **the worst mountain bikes in history** at the ticket booth and pay our entry fee. The Bocas Del Toro bike-hire-fail just got knocked off its perch!

Suddenly I hear an almighty scream:
"*LOOK OUT TONY!!*"
A snake has fallen off the roof of the ticket booth and landed between us, missing us by about a metre! I turn just in time to see

it slither over my bag and disappear under the building. After removing a tailless whip scorpion from our bathroom the night before, I'm left wondering what Nica has against us.

It's not long until we realise the four hour trek mentioned in the travel guide is only a four hour trek if you've arrived on a bike. Walking up the road towards the falls, we're passed by cars and motorbikes and eventually reach a carpark before the real trail begins. We could've biked it- if we had bikes that could cope with a steep climb. You know, like mountain bikes?!

From the carpark we walk for another 30 minutes through the jungle, barely stopping to check out the local monkey population. Again, we've seen it all before, and we're not really in the mood after a tough cycle and a 4km uphill struggle. Our efforts are rewarded with a view as we arrive at Casacada San Ramon but:

"It's not as good as Iguassu." Amanda sums it up for both of us.

I go for a swim in the freezing cold, knee-deep, muddy water at the base of the trickling cascade anyway.

The cycle home is no less frustrating but memorable for the fact that we actually pass a couple on a motorbike! It looks like they've never ridden one before either. We arrive back at the hostel completely shattered.

Two days of recovery later we decide to move on, still in search of a place that will fulfil us.

The chicken bus that arrives to take us back to the ferry is SO FULL that it takes 15 minutes of shuffling to get the ten people waiting at our stop boarded. One guy even decides to travel on top of the luggage tied to the back of the bus! And we STILL pick others up. It's seriously touch and go as we attempt to climb a small hill. With my face practically plastered to the windscreen I give a running commentary...

"Nearly there!" I yell.

Five minutes later...

"Nearly there!" And so on. Fellow gringos are mildly amused by my antics; the locals wonder what all the fuss is about.

When we finally reach the top of the hill, we come to a bus stop where we change buses. It's a bit quieter this one; Amanda gets a seat but I remain standing. Towards the end of the trip I've been pushed so far back, as more and more people get on, that I'm actually pushed out the back door and end up running behind the bus for the final ten minutes. Wearing my pack. Wellll ok, not *quite*, but if I never see another chicken bus for as long as I live, it'll be too soon. Next stop Leon. Probably on a chicken bus.

Unfortunately in Leon things go from bad to worse. After tipping the cycle-taxi guy well for his extraordinary effort getting us up the hill to our hostel, we find the hostel has lost our booking. Oh, and the place is full. It's a short walk to our second choice.

The next day Amanda has such a bad migraine she can't get out of bed. For three days she lies in bed in our small, stiflingly hot room, attempting food and drink when she has the energy. Assuming nursing duties, I don't venture more than a block from the hostel. And that's where we spend our one-year-travel anniversary, celebrating with a bowl of instant noodles cooked on our little stove in our room- after I find that the kitchen doesn't even have plates. We make a toast with a bottle of water. It's a special moment.

By day four with Amanda no better, I decide enough is enough.

"We're moving to a hotel darling. Do you think you can walk 800 metres?"

"No."

"50 metres to a taxi?"

"No."

Two days later, when building renovations commence, she finally summons up the energy to move. In a genius moment of forward planning, I arrange for an early check-in and the luggage arrives before she does.

That is how we end up staying at what is easily the most expensive and luxurious accommodation (Costa Rica aside) in all our travels. A double bed...each. Air con, onsite restaurant, a pool, a hot water shower, cable TV. All in all, it's just the place for a speedy recovery.

For two more days Amanda lies in bed, the air conditioning aiding her recovery, while I hang out in the pool or at the gym. Judging by the looks from staff, I may well be the only person to have ever used the latter! Eight days after arriving in Leon, we finally emerge our ill-health exile and venture out into this authentic Nicaraguan city.

One of the stops on our self-styled walking tour is a highly rated art gallery, apparently the most comprehensive in Central America. It's safe to say I'm not a huge art fan though.

"I did better paintings than this at the Waikato Winter Show, when I was three." I observe as we walk into the abstract art room. Amanda, finally returning to her old self, hits me.

Five minutes later:

"It looks like a kindergarten did this one." Amanda this time, getting in on the act.

I guess we just don't get it.

In the next room though, I find out what it's like to appreciate art. For ten minutes I stare at a painting of some wood-grain floorboards. I'm certain they are real. Amanda sits down beside me.

"There's no way they're real." she says.

Art gallery etiquette goes out the window and I brave the cameras to do some close up investigation. No, they're not real but the painting has a real wood-grain feel. Perfect art for the wood worker.

Then the paintings take a break as we enter a video "art" exhibition Not since I walked into a room at the Tate gallery in London (and walked out again thinking the room was being renovated) have I seen such an incredible amount of shit that apparently passes for art. Amanda sits down to watch a video, that turns out to be of a woman getting drunk and killing herself. I watch a bizarre video of someone digging a hole, making a fire in it then burying the fire. At least this one is being shown on a gas powered iPod. Finally, though, I think we get it: these are the artists that need psychiatric help.

Our last day in Leon sees us heading to the museum of the revolution. It's not much of a museum but it's brought to life by an awesome guide. Standing on the roof of the museum building, which was a stronghold of the National Guard until revolutionaries took control, our guide, a fighter for the revolutionary forces, brings the battle to life. We see bullet holes, and he points out various strategic points around Leon as he describes the day's happenings.

"See all those bullet holes in the corner of the building?" Nicaragua's answer to Che Guevara points out. "There was a National Guard sniper there. He was a very good shot and killed many men before our mostly untrained soldiers managed to kill him."

The battle rages on in our imagination, and in the guide's memories, for the hour we are up on the roof, Amanda furiously translating for me the whole time. After our less than fulfilling experiences in Nica so far, it's great to find a little gem like this to spur us further along the road.

And that road leads us directly to the beach.

Surf's up!

"Nicaragua is a very safe place these days, not like Guatemala, which is very dangerous." The local taxi driver is most informative on the ride to the beach. "But I have this just in case." He then pulls out an enormous, and lethal looking, machete from beside his seat.

"Nicaraguans don't back down, they like a good fight."

The beach can't come quick enough! We tip the taxi driver well...just in case.

Jiquilillo is a quiet little fishing village that's not really been discovered yet. It's an authentic slice of Nica beach life, complete with Crazy Fish Lady, who shouts at us every time we pass her, and always seems to be holding a fish. Swap the fish for cats and you have the real-life version of The Simpsons' Cat Lady.

Back when we were in the planning stages of this trip, I envisaged a nice, easy month in a seaside village, running down the beach every morning, eating fresh fruit from the local market, and learning to surf, waves permitting. Running well behind schedule, I've condensed that dream down into a week. Amanda is hoping a stay at the beach, and some more Spanish lessons will renew her sense of purpose, so she's pretty keen to stay put too, at least for a while.

On our first day here, there wasn't a single bloody wave to be seen. But on the second morning, the swell's picked up so I hire a board. After an hour of paddling to catch waves, wiping out A LOT, *and* standing a few times, I'm absolutely knackered and retire to the hammock "to wait for my next set." Just on dusk, with the tide on the rise, the waves return so I'm out for the evening session. I don't even last an hour; do I really think I can take a whole week of this? Absolutely not! But having stood on a board for the first time in my life, I decide to quit while I'm ahead and retire happy. Respect to the surfers of the world for the patience, skill, fitness and enthusiasm necessary to succeed in this sport. Or even to do it.

Amanda's Spanish lessons don't last much longer. During her very first lesson it becomes obvious that her teacher isn't actually a teacher at all, and hasn't, in fact, ever taught anyone more advanced than an absolute beginner. When they part, he says he'll have to find his text books for the next lesson then simply doesn't turn up for it. Once again Amanda is without purpose.

On day three I'm sitting happily on the composting toilet in our room when something strange happens. Midway through my "ablution," I realise I haven't yet heard the usual sound associated with a poo hitting the water below, or in this case, the saw dust shavings. To my horror, I realise the bowl is nearly full and there's literally nowhere for my "ablution" to drop; we are still connected! As I stand to see what's going on, a very determined poo decides to come with me! Crisis narrowly averted by some of the best toilet acrobatics Latin America has seen since Amanda's "World's most dangerous toilet" episode. Rather than deal with our now full composting toilet, we decide to leave.

Decision time

With Amanda's sense of purpose extinguished again, new plans are hastily concocted. Plan A involves taking two separate chicken buses to the tiny port town of Potosi and boarding a fishing boat, destination La Union, El Salvador. But we doubt we have the energy left to take in another country. Bring on Plan B...

"Let's go back to that five-star hotel in Leon and research this properly with the good Wi-Fi," I suggest. Amanda agrees immediately and wholeheartedly.

Unfortunately getting back to Leon also involves two chicken buses. As we sit on the first one, waiting for the local villagers to load up their fish and board, I ponder the real meaning of our spontaneous decision to backtrack to a five-star hotel. Amanda doesn't look like she's pondering anything much and sits contentedly in her window seat as fish juice from the roof "luggage" drips on her head through the open window.

Sitting in air conditioned comfort back in Leon, it's time for us to really take stock.

Being surrounded by poverty in nearly every country we've visited has been hard on Amanda, and she feels the overwhelming need to get back to work and start contributing to society once again. But she's also very mindful of the fact that I'm not ready to go home just yet. And we're both quite keen to see Guatemala. The more we talk, the more torn she becomes.

By now, I realise that she's felt this way for quite a while, and the family Christmas in Costa Rica is the only thing that's kept her going this long. It's also become clear to both of us that the further we get into Central America, the less excited we are by the usual attractions. Once you've seen your share of ruins, volcanoes, and wildlife, and experienced your share of culture, you reach a point where you need no more.

We're also tired. Tired of moving on every few days; of packing and unpacking; finding accommodation and transport; being crammed onto another bus with 20 too many people already on it; listening to bloody roosters all night- or dogs- or both; and of having to constantly be on our guard, of being "rich" Westerners travelling through developing countries. The decision seems to have made itself for us.

"You know you've had enough when you find yourself staying in a five star hotel. Maybe it's time to go home..." I ponder aloud, testing the waters.

Amanda bursts into tears and hugs me. Just like that our adventure is over. And I just inadvertently acquired at least a decade's worth of brownie points!

It took Nicaragua to finally break us...

23- Epilogue

When word gets out, messages come in from around the world from friends and family, congratulating us on our decision to quit travelling. Now heading to a northern hemisphere winter, I'm not so sure. It's the messages from the friends we've met along the way that really get my attention.

As Aussie Jen puts it:

"You guys are travelling the wrong way!"

She's just reached Patagonia. It seems like an age since we were there, that beautifully rugged part of the world, trekking to our hearts' content.

And Phoebe from the Huayhuash trek writes, her advice a little more specific:

"So you're back to the real world? Take it slow: the northern hemisphere can be surprisingly confusing- they actually follow rules. No more *"I'm sorry, I'm a tourist;"* people *actually* stand in line; no cheap street food; you can't fill cars with 20 passengers; people understand you if you talk behind their backs; police don't accept bribes; no more cockroaches... Best to take a holiday to help acclimatisation! All the best! Take care."

Michael from the Dientes trek is short and to the point...

"Do you wish you were in Europe ***now***? Sleeping in a comfy bed? Paying €5 a beer and €15 for hand-sliced ham?"

Faced with those arguments it's a definite no for me. This hits home in a big way when we touch down in Copenhagen leaving 40°C (104°F) in Nicaragua. The snow ploughs are out on the runway and it's not even 40° *Fahrenheit*.

We try and cheer ourselves up with a soy hot chocolate each; *epic* fail when they total more than double the average price of a night's accommodation in Bolivia. But we have to live with the choices we've made.

One choice that Amanda made more than ten years ago was marrying me. Another choice was to live with me in New Zealand, a long way away from her family. The third choice is the one that has brought us to this moment: quitting our jobs to travel Latin America for a year, *without* knowing anything about UK immigration requirements before we left. It turns out that Amanda is now deemed unemployed by the UK home office, which in turn means that I am ineligible for the spousal visa to live and work there. Foiled by a xenophobic law. The Government's tough stand on Immigration actually denies British Citizens the right to live in their own country if they're married to foreigners. This is how we wind up back where we started our trip, mid-winter in Scotland for another visit. The weather hasn't improved any!

And *this* is how we end up in the Netherlands, where Amanda uses her status as an EU citizen to settle. I too am welcome. After a year in chaotic Latin America, the highly orderly Netherlands is a breath of fresh air. Public transport is plentiful, as, to be fair, was the case in Latin America, but it's also reliable and animal free! There are no roosters crowing all night. The dogs are obedient- and have owners. The tap water is drinkable. There is *hygiene*!

The list could go on... and on, but the one thing that stands out above all?

Not having to put my toilet paper in the bin provided...

24- Other interesting stuff

Travelling light...*ish*

Gunning for a bag weight below 15kg, I cut the excess strapping off my backpack, while Amanda watched on in amusement, and I proceeded to weigh everything that went into it. Should I take my All Black rugby jersey or my Waikato one? Tough decisions to be made: in the end, the All Black one was lighter. Included in the 15kg was a tent, a sleeping bag, a sleeping mat, a gas cooker, cooking gear (-one pan, two bowls and two sporks), a day pack, a water filter bottle and a seven inch tablet. Clothing consisted of one down jacket, two fleeces, a long-sleeved thermal top and bottom, one pair of short trousers, one of long, with zip-off legs, two t shirts, three pairs of undies, three pairs of socks, one woolly hat, one sun hat and one pair of gloves.

> Amanda- I was appalled that Tony was only taking three pairs of undies and highly dubious that they would be washed often enough to meet basic hygiene standards!

Footwear: lightweight trail-running shoes, plus a pair of jandals. It took me half a day to pack but I'm happy to say I came in under my goal weight. However, it must be said that, because of my lack of sewing skills, the strap cutting wasn't that good an idea. The safety pins I had to add to my pack to keep everything from falling off probably ended up weighing more than the weight I saved!

Amanda's weight limit was 10kg and it was my turn to be amused when, in an effort to get everything into her bag (at the last minute, as usual) she resorted to compression sacks. I witnessed ten pairs of socks and ten pairs of knickers go into one of these sacks. That was when I decided not to get involved! I did, however, convince her *not* to take her heavy, slow drying jeans, and to this day, she's yet to forgive me.

By the end of the year my pack weighed closer to 20kg.

> Amanda- I regret not having the camera that Tony made me leave at home. The pictures I got on my phone were pretty good but it was hopeless for wildlife or fast moving shots, and we really missed some good ones. I also found it hard to live a whole year with only one change of clothes. I felt a bit like a tramp towards the end. However, if you'd asked me whether I regretted either of these decisions as I slogged up some of those mountains, the answer would be a definitive no!

Tone-style

> Amanda- Those of you that know Tone know that he's "a man who goes his own way." Nowhere is this more evident than in his unique sense of "style." On this trip, it's fair to say he felt free enough to take his style to the next level. Some of his ensembles included:
> -Shorts held up by the luminous yellow string he took off the compass.
> -Shorts and a giant puffer jacket, topped off with a woollen hat- and all the other winter extras. Actually he doesn't wear anything but shorts no matter how cold it is.
> -Baggy-bottomed long johns- that somehow he's failed to notice are actually a form of underwear.
> -Jandals (flip-flops, thongs, whatever) and socks. My particular favourite.
> You might think there's nothing wrong with such outfits- and that's probably quite true in the Patagonian wilderness. But Tone considers himself something of a trendsetter, and dresses like this to go out to dinner with new friends too! This has resulted in many glances (that Tone interprets as admiring) and a few comments but, to date, no actual trend followers. I have mentioned to Tone that to be a style icon, one must have followers but he feels it's just a matter of time 'til everyone else catches on. I think he's just too avant guarde for these conservative Latinos!

Spanicdotes- When Spanish goes wrong...

Arriving back at the hostel after the Dientes trek I found myself looking to dispose of some *basura* (rubbish). I walked into the kitchen holding up the rubbish and said:

"El bano?"

That left the hosts wondering why I wanted to put my rubbish in their toilet...

***

Also after the Dientes trek Amanda was doing some laundry. When one of the hostel owners tried to help her hang out the clothes she said:

"Puedo coger mis ropas"

The hostel owner looked a bit startled.

Amanda later realised that she had confused *colgar* with *coger* and thanks to South American Spanish slang, she'd essentially informed the hostel owner of her intention to fuck her own clothes...

***

Out for a meal one night, I had no idea what the Spanish word for 'menu' was, so decided to go with the duel 'Spanglish' approach and asked for:

"*El menu, por favour?*

I was somewhat surprised when the waitress returned to the table with the toilet key...

***

Amanda woke up one morning in Valparaiso, Chile, with a rather nasty mosquito bite on her eye lid. Already booked on the bus to Santiago that day, we decided to forge ahead with me as her guide. Arriving in Santiago, we decided that her eye had swelled up enough to warrant medical attention so I guided her to the hospital. Unsure where to go, Amanda approached the information desk:

"*Tengo un problema con mi hijo.*"

The lady looked at me strangely, then back at Amanda.

"You have a problem with your *son*?"

"Oops! *Ojo!* Not *hijo*! *Ojo!* I have a problem with my *eye*!"

***

After six weeks of one-on-one Spanish lessons in Bolivia, I wasn't exactly proficient- far from it in fact. I learned more from The Simpsons:

"*Donde esta la biblioteca?*" -Where is the library?

However, I *did* pick up the following, extensively used, go-to line at language school:

"*Cuantos zanahorias tienes?*".-How many carrots do you have?

Very useful...

***

Finally, there's the moment where you think you've mastered Spanish:

"Wow!" This is me: "I actually understood exactly that *entire* conversation!"

"They were speaking English Tone."

Amanda TV

After walking the streets of Valparaiso for a couple of days looking at the awesome street art, we are in dire need of some beach time so we jump on the local train and head over to check out one of Chile's most popular beaches, Vina del Mar. It's a scorcher and we are dressed accordingly.

After jumping off the train and walking through the centre of Vina del Mar, beside one of the most disgustingly polluted rivers I have ever seen, we're no longer in the mood for a swim so content ourselves walking down the boardwalk looking out over a beach covered with rubbish.

Wandering along, we're approached by a reporter with a cameraman in tow and, before you know it, Amanda's being interviewed, live on TV, about the unseasonably warm weather in Chile at the moment.

As Amanda does her very best to answer the reporter's questions in the wider context of climate change, in very limited Spanish, the cameraman zooms in for a close up...of her jandals.

Amanda- It's the fact that I hadn't shaved my legs that concerned me more!

Nicaraguan humour
Spotted on a placemat in a restaurant:
"What does Santa give children in the desert?"
"Milk powder!!"
And another:
"Dear Santa, please bring me a fire truck for Christmas, thanks, Luis."

"Dear Luis, I will set fire to your house whilst you're sleeping then you can have all the fire trucks you want, Santa."

And I thought *my* sense of humour was weird.

International culinary delights

Best Mexican food- Taco Bello; Otavalo, Ecuador.

Best curry- La Eliana; Salento, Colombia.

Best pizza- Inti Wasi; Isla de sol, Bolivia. (*If* you can track down the owner)

We'd elected to stay at Inti Wasi on Isla de Sol but we found it closed when we got there. A few days later we decided to have a meal there but it was still closed- until a friendly local lad spotted our dilemma. He sped off to rouse the owner, who was only too happy to open for us. What followed was the BIGGEST and BEST pizza we have **ever** had! We recommended this place to all our travel friends; all, bar none, were grateful.

Top tech tips

To keep friends and family informed I used the top notch travel blog site:
http://www.travelpod.com

Boldly go where someone has gone before with this great little outdoor navigation app:
http://www.wikiloc.com/outdoor-navigation-app

Worried about losing your phone with all those awesome photos you've taken? Set it up to upload them straight to:
https://www.dropbox.com

Currency conversion app, a must have:
http://www.xe.com/

Accurate and up to date weather predictions for mountains around the world:
http://www.mountain-forecast.com/

Find the cheapest flights and/or the best options:
http://www.skyscanner.net/

Don't leave home without a kindle, or whichever eBook app you prefer; you'll find it's a lot easier to carry those ten or so travel guides! It surprised us how many people we met *didn't* do this.

Bolivia gets the final word

Bolivians are known for their blockades, protesting against one thing or another. These can sometimes hold up traffic for days. Thankfully the closest we came to experiencing this was on Isla del Sol when Amanda spotted a fantastic photo opportunity: five young girls walking a llama down the trail.

"Can I take a photo *chicas* (girls)?" Amanda asks.

Quick as a flash the youngest one, probably about three years old, starts the negotiations.

"Two bolivianos."

Amanda agrees to the price and takes the photo. Next thing ya know the kids are blockading the path and demanding two bolivianos each. I'm already past so Amanda has two options, pay up or run the blockade, a risky proposition in Bolivia. But not so risky with five kids under-5 and she sneaks past as they try and hit the next people up. The llama asks for nothing...

Printed in Great Britain
by Amazon